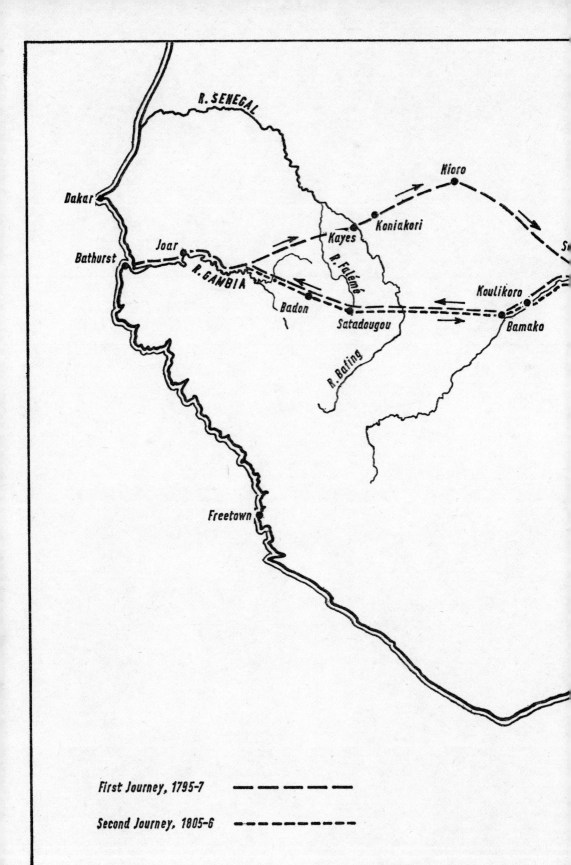

R. SENEGAL

Nioro

Dakar

Koniakori

Kayes

Joar

Bathurst

R. GAMBIA

R. Faléme

Koulikoro

Badon

Satadougou

Bamako

R. Bafing

Freetown

First Journey, 1795-7

Second Journey, 1805-6

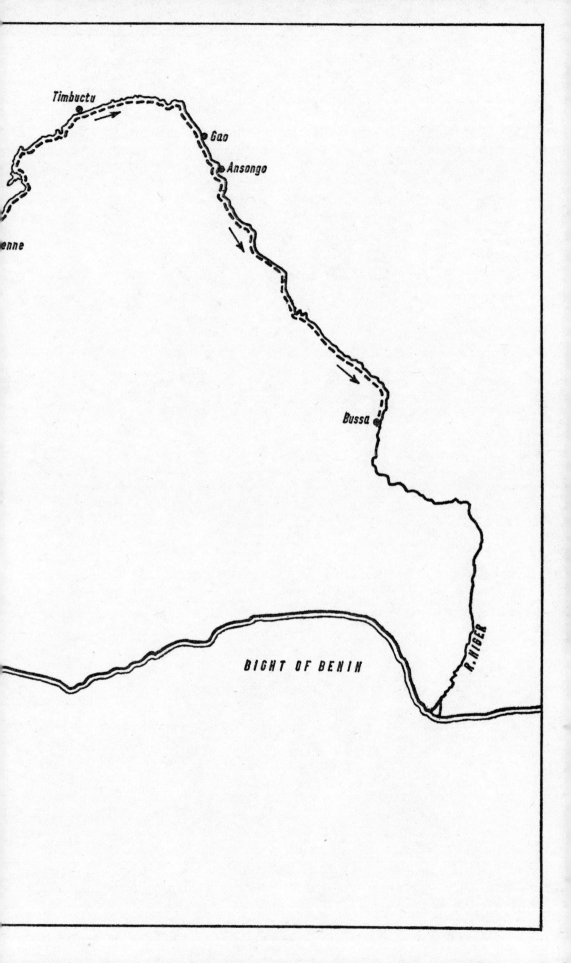

BLACK NILE

ABOUT THE BOOK

Mungo Park was the first of the great, classical African explorers. Before his expeditions, the course of the Niger had for centuries been a mystery teasing and confusing the geographers of the West. It was Park, a crofter's son from the borders of Scotland, who was chosen by the great Sir Joseph Banks to solve that mystery. In time, that mystery came to obsess him.

Peter Brent tells of his months of struggle in the wilderness—with hunger, with terrain, with climate, with fever and and sickness, with religious fanatics and avaricious local tyrants. There are the African men and women from whom he so often received food and shelter and the thieves and robbers who beset his path, his last ferocious dash down the Niger, over a thousand miles through Mandingo country and the slave traders to the rapids of northern Nigeria in a death that will never now be totally explained.

Peter Brent traces the connection between exploration and the colonialism it presaged, and shows that the ideas underlying the whole concept of "Exploration" were, despite the liberalism and humanity of some of the explorers themselves, inevitably both racist and exploitive. While vividly recreating the arduous and dramatically dangerous; journey of Mungo Park and his successors, he raises issues that remain directly relevant to the way in which, even today, the West regards the countries of the Third World.

ABOUT THE AUTHOR

Peter Brent was born in 1931 and educated in Wales. He is a full-time writer and has written a number of extremely successful travel books: *Antarctic Tragedy, T. E. Lawrence, The Viking Saga, Gengis Khan, God Men of India. The New York Times* said of him in a recent review, "He is a professional writer and a good one."

Mungo Park and the Search for the Niger

BLACK NILE

by Peter Brent

Gordon & Cremonesi

Designed by Heather Gordon
Set in 11pt on 13pt Bembo and printed in Great Britain by
The Anchor Press Ltd and bound by Wm Brendon & Son Ltd
both of Tiptree, Essex

British Library/Library of Congress
Cataloguing In Publication Data

Brent, Peter

    Black Nile
    1. Park, Mungo
    1. Title
    916.6'04   DT356   77-30052

ISBN 0–86033–017–6

Gordon Cremonesi Ltd
London and New York
New River House
34 Seymour Road
London N8 0BE

For MARITA

Contents

Introduction

Real Niger, Niger Myth

Its first waters come trickling or gushing into view some 3,000 feet up among the ridges and gorges, the escarpments and eroded plateaus of the Futa Jallon mountains. To the south-west these highlands step slowly down towards the sea, some 200 miles away; to the north-east they sweep, dwindling, across Guinea and deeper into Africa. This is the direction the river follows, north-east towards the Sahara, collecting up its tributaries as it flows, widening, deepening, gathering momentum for the 2,500 miles or more that it must cover before it reaches its final vast outpouring into the sea.

On the banks of its upper reaches market-towns have grown up—Faranah, Kurussa, Bamako, Segu. These have for their hinterland a wide, monotonous countryside of woods, open scrub and pasture, dotted with the many villages, the fields and plantations, of an industrious peasant people. By them, the river is called the Joliba. Beyond Segu, both land and river alter. Losing its earlier certainty, the current flags; the river wanders into a multiplicity of channels, turning at flood-times into a vast inland delta that covers some 30,000 square miles (though irrigation engineers have seized their opportunity, and under their ministrations the water these days stretches in ducts and lakes purposefully across these lowlands). Here too the Niger is joined by that tributary upon the banks of which stands Jenne (or Djenne), centre of an ancient trade in gold.

Endless downpours sustain the green trees and opulent vegetation that line the most southerly of the river's early reaches. After the inland delta, however, the Niger flows slowly on into the semi-desert, lucky to see five inches of rain in a year. It pushes even further, seemingly prepared to challenge the powerful aridity of the desert itself. But soon it begins to give way, as though repelled by the infertile wasteland facing it. It flows by Timbuctu (once on its very banks, now separated from it by seven miles of the constantly-deposited desert sand) and its port, Kabara, reaching towards that great northern bend that for so many centuries deceived the learned. From its left bank almost to the shores of the Mediterranean stretch the barren plains and dunes of the Sahara.

As at last it swings away towards the south-east, it is established as a great river, the Niger, claiming that name from those who live on its banks, giving it back to two of the states through which its waters pass. It sweeps past the ancient Songhai capital, Gao, where millennia ago streams fed it from what are now the Sahara uplands. Strengthened by the river Kebbi, which flows down to it from the Hausa territories, the river moves on, from Niger into Nigeria; sometimes it spreads wide, its progress languid, sometimes it howls, foam-laced, between confining cliffs. For rapids here make it almost impassable; the worst are near the town of Bussa. But sixty miles below Bussa lies Jebba, and from there to the endless bifurcations of its delta the Niger is navigable—at least from July to October, when its waters are high. From the left more tributaries flow in, the largest of them the Benue. It is after this confluence that the river turns due south, as though ready at last to head directly for the ocean.

The banks here are lined with heavy vegetation, though they are far apart—travellers need feel no sense of rain-forest oppression. The final delta begins at Abo, some eighty miles from the sea. It spreads the Niger into streams that reach the Atlantic along 200 miles of coastline, their courses often tangled by the endless, tentacular archways of vast mangrove swamps. Down these streams—the Brass, the Bonny, the Sombrero, the Nun and the rest—slavers for century after century brought their desperate cargoes. Today it is oil, drawn from the fields beyond Port Harcourt, that has superseded slaves in the economy. Palm oil, too, once helped to keep these coastal territories wealthy—sixty inches of rain fall every year over the delta to sustain the trees. Rooted in that damp fertility, the groves still stand, like waiting crowds, like patient reserves in some long battle. The tankers inch closer and the derricks lift towards the clouds, but the rain still falls. Like the Niger itself, it will continue long after the earth has been savaged for the last drop of its oil. The rain, the palm trees, the river—they can bide their time.

The course and direction of the Niger, indeed its very existence as an independent stream, were at the beginning of the nineteenth century the focus for much speculation and argument in Europe, and had been so for hundreds of years. The states that rose, struggled and fell on its banks were practically unknown outside the Muslim world. Hardly a single European, in all the years during which the coast of Africa was charted and trade with the inhabitants pursued, had ventured to strike inland and try to settle the question once and for all. There had been an embassy or two by the Portuguese in the sixteenth century, their purposes diplomatic and commercial, and their reports restricted to Authority's chosen. The rest was the silence of ignorance, fear and unconcern.

In 1447 a Genoese trader, Antonio Malfante, wrote from the oasis of Touat, halfway between Algiers and Timbuctu, to the merchants who employed him. He mentioned such Muslim states as "Thambet [Timbuctu], Mali, Sagoto and

Bamba. . . . To the south of these there are many states and territories solely inhabited by idolatrous negroes, incessantly at war with each other. . . . A very great river flows through those territories and at a certain time of year pours its flood over the land; that river passes the gates of Thambet and runs through Egypt and it is the river which passes through Cairo. They have upon it many barks in which they carry on their commerce."

This confusion of Nile with Niger was an old story among the speculations about Africa. The twelfth-century geographer al-Idrisi attributed a joint source to the Nile and the Niger. He knew, however, that there was a great river flowing towards the Atlantic (although he seems to have been uncertain about where its mouth was and thus about the direction of its flow) and that on its banks stood states and cities of great power. The thirteenth century saw an expansion of the trans-Sahara trade, so that cities such as Gao and Timbuctu became familiar to Moorish and Arabic travellers like ibn-Battuta, their accounts opening these regions to the interest and curiosity of the literate. This was knowledge, however, largely confined to the Muslim intelligentsia; it was not until 1619 that al-Idrisi's account, for example, was translated into a European language.

Three centuries before that translation, the Jewish cartographers of Majorca, primed by Arab travellers and merchants, had displayed in their magnificent maps a knowledge of Africa no European geographer was to match for 400 years. Nevertheless, for them, too, the true course and outlet of the Niger remained a mystery. In 1600 the *History and Description of Africa* by Leo Africanus helped to dispel some of the ignorance that made Africa such a darkness to North Europeans. He had been born in Granada, a Moor like al-Idrisi, but one who belonged, not to the heyday of a culture, but to the last secure generation before his people's final expulsion. The pious lances of Christian knights having cleansed the land of all those who would not accept the religion of divine compassion, he became a traveller whose eyewitness accounts give us some indication of the wealth, dignity and organisation of the Hausa kingdoms of his time. Later, he was captured by corsairs and forcibly baptised. Taken to Rome, he fell happily under the patronage of Leo X; it is because of this that we still know him by his grandiose Latin name. He certainly seems to have travelled as far south as northern Nigeria, leaving us a description of the city of Kano as it was in the sixteenth century. Nevertheless, his description of the Niger and his conviction that it flowed westward through Mali must have been based, despite his assertion that he had sailed the river himself, on inaccurate hearsay. This assertion, however, and the corollary he drew from it that the Niger was a branch of the Nile, were to confuse many of those who came after him.

He was, whether knowingly or not, only following classical masters in this. Despite a Roman expedition under Julius Maternus that reached the Fezzan and perhaps even further, the area south of the Sahara remained almost totally unknown to the old Mediterranean empires. Both Herodotus and Pliny had been adamant that Nile and Niger were connected, although Pliny had laid it

down that Niger (for him the Gir or Nigir) flowed into Nile and so out into the
Mediterranean. Malfante, as we have seen, thought the same, but the Moorish
geographers, though retaining the connection between the rivers, reversed the
Niger's flow and made the Senegal, the Gambia or the Rio Grande its outlet to
the sea. In this, they ran counter to another ancient authority, Ptolemy, who
insisted accurately that the Senegal was a quite separate river. He, however,
denied that the Niger had an outlet at all, imagining that it fluttered and stuttered
away into a series of lakes and swamps somewhere deep in the African interior.
By the eighteenth century other experts were convinced that it was the Congo
with which the Niger was in some way connected—Mungo Park himself was
to believe this.

An attempt to gather up known opinion into a single comprehensible theory
was made by the great Jean-Baptiste D'Anville, who, born in 1697, had
been appointed a Royal Geographer at the age of only twenty-two; when he
died, aged well over eighty, he left behind him 211 of the most accurate maps
produced in the eighteenth century. In 1727 he first published a map of Africa
(he followed it by an atlas of China and a geographical analysis of Italy, an
attractive display of geographical catholicity); then and later he considered the
Niger as separate from the Senegal, following Ptolemy in this as in his conviction
that the river flowed in an easterly direction, spreading into a series of lakes and
marshes somewhere to the north-east, there largely to evaporate under a
Sahara sun strong enough to bring even the greatest river to futility. He thought
that it did not entirely evaporate, however; flowing underground or in some
other inconspicuous manner, some of its waters continued eastward until linking
at last with the upper reaches of the Nile. So two theories were accommodated
in one.

It is curious that Europe should have remained in such confusion for so long.
(West Africans, of course, found the Niger rather less of a puzzle.) For, whether
Hanno the Phoenician really entered the mouth of the Gambia in 500 BC or
stopped at some other, nearer, river, the Portuguese navigators of the fifteenth
century certainly reached it. In 1444, Diniz Dias cautiously observed the mouth
of the Senegal, the furthest then of the series of nibbles with which the Portuguese were chewing their way carefully towards the southern tip of the continent.
Two years later Nuno Tristão probably died in the mouth of the Gambia. In 1460
Pedro da Sintra saw and named the mountains of Sierra Leone, moved to call
them that by the savage growling of the thunders that lurked and echoed among
those peaks. The Venetian captain Alviso da Cadamosto, sailing in the service of
Portugal's Prince Henry the Navigator, described the coast they were discovering and the people who lived on it. Its estuaries and inlets were heavily tree-
fringed; elephants shouldered their way through its forest clearings; hippopotami sank in luxurious stillness into its waters; monkeys yelled and
chaffered through its branches. About the village markets stalked white-robed
Muslim traders, while hunkering on the ground the gleaming inhabitants of the

coastal lands offered their produce for sale—furs and skins and ostrich eggs adding variety to the usual trade in necessities.

After Henry's death in 1460, there was some confusion, some loss of purpose, in the Portuguese exploratory effort, but nevertheless, little by little, the West African coast was opened up to trade. This process received a renewed impetus when a venturer named Fernão Gomes leased all commercial rights for an annual rent and the promise to finance future exploration. It was captains in the pay of Gomes who charted the Bight of Benin, sailing by the endless streams and ponds and stinking flats, the heaving undulation of root and branch arching darkly across ooze, of the largest mangrove swamp in the world. They had no suspicion that they were passing that long-hidden secret, that abiding mystery, the mouth of the Niger.

Gold altered the attitude of the Portuguese crown. Once it was seen to be available in the villages that lined the Bight of Benin, the contract granted Gomes came to an end. In 1482 Portugal sent an expedition to what would become known as the Gold Coast (the Portuguese themselves called it *Mina de Ouro*—The Gold Mine) and after some skirmishing built a fortress there to safeguard its trade. For over a hundred years, although French, Castilian, English and Italian merchant venturers sent their ships into these coastal waters, the Portuguese were the only ones to establish a foothold on land. They used the navigable reaches of the Senegal and the Gambia to spread their influence in those regions, while they extended their garrison system on the Gold Coast in an effort to hold their early monopoly there.

By the early sixteenth century, the Portuguese middlemen and merchants were sending back to Lisbon one-tenth of the world's gold supply. It is no wonder that they made every effort to remain on good terms with the peoples they traded with; there may even have been a Portuguese embassy in Timbuctu in 1565 and there was certainly one in Mali some thirty years earlier. Yet, perhaps because of the jealousy with which they guarded their West African trade, whatever knowledge they gained of those countries never became widespread.

The coastal people meanwhile resisted all attempts at cultural and religious infiltration, as well as any hint of Portuguese efforts to dominate them. (The punitive expedition sent by the Portuguese to punish those who dealt with Europeans of other nationalities tended to harm rather than improve their diplomatic position.) Though their forts and warehouses gave the Portuguese certain advantages, the inhabitants of Benin or the Volta valley never recognised their claim to special consideration. On the coasts further west, near the mouths of the Senegal and the Gambia, cultural infiltration tended if anything to flow the other way, with Portuguese traders marrying black wives and settling into the local communities. If Christians in the homeland were horrified and hoped for swift missionary penetration to alter this deplorable state of affairs, for the traders it probably brought advantages no fort could have achieved for them.

Early in the seventeenth century, the English took a brief part in the attempt to seek out the mysterious riches that everyone was certain lay hidden in the interior of West Africa, adventuring, as one such explorer, Richard Jobson, was to write, "upon these promising rivers that fall into the maine Ocean upon that South-West side". In 1618 a Barbary Coast merchant named George Thompson led a party up the Gambia, the expedition rowing their small boats gamely against the current. He established a trading post, then sent a group back to the coast. They found their mates dead and their ship, the *Catherine*, gone: there had been an attack by the Portuguese and mulatto poor of the region, perhaps egged on by commercial rivals. They managed nevertheless to scramble a passage home—their good fortune itself an indication of the volume of traffic in those days—and in time a fifty-ton pinnace, the *St John*, was sent upriver to relieve Thompson. He refused to embark, however; instead, with eight companions, he set off to keep a rendezvous with a noted local trader, Buckor Sano. The latter never appeared, but recurring rumours of gold all about inflamed Thompson's greed and apparently made this already difficult man intolerable. At last one of his companions rounded on him and killed him. Secretive always, whatever he knew vanished with his soul.

In 1620 the *St John* was back, escorting the larger *Lyon* on the expedition led by Richard Jobson. He took his two ships up as far as the Barraconda Falls, some 200 miles from the coast, and there settled to trade. Salt, as always, was the commodity in demand—and slaves, he found, the goods most freely offered. Jobson recoiled, finding that trade abhorrent; textiles and ivory were more to his taste. He talked to that Buckor Sano who had so tantalisingly failed to meet Thompson, and from him learned a little about Timbuctu, "a great Town the houses whereof are covered with gold". From the Falls, Sano told him, a pack train could travel there and back in the space of four moons.

Richard Jobson was never to reach Timbuctu. Instead, he returned to England and wrote *The Adventures of the Golden Trade*. Published in 1623, much of what it recounts of West African places and people has been confirmed by later travellers. But little commerce followed: England's influence in Africa was about to wane for almost a hundred years. And in any case the gold trade was beginning to be superseded by a less complicated and more profitable traffic. Not everyone was as honourable, or as squeamish, as Richard Jobson. The Americas' insatiable demand for slaves—each with a working life of at most thirty years—soon overcame all but the most obdurate of scruples. It was in about 1530 that the Spanish began to import slaves in large numbers to work the silver mines of Mexico and Peru. From that moment, the appalling flow of human beings across the Atlantic seemed to increase year by year, and each increase to bring West Africa more and more prominently into the European world-picture.

Slaves had of course always been traded, sent north along the caravan routes to serve the wealthy nobility of the Mediterranean states and the Middle East.

The first century of the Atlantic trade to the Americas saw some 200,000 people torn from freedom and sent to the mines and plantations waiting to devour them. A rate of 2,000 a year, though dreadful enough, would hardly have altered the numbers of those normally sent into servitude. But the figures increased as the economies west of the Atlantic came to rest more and more heavily upon sugar, tobacco and cotton. The new demand produced not only new supplies, but also new suppliers. The Dutch in the early part of the seventeenth century, their efficiency at last ousting the Portuguese, traded in West African slaves as they did in everything else that ships could carry.

By the second half of that century, however, the slave trade, lucrative and, with the normally favourable winds, uncomplicated, had become a scramble. Soon half the countries in Europe seemed to be trying to grab their share. Danes competed with Swedes; Germans with Dutch; British with French; Spaniards —still—with Portuguese. In West Africa, national monopoly companies from the various countries struggled for preferential treatment, favourable terms, better sources of supply. They set up forts and trading posts, warehouses for the goods they brought in, depots where slaves could be kept like cattle until whipped away to board the waiting ships.

War in Europe altered the situation elsewhere in the world. The emergence of France and England as the strongest European powers was reflected in their West African holdings. Senegal became the centre for French activity, where Gorée (captured from the Dutch in 1677) became their chief mainland base, supported by their strong presence on the island of St Louis. Alas, Senegambia was not as truly profitable an area for slavers as were the coasts a little further east. Although supported by hides and ivory, gum arabic and wax, and despite a volume of trade which reached £500,000 in some years, not more than 1,000 slaves could be taken from the region annually—only a little more than one-tenth of the total French shipment of slaves across the Atlantic. By the mid seventeenth century, the British, on the other hand, were energetically sending 25,000 souls westward to the plantations every year. Small wonder that the French companies in Senegambia had a record of failure and bankruptcy.

The Gold Coast presented a more buoyant picture. As the eighteenth century began, its exports of gold dust were still worth some £250,000 annually. Its trade with Europe was so well established—some fifty fortified trading posts, large and small, jostled on the 250 miles of its coastline—that to set up a supply-line for slaves presented few problems. By 1785, the Gold Coast was exporting 10,000 slaves every year, most of them marched to waiting British traders and brought in chains on board British ships. For by this time Britain was the premier trading nation of the world. It had reached that point of economic take-off that would keep it flying—though after a while, almost imperceptibly, lower and lower—for almost another 150 years. Its wealth was still building steadily, based as it now was on that triangular trade that the defenders of slavery found so pleasant to contemplate: British manufactured articles sent to West Africa paid for the

slaves sold in the Americas to obtain the raw materials that made the manufactured articles for buying yet more slaves. The profits made on each leg of this
three-party journey went on luxuries—the food and drink, the spectacular
entertainments, the academies and museums, the arts and the adornments that
created in late eighteenth-century England so early, and often so unappetising,
an example of conspicuous consumption.

The dominance of the British position in West Africa was consolidated when,
after victory in the Seven Years' War, Britain took over the colony of Senegambia. Although this was returned to France after 1783, it left Britain holding
as large a share of the West African trade as all the rest of her European rivals
put together. This meant, in brutal flesh and blood, that British ships were carrying 38,000 men and women across the Atlantic to slavery every year, half the
world's total, and that 26,000 of these came from West Africa; French and other
traders dragged away perhaps the same number.

When the Napoleonic wars began, the French trade died away, while the
rest of the European trading nations were blockaded by the British navy. As a
result, the number of slaves carried by British ships increased to 50,000 a year,
well over half of them from West Africa. It has been estimated that, from the
beginning of the seventeenth century until the end of the slave traffic just over
200 years later, something like 6 million people were carried away for ever from
West Africa alone (the total for Africa as a whole is given as almost double this).
In the eighteenth century, $4\frac{1}{2}$ million men and women were dragged in chains
to the shore and the waiting slave ships.

Despite the declining trade in gold—a decline due in part to the new
prosperity of the slave-dealing coastal nations, who now preferred to keep their
gold rather than sell it—it is clear from these figures that West Africa at the time
when Mungo Park first set foot in it in 1795 represented enormous business for
the merchants of Bristol, Liverpool and London. Remembering the long and
profitable connection with the area through which this business had been built
up, one might ask why, except briefly in Senegambia, no attempt had been made
during that embattled eighteenth century at the colonisation and annexation
that by 1800 had become a commonplace elsewhere in the world.

As might be expected, the first explanations are physical. The country was
believed, not without reason, to be dangerous to the stranger's health. It was
here that the White Man's Grave stretched, dank, miasmic, treacherous. Yellow
fever, dysentery and malaria all awaited the unprepared European, infiltrated his
bloodstream and laid him low in a matter of days. Inland, there were swamps,
forests, mountains and great streams (as well as open plains, scrubland and
savannahs). Dangerous diseases, therefore, and difficult country—a forbidding
combination. To them may be added the intransigent bigotry of the Islamic
states and communities, societies filled with a hatred for all infidels—and especially for Christians, over so many centuries Islam's prime enemies. This religious
attitude was reinforced by the commercial defensiveness of the middleman

determined to keep in his own hands the sources of his trade. Since, moreover, the middleman operated with great efficiency, Europeans had no great incentive to face the rigours of inland travel in the hope of augmenting their already adequate profits. As long as the money poured in, it was best to leave things as they were.

As the eighteenth century moved towards its close, however, new forces began to work on this static, though comfortable, situation. Changes were in the offing. In Europe, nations had become more self-aware, their dynasties local, their divisions patriotic and not, as they had been 100 years before, religious. With the Seven Years' War, their rivalries had become worldwide, battles in India or America having the same significance as those fought on Continental fields or across the waters of the Atlantic. This developing identity may have received an increased urgency from the rise in population: between 1600 and 1800, the number of Europeans doubled, to double again in the centnry that followed. The slave trade, on the one hand, and new agricultural and industrial methods on the other, were between them bringing Europe greatly increased wealth; Britain especially was achieving an unprecedented strength. It was natural for her, and for her nearest rivals, to search for arenas where this wealth might be used and this strength tried. Africa seemed to provide one.

The great empires that had one after the other given a certain homogeneity to West African politics and commerce were making way for a number of smaller kingdoms and conglomerations. Raiders from the north, unrestrained by a weak Moroccan suzerainty, were spreading their own kind of anarchy. The front against the interloper had, therefore, greatly weakened. At the same time, these new conditions made trade for the traditional merchants much more difficult than it had been. Thus the barriers against European expansion from the coast had been crumbling to some extent throughout the second half of the eighteenth century. (Within a couple of decades or so of its end, moreover, quinine would have broken through the barricades of fever.) Meanwhile, the image that Europeans had of Africa had also been changing; it was, among other things, coming into much sharper focus. The trade figures make the point statistically, for, by the beginning of the French wars, exports from Britain to Africa were six or eight times greater than in 1720. Northern English textile manufacturers discovered the African trade, as did their gunsmith colleagues in the Midlands (though Leo Africanus writes as early as 1513 of a handsome pistol that he saw being presented to the sultan of Bulala). The merchants who were growing wealthy with the new wealth of the Atlantic ports were also becoming more and more interested in exporting to this hitherto mysterious continent.

Men of this new middle class, consciously thrusting and energetic, many of them self-made on a pattern that the nineteenth century would copy and extend, were not to be put off by tales about the impenetrability of the African interior. They were becoming used to regarding the world as their market-place and had begun to think no area so obdurate or remote that it might withstand their intention to penetrate it. Their interest, based on commercial ambition, here coincided with a purer stream—travel and exploration were beginning to engage the stay-at-home curiosity of the increasing numbers of literate middlebrows. To satisfy this readership, a large variety of books and periodicals disseminated information of differing reliability about many parts of the world—Africa among them. Accounts of faraway places by travellers such as Cook and Bruce were adding to the romanticism of voyaging the precise practicalities of science—a combination irresistible to the strained seriousness of the new commercial classes. The world was full of wonders, of incredible animals, magnificent plants, and people of an almost incomprehensible variety. As the light of Western curiosity shone more and more brightly about the world, making "real" what had in the past been the possession of only the people who lived there, the darkness that was inner Africa became increasingly noticeable, increasingly anomalous.

Meanwhile, the ancient institution of slavery and the political struggles that were beginning to be fought over it also were focusing clearer attention on the continent that was the home of slaves. Blacks were no longer a real novelty in England—there were 10,000 slaves in the country by 1770. Two years later, the courts decided that slavery in England was illegal, a judgement indicative of changing attitudes. Before another twenty years had passed, the attack on the whole appalling business had sharpened, with a Quaker nucleus, weighted by such public men as Wilberforce, forming a crusading group that did not take long to mobilise liberal opinion. Suddenly, in speech, sermon, pamphlet and Parliamentary debate, Africa had become the subject of the day. And still, despite everything, the European ignorance about most of the continent's interior, its peoples and countries, its mountains, forests and rivers, its present condition and its potential for development, remained almost unaltered. It was a situation that had to be put right. Among those determined to see to this was the body known as the African Association, one of those busy conglomerations of amateurs which have so often sponsored action among the British, or have stung governments into sponsoring it for them. Among the earliest of those whom they sent into Africa to disentangle the mysteries surrounding the river Niger was a tall young Scottish medical man, personable, intelligent and resourceful, already with experience of travel as a ship's doctor and anxious to make his reputation. His name was Mungo Park.

PART I

THE SOLITARY QUEST

MEDINA, CAPITAL OF WULI.

Chapter One

Preparations for a Journey

Mungo Park was a Lowland Scot, a man of the Borders. Later, fashionable London was to find him dull, but he had learned taciturnity early, and in an accomplished school. His people were hard, they understood land and weather, their concern was for their own survival and the survival of their crops and flocks. His father was an upland farmer, holding several hundred acres of sloping pastureland from the Duke of Buccleuch, the land rising from the undramatic but beautiful banks of the river Yarrow. The farm was named Foulshiels and stood not very far from the town of Selkirk. There Park was born, on 10 September 1771.

His father, also called Mungo, seems to have been sober, industrious and by no means poor. In 1757 he had a brush with the law, but this was probably a political matter, a consequence of the turbulence still afflicting Scotland in the wake of the Jacobite storms of 1745. Eleven years before the birth of his son he was able to lend the borough of Selkirk a fairly substantial sum of money, so he was clearly not only a man of some small wealth, but also a man of some standing. It is no surprise, therefore, that he made sure that those of his children who survived infancy—eight of the thirteen born—should have a thorough early schooling. Mungo was the third son of the house, and the seventh child, which means that he passed a by no means solitary youth. His father, however, fifty years old when he married a girl half his age, may well have been a somewhat forbidding figure to a young boy. In any case, the private tutor the elder Mungo Park engaged—whether on his own or as part of a hard-headed consortium of ambitious parents is not quite clear—saw to the younger Mungo's education as to that of the other children. Showing by the work he did that he might benefit from the move, the boy was sent out into the more competitive atmosphere of Selkirk Grammar School.

He responded well to school. He worked hard, his determination already clear, and was soon installed at the head of his age group. Encouraged by this, his parents began to see in him material for the ministry. Mungo himself, whether looking within himself or in more practical directions, did not agree.

His eldest brother, Adam, had studied medicine and worked for a while for the East India Company. Later, he had made his home in Gravesend, but it may be that already the idea of travel, those half-legendary coasts and islands where "John Company" traded, had helped to structure Mungo Park's ambitions. He too, he said, would study medicine. Already somewhat withdrawn, he walked often, stepping alone over those low, solitary hills. He read and heard with great avidity the tales, poems and ballads of the Border, and mixed with these a handful of novels. It is clear that he was imaginative, able to spin for himself some universe alternative to the mundane one that he inhabited. Outwardly, however, he seems to have been cold and reserved; it is unlikely that with such a temperament, with his record as a hard worker and avid reader and his place at the head of the class, he can ever have been very popular with his schoolmates. Despite this slightly precocious gravity, however, which might well have been designed for the manse and the reproving sermon, he resisted his parents' pressure and clung to his decision.

He seems to have held other ambitions, however, secretly arrived at and shyly maintained. In his biography of Park, Lewis Grassic Gibbons tells of a day when the farm servant, sweeping up among other rubbish the leaves of a fallen book, was reproved by young Mungo. "You're destroying the book!" he cried.

Unmoved, she made some gesture of indifference, some remark about their only being the work of a writer hardly worth considering. "Aye," said Mungo, "you or somebody else will one day be sweeping up my book leaves and saying, 'They're only old Mungo Park's'."

It was left to his mother to puncture the effect of this self-dramatising response. "You poor useless thing, do you think you will ever write books?" It is likely that after this, if he still clung to literary ambitions, he kept his own counsel about them.

When he was fifteen he moved to Selkirk, settling into the house of surgeon Thomas Anderson, who took him as his apprentice. From time to time he continued working at the Grammar School, but in 1789 he went up to Edinburgh University to continue his medical studies there. It was in this year, too, that he made a tour of the Highlands with a man whose contacts in London would utterly transform his life—his brother-in-law, James Dickson. Now a botanist of some distinction, Dickson had come out of poverty and risen above the drawbacks of an inadequate early education. As a boy he had worked in the gardens of the great house at Traquair, the Border village where he was born, but when still very young he made the long journey of ambition south. He soon found work as a gardener in a large Hammersmith nursery, and while there was noticed by Sir Joseph Banks. This was the beginning of a connection that was to prove crucial for his own career—and for that of Mungo Park. Because Sir Joseph was a very important man indeed.

Educated at both Eton and Harrow, and subsequently at Oxford, Banks seems at the age of fourteen to have undergone an almost mystical conversion to the subject of botany. It was as a botanist that he travelled on Cook's first voyage, he himself having fitted out his ship, the *Endeavour*. Surviving the severe cold at Cape Horn, a mishap when his ship went aground on the Great Barrier Reef, and a fever epidemic that killed thirty of those who were with him, he returned with a reputation as an explorer and as a meticulously scientific observer. This he was to extend by his lifelong patronage of travellers and scientists.

In 1778 Sir Joseph became President of the Royal Society, a position that allowed full scope for both his generosity and his often autocratic, not to say irascible, temperament. Indeed, his reforms at the Society, involving as they did his gathering of more power into the presidential hands, threatened to split that theoretically equable and rational body; enlightened despotism carried the day, however, and, despite a number of resignations, Banks remained enshrined in authority until his death in 1820. He was a man of great ambition, much of it expressed in his single-minded patriotism, and had wide influence and swift perception. Those whom he befriended, or whose careers he decided to further, soon came to realise the very practical value of his support.

Since Banks's passion for botany easily transcended any barriers of class, he and the young Scottish gardener, Dickson, often spoke together when they met among the seedlings and potting-sheds of a still-rural Hammersmith. After Dickson had worked as a gardener in the grounds of several of London's big houses, he set himself up in business on his own, as a seedsman. This, however, only guaranteed his income; it was botany that had by now seized his interest. His friendship with Banks developed, this energetic knight becoming, in a way, his patron. It was through using Banks's library that Dickson was able to study the theoretical basis of the practice that he had always undertaken so well. As a result, he soon became a botanist with a considerable reputation: he was a founder-member and Fellow of the Linnaean Society, and later became Vice-President of the Horticultural Society. In the most important of his several works, he was able to describe for the first time over 400 British plants. It was presumably while collecting specimens in the Border country that he met the Park family; in any case, although a widower by no means young, he eventually married Park's sister and, during that first student summer, took Mungo with him as he travelled, and searched, and minutely described, among the cloud-dappled wildernesses of northern Scotland.

It is not quite clear what degree, if any, Park took at the end of his three sessions at Edinburgh University. Doubts have been expressed whether he was in fact fully qualified when he arrived in London in 1791—there is certainly a curious absence of medical expertise in his accounts of his travels. However, he was later to practise and it is likely that he knew as much as the contemporary state of medicine made necessary. Certainly it was as a surgeon that he offered himself to the world, and as such, doubtless, that James Dickson presented him to Sir Joseph Banks. That benevolent spider manipulated one strand in the intricacy of his worldwide web and, early in 1792, Mungo Park was installed as assistant surgeon on the *Worcester*, an East Indiaman bound for Sumatra.

At this time he clearly felt he was on his way towards making some sort of mark in the world, yet striving to temper ambition with the modesty that seemed decent to a devout Lowland Scot. In January he wrote to Alexander, the son of his old master, Dr Anderson, "I have now got upon the first step of the stair of ambition. Here's a figure of it. [A hasty little drawing of a step-ladder illustrates his point, a small figure standing on its lowest step.] It very nearly resembles one of Gordon's traps which he uses in the library. Now, if I should run up the stair, you see the consequence. I must either be mortified by seeing I can get no further, or, by taking an airy step, knock my brains out against the folio of some succeeding author. May I use my little advantage in height to enable me to perform the office of watchman to the rest of mankind, and call to them, 'Take care, sirs! Don't look too high, or you'll break your legs on that stool. Open your eyes; you are going straight for that fire.' "

After reaching a sort of crescendo of self-congratulation—"Passed at Surgeons' Hall! Associate of the Linnaean Society!"—he drew back into a more sedate attitude of pious humility: "The melancholy, who complain of the short-ness of human life, and the voluptuous, who think the present only their own, strive to fill up every moment with sensual enjoyment; but the man whose soul has been enlightened by his Creator, and enabled, though dimly, to discern the wonders of salvation, will look upon the joys and afflictions of this life as equally the tokens of Divine love." A little more in this vein precedes the afterthought, "I sail in about a month." Nowadays, such sentiments are no longer expressed and we look with suspicion on those, even in the past, who have so unself-consciously voiced them. We struggle to understand them, for all the plainness of their speaking, but something eludes us—the straightforward, undefensive simplicity of their faith. Later, when he wrote about his travels, Park made no great mention of his religion, yet there is no doubt that, like his patriotism, it permeated his ideas, his view of the world, his character.

There is, nevertheless, an unpleasantly sententious note in his last letter to Alexander, written just before he sailed. It is almost as if, though he had refused to go into the ministry, he was loath to give up the luxury of preaching—though that too was a delight that almost everyone who could put pen to paper allowed himself at one time or another. "I have now reached that height," he wrote, "that I can behold the tumults of nations with indifference, confident that the reins of events are in our Father's hands. . . . I wish you may be able to look upon the day of your departure with the same resignation that I do on mine. My hope is now approaching to a certainty. If I be deceived, may God alone put me right, for I would rather die in the delusion than wake to all the joys of earth. May the Holy Spirit dwell for ever in your heart, my dear friend, and if I never see my native land again, may I rather see the green sod on your grave than see you anything but a Christian." One hopes that the young medical student in faraway Edinburgh, thus addressed by his father's ex-apprentice, had the humour to smile.

So the *Worcester* left, and for a year Park discovered the long tedium and occasional excitements of world travel. As reading for the voyage, he took with him Dugald Stewart's *Philosophy*, a choice of book that suggests that his reputation while at Edinburgh University for delighting in solemn literature was fairly earned. He also remembered his connection with the Linnaean Society; when he returned, early in 1793, he brought with him detailed descriptions of eight fish new to the West. He gave a paper on them at the Society, and in volume 3 of its *Transactions* the paper was published. One may imagine the struggle between exuberance and Christian indifference that its appearance induced in him.

By then, however, much had changed for him. For Mungo Park was known to Sir Joseph Banks, had in some measure been picked out by him; and Sir Joseph Banks was the leading light in the African Association. This powerful grouping of energetic men had arisen almost by chance, but it played so decisive a role in Mungo Park's life that it is now necessary to give its history some further attention. It had been started in 1788, when twelve gentlemen, members of the Saturday's Club—a regular gathering of diners of the sort then common in London—decided to give their meetings a more romantic purpose than a prosaic, if convivial, weekly meal. Early in June of that year they formed the Association for Promoting the Discovery of the Interior Parts of Africa. From the beginning its most important member was Sir Joseph Banks, whose position at the very centre of the intellectual and scientific ferment that Britain's, and Europe's, new wealth and power had so energetically stirred up made it certain that, even if he had not been a founder-member of the African Association, he would in some manner have been co-opted.

Henry Beaufoy, a Member of Parliament, and as a Quaker an opponent of slavery, became Secretary of the new Association; among the rest were members of the landed aristocracy, military men, administrators, men who had served in various arms of government with some distinction, one or two of the increasingly important professional class—a lawyer, a doctor—and the Bishop of Llandaff, a polymath of free-ranging intellect and undogmatic views. All were united in their liberal opinions and in the breadth of their interests; all were noted for their opposition to slavery and to the coercive war against the American colonists; all took a keen interest in the intellectual, and especially the scientific, notions of their day.

In deciding how to give their fascination with Africa its best expression, they had before them the recent example of James Bruce, a Scotsman who had once been destined for the church, but had instead opted for a more unsettled life, being at times a merchant, for a while British consul among the corsairs of Algiers, but all the time a traveller. At well over six feet tall and with a character of vigorous firmness, he had travelled to Ethiopia in 1769, almost the first European for 150 years to do so. His medical skill brought him the approbation of the court, which in turn led him to obtain domains of his own, discovering there the source of the Blue Nile and so solving at least one minor mystery in the continuing puzzle of the Nile's origins. He had returned to Egypt in 1772, to England in 1774; in 1790 he published the lengthy but fascinating account of his travels, thus seconding by his example on the land-mass of Africa what had already been proposed in the sea-voyages of Cook and such French explorers as Bougainville and La Pérouse—that it was individual courage and enterprise that would unlock the dangerous secrets of the globe. For the African Association, the publication of Bruce's five volumes made their own task immediately both more plausible and more fashionable, for, if Bruce had been received on his return with little attention and no honour, his books caused a discernible stir of interest.

That the Association's interest should be focused on West Africa is understandable. Bruce himself (the first volume of his travels was eagerly awaited at the time of the Association's formation) had to some extent opened up the eastern sections of the continent. The north was reasonably well known, while the south, dominated by the safe and heavily-used harbour of Cape Town, had seen a whole clutch of travellers move fitfully inland. Boer farmers, desperate searchers for a bucolic solitude in which to rule their own domains unhampered, had already crossed the Orange river as early as 1760, at least on hunting expeditions. Another fifty years or so would see them press restlessly deeper into the interior, intent on outdistancing British rule and its burdensome directive to abolish slavery.

Meanwhile the land-mass south of the Sahara and north of the Kalahari remained almost totally mysterious, a place from which came, on the one hand, stories of imperial organisation and steady trade, of disciplined armies and peaceful towns; and, on the other, seeping out like the area's own fearful miasmas, rumours of religious sacrifices, cannibalism, feud, revolt, Islamic intransigence, and tyrannous cruelties. More prosaically, there was the mystery of the Niger, and the need to clarify and extend what al-Idris and Leo Africanus (virtually the sole authorities) had said of the region. In short, as Henry Beaufoy's "Plan of the Association" put it, the interior of Africa was "but a wide, extended blank, on which the geographer . . . has traced, with a hesitating hand, a few names of unexplored rivers and of uncertain nations". He went on, "The course of the Niger, the place of its rise and termination, and even its existence as a separate stream, are still undetermined. Nor has our knowledge of the Senegal and Gambia rivers improved upon that of De la Brue [one-time Governor of Senegal] and Moore [an employee from 1730 to 1735 of the Royal African Company]; for though since their time half a century has elapsed, the falls of Felu on the first of these two rivers, and those of Baraconda on the last, are still the limits of discovery."

There followed a series of resolutions: a committee should be chosen and "entrusted with the choice of persons who are to be sent on the discovery of the interior parts of Africa" and any information such persons sent back to London should not be disclosed "except to the members of the Association at large". It was not long before persons began to offer themselves. The first was Simon Lucas, a man who had once been a slave in Morocco, following, as so often, capture by corsairs; later, he had been British vice-consul there. Now, as an interpreter at the Court of St James, he had made a number of useful contacts, one of them the Foreign Minister of Tripoli. As a result, he suggested himself for a trans-Sahara journey beginning in Tripoli, making the Fezzan to the south his final stopping-place before travelling on towards the Niger. The Association having agreed to continue his salary of £80 a year while he was on his hazardous travels, he duly set off.

The other early explorer was an American, John Ledyard, who had sailed on Cook's last voyage and published an unauthorised account of it, and who a little later had set out to cross Siberia on foot. He made his way eastward until beaten by winter and the Czarist militia, who sent him by sledge "through the deserts of the Northern Tartary", as Beaufoy reported, and left him at last "on the borders of the Polish dominions". This seems an extravagantly long journey, but no one appears to have questioned it. "In the midst of poverty", Beaufoy went on, apparently rather taken with the picture he was conjuring up, "covered with rags, infested with the usual accompaniments of such cloathing, worn with continued hardship, exhausted by disease, without friends, without credit, unknown, and full of misery, he found his way to Königsberg." Beaufoy, indeed, was in many ways overcome with Ledyard's accomplishments and person. Sir Joseph Banks had sent the American to see him, and Beaufoy tells us that even before he knew who his visitor was or what he wanted, "I was struck with the manliness of his person, the breadth of his chest, the openness of his countenance, and the inquietude of his eye. I spread the map of Africa before him, and tracing a line from Cairo to Sennar, and from thence westward in the latitude and supposed direction of the Niger, I told him that was the route, by which I was anxious that Africa might, if possible, be explored. He said, he should think himself singularly fortunate to be entrusted with the adventure. I asked him when he would set out? 'Tomorrow morning', was his answer."

Alas, the Association's hopes were not yet, and not by these frail means, to be brought to fruition. "Great was . . . their concern, and severe their disappointment, when letters from Egypt announced to them the melancholy tidings of his death. A bilious complaint . . . had induced him to try the effect of too powerful a dose of the acid vitriol; and the sudden uneasiness and burning pain which followed the incautious draught, impelled him to seek relief from the violent action of the strongest tartar emetic." So perished Ledyard. Lucas, for his part, set off from Tripoli on 1 February 1788, spent a week travelling along the coast for a distance of a hundred miles or so, and then found he could not continue to the Fezzan without a caravan of some 120 camels, which were not to be obtained. His only information of value came, as Ledyard's had done, through hearsay, one of his companions, at one time a factor to the ruler of the Fezzan, having often travelled as far as Bornu at least. This was thin stuff for the waiting Association in London, who must have imagined that a year or so might have brought them more definite news of the Niger and of the West African states. What they learned instead was that Lucas had sailed away from Tripoli, had been tediously confined by quarantine regulations, had arrived in Marseilles and was on his way back to London. On 26 July he was home again; without much exerting itself, the interior of Africa had repulsed the first assault.

There followed much gathering of the scanty information about the lands south of the Sahara, all from men who had never been there, but who had met people who had. British consular officials in North Africa offered the knowledge they had gathered of caravan routes southwards, while in London a Moor named Ben Ali claimed to have visited Timbuctu in his youth and put himself forward as guide and interpreter for any new expedition the Association might plan. Meanwhile, he was prepared to relate all he knew about those mysterious regions and was, as a result, placed on a stand-by salary of three guineas a week. While the Association debated Ben Ali's terms—he wanted £300 for trade goods and a pension of £200 a year after his return—the man himself went missing, as Sir Joseph Banks noted in a hectic paragraph or two. "The Moor is missing Augt 6 1789 Mr. Dodsworth tells me that he has left his Lodgings and cannot be heard of that he had taken nothing with him & from his uneasiness of mind it is to be feared that he had made away with himself." Unsavoury revelations attended this disappearance, for Ben Ali had been "attacked various times by women who come with constables to swear children to him one of whom having no appearance of being with child lately swore she was 4 months gone . . . how is this Consonant with an intention of travelling in our service."

The first two years of the African Association had been, on the whole, frustrating, although, in the *Proceedings* of 1790, Beaufoy put a good face on it by setting out what had been gleaned about those territories upon which no emissary had so far been able to intrude. He wrote about the Niger, "Of this river, which in Arabic is sometimes called Neel il Kibeer, or the Great Nile, and at others, Neel il Abeed, or the Nile of the Negroes, the rise and termination are unknown, but the course is from east to west. So great is the rapidity with which it traverses the empire of Cashna [Katsina], that no vessel can ascend its stream; and such is the want of skill, or such the absence of commercial inducements among the inhabitants of the borders, that even *with* the current, neither vessels nor boats are seen to navigate." Despite his lack of information about the Niger, however, some of Beaufoy's painstaking collation of such facts as were available did both codify and increase what was known of Bornu and the other states on the southern edges of the Sahara.

In his "Conclusions", he painted a rosy picture of the commercial possibilities that lay beyond the successes of exploration: "associations of Englishmen" should set out with caravans "from the highest navigable reaches of the Gambia, or from the settlement which is lately established in Sierra Leone", the consequence of which would be that "countries new to the fabrics of England, and probably inhabited by more than a hundred millions of people, may be opened to her trade". More importantly, these shorter routes would make trading cheaper than it was for the merchants of the Fezzan, whose goods had to cross desert both ways before reaching their outlets to the sea. The English would therefore be able to undercut them and so capture their markets. Climate, he felt, would be no bar to success, for the fact that rivers flowed to the sea on those coasts argued higher, and therefore more temperate, areas further inland; while religion was of little significance south of the Muslim belt, for "in the judgement of the Pagan, the Crescent and the Cross are objects of equal indifference". The gold to be found inland "to an unknown and probably boundless extent" would provide a gratifying recompense for all this effort. As yet, however, exploitation had to wait upon exploration—and that in turn upon the envisaged, but not yet discovered, explorer.

More information became available when Beaufoy met a Moor named Shabeni, from whom the Association first learned of the Hausa. Beaufoy spelled it Housa, set down Shabeni's opinion that it was a kingdom with a capital the size of Cairo, added to this a detailed description of Timbuctu and its ruler and administration, and gave details of a voyage that Shabeni said he had taken from Timbuctu to "Housa". He had travelled by river, and could therefore give a description of the Niger, this section being headed by Beaufoy, "The River Neel or Nile". It describes August floods that lasted ten days and so assured the rice crop. "He always understood that the Nile empties itself in the sea, the salt sea or the great ocean. . . . He saw no river enter the Nile in the course of his voyage. It much resembles the Nile of Egypt, gardens and lands are irrigated from it. Its breadth is various; in some places he thinks it narrower than the Thames at London, in others much wider. . . . Ferry boats are to be had at several villages."

Despite the increase in at least hearsay knowledge, the confusion of names between Niger and Nile, the contradiction of evidence—did people sail on the river or did they not?—the continuing mystery of both source and outflow must all have helped stimulate the Association's irritable curiosity. The time was ripe for someone else to be sent out as their reliable eyes and ears, and in the summer of 1790 they thought they had found him. Major Daniel Houghton, a retired officer, offered his services and at a meeting of a small committee held on 5 July it was resolved "That Major Houghton be requested to take passage for the Gambia by the first vessel which shall sail. . . ."

The Association was influenced in its choice by Houghton's experience; he had eighteen years before been on a mission to Morocco, and after the capture of Gorée from the French had served there for three years as Fort-Major. On the other hand, he was already fifty years old and perhaps rather desperate, a bankrupt with a family to support and no employment to give him the means. The fact that he asked for only £260 as his expenses—his modesty may explain

B

his circumstances—probably had an influence with the committee (only Andrew Stuart, a lawyer, sat with Banks and Beaufoy on this occasion, so there would have been little argument).

Houghton set off early in the autumn of that year, West Africa's dry season, with the Association's instructions in his pocket. He was to search for "a considerable Empire, distinguished by the name of *Houssa*", he was to determine "the Rise, the Course and the Termination of the *Niger*" and he was to try to take a long, close look at "the wealth and population of the city of *Tombuctoo*". In addition, he was given a long questionnaire with which he might plague anyone who possessed the sort of information that the Association was so anxious to learn; the headings are tidy—"Government", "Administration of Justice", "Regulations with respect to Property" and "Revenue of the State" begin the list, with "Manners" following on "Language" and "Musick". The last section of the questionnaire, after that headed "Gold" ("Is any found in the Dominions of Houssa? In what manner is it collected?"), deals with the Niger, and asks plaintively all the questions that so plagued the gentlemen in London.

Houghton reached the mouth of the Gambia in mid-November and there renewed his acquaintanceship with the king of Bara, whom he had met when he was stationed on that coast a dozen years before. He moved inland, to a place named Junkiconda; there, he circumvented a plot against his life devised by the far-sighted mistresses of local traders, who quite properly suspected that his arrival was the portent of dangerous commercial rivalries to come. He swam his pack train across the river to safety and soon reached Medina, the capital of a small country named Wuli. From there, Houghton wrote a letter to his wife: "I am now perfectly safe, and out of all danger. . . . On my arrival here I was received in the most friendly manner by the king and all his people." With his memories of family life to keep his observation sharp, he comments on the abundance of "fowls, sheep, milk, eggs, butter, honey, bullocks, fish and all sorts of game; I am tired with killing them. . . . I wish I could send you only what I have to spare, which would more than supply your family at home."

The contented, almost elegiac, tone, however, undergoes abrupt alteration. "I have met misfortune here," he suddenly announces, as if disaster had struck between full stop and capital letter. In fact, he says, he was in the middle of a report to Beaufoy at the time. Medina had fallen into flame, the noon-day heat having made kindling of the grass thatch, the bamboo-cane roofs. Lit in sequence by a busy wind, a thousand houses—the entire town—burned within an hour and with them the hut in which Houghton lived. A large proportion of his possessions and trade goods turned to ash. He remained eager, nevertheless, to journey on, assured as he had been by the local ruler that he could "travel with his people to Tombuctoo with only a stick in my hand; no one will molest me".

On foot, with two asses to carry the remainder of what he owned, Houghton set out north-eastward, towards the neighbouring kingdom of Bundu. There, the ruler proved less obliging than those he had met hitherto, was not pleased with such gifts as Houghton was able to place before him, and sent him back to the frontier to await the royal pleasure. A prince paid Houghton a visit, if the Association's *Proceedings* are to be believed, "and, to the Major's extreme disappointment, took from him the blue coat in which he hoped to have made his appearance on the day of his introduction to the sultan of Tombuctoo".

Now there were delays: Houghton's guide, a slave trader, was forced by a rice shortage to remain at home to tend his own fields; Houghton made a visit to neighbouring Bambuk, lost his way, was drenched by rain and contracted fever; and, finally, he had to wait at the friendly court of Bambuk while "all business was suspended by the arrival of the annual presents of mead, which the people of Bambouk, at that season of the year, are accustomed to send to their king; and which are always followed by an intemperate festival of several successive days". Not all was loss, however: while waiting, he made yet another arrangement to be guided on to Timbuctu, and at the moment when he sent his dispatch to London, on 24 July 1791, he seemed full of optimism.

This mood was matched by that of his sponsors. "From his poverty, which affords but little temptation for plunder, and from the obvious interest of his guide, whose profit depends on the faithful performance of the contract, he derives an assurance of success." Thus, comfortably, Beaufoy, his certainties flourishing a long way from where the danger was. He continues, in hopeful flattery, "The obstacles he has surmounted, and the dangers he has escaped, appear to have made but little impression on his mind; a natural intrepidity of character, that seems inaccessible to fear, and an easy flow of constitutional good humour, that even the roughest accidents of life have no power to subdue have formed him, in a peculiar degree, for the adventure in which he is engaged; and such is the darkness of his complexion, that he scarcely differs in appearance from the Moors of Barbary, whose dress in travelling he intended to assume."

On 1 September the explorer pencilled a note to Dr Laidley, a Scotsman from Dumfriesshire who was stationed on the river Gambia. "Major Houghton's compliments to Dr. Laidley, is in good health on his way to Tombuctoo, robbed of all his goods by Fenda Bucar's son." Although the name of the place where the note had been written was largely indecipherable—all Laidley could make of it was "Simbing"—it appeared that Houghton was well on his way to Timbuctu. Jubilation in London was, however, cut short by a series of distressing rumours. Trickling out of the interior to the coast, they contradicted each other only about the manner and not about the fact of Houghton's death. Rapacity or dysentery, it hardly mattered which: someone or something had killed him and his body lay under some unmarked tree near an unknown town, his own ambitions and London's hopes in the grave beside him.

The Association drew swift lessons from the failure. "It was stated, on a

former occasion, that he derived an assurance of safety *from his poverty*; but unhappily he had no such security . . . the Major had encumbered himself with an
assortment of bale goods, consisting of linens, scarlet cloth, cutlery, beads, amber
and other merchandize, which presented to the ignorant Negroes such tempta-
tions as savage virtue could not resist." The sanctimonious pomposity of tone
was typical (and would by no means diminish even when those who used it had
deprived "the ignorant Negroes" of both their lands and their independence in
the century to come), but the conclusions drawn from "the melancholy issue
of this unhappy expedition" were interesting. Houghton's failure, the Association felt, "furnishes no proof that the difficulties of proceeding to Tombuctoo,
by way of the Gambia, are insuperable; on the contrary, there is reason to
believe, that a traveller of good temper and conciliating manners, who has nothing with him to tempt rapacity, may expect every assistance from the natives,
and the fullest protection from their chiefs."

While awaiting this ingratiating paragon, however, the Association felt that
the time had come to capitalise on what they had learned and Houghton had
discovered. In May 1792, the members empowered their committee to make
"whatever application to Government they may think advisable for rendering
the late discoveries of Major Houghton effectually serviceable to the Commercial Interests of the Empire". The decision arrived at was that a British official
presence on the Gambia would do much to strengthen the bonds of trade. A
consul in Senegambia was proposed, and a name for the post very soon put
forward—James Willis. Beaufoy wrote to Banks that "his Habits are Commercial . . . his age, to all appearance does not much exceed Thirty—but his
attainments Classical & in some degree Scientific; & his Understanding, as far as
I can judge is of no ordinary Class".

As Beaufoy wrote, however, war was quartering France. Within months,
Danton would rise to his brief, bloody, yet splendid dictatorial power, and the
surge of his defensive campaign would spill into that assault upon the Low
Countries that was to arouse the urgent and traditional suspicions of the British
Government. The French wars, which would drag on for over twenty years,
had begun. Against this background, the Association's concern over trade with
West Africa began to seem increasingly irrelevant. Willis had influential connections, his friend Alexander Brodie being an MP and a close associate of
Henry Dundas, who as Secretary of State was one of William Pitt's most
trusted supporters. It was to Dundas that the Association submitted a paper on
the subject—"A lucrative Commerce" were its first words—and it was from
Dundas and Pitt that they received a response favourable enough to persuade
them to set out detailed plans of their project. They wanted to establish a mud
fort at Fatetenda, and station there a garrison of fifty Europeans "exclusive of a
Surgeon and Surgeons Mate", these to be supported by two 40-ton sloops.
There the consul would be established and, having gained the support of
the king of Bambuk by making him a gift of muskets, would "open communi-

cation between the Niger and the Gambia", a move that would, it was hoped, open up for trade all those gold-rich lands of the interior which undoubtedly lined the Niger's banks.

Willis was appointed on 10 April 1794 and hoped to be installed that winter. With him would travel the latest in the line of adventurous aspirants for the Association's patronage—a young Scottish medical man named Mungo Park. There were, however, delays, for, as Beaufoy wrote to Banks in October, "in times like these . . . it is not easy to excite . . . solicitude for the concern of a Scientific pursuit, however blended with important, though distant, Commercial considerations". Willis "had purchased a vessel, which Park describes admirably suited to the Voyage", but had entrusted to an officer named Barbauld the task of recruiting the detachment of fifty men that was to ensure his honour and safety on the banks of the Gambia. Barbauld, however, proved devious and lax; months passed by, but no detachment formed. Beaufoy fiercely pointed out that, "whether the conduct of Barbauld was to be ascribed to his fear of the African climate, or to the hope that if he Wintered in England, his Captain's Commission might smooth his way to a fortunate matrimonial connection, was to us immaterial". A contractor was put to work and soon rounded up the necessary men; a second ship was purchased, since there were now both troops and supplies to accommodate.

By the summer of 1795, everything was ready; but in West Africa the season was, it had been discovered, more unhealthy than others and a delay was recommended. Final instructions were awaited from the Government, but awaited in vain. Instead, Willis was asked to submit an account of all he had spent. It amounted to £5,816. Early in 1796, his instructions came, given by Dundas; meanwhile, Willis had handed his accounts for scrutiny to Sir Joseph Banks. The Government now wanted him to sail as soon as possible, but Willis had not only the auditing of his accounts to make him hesitate, but also other worries, born of the belligerent times through which Europe was passing. He wanted, he wrote to Dundas, an escort to convoy him to West Africa; "Authentic Intelligence has been lately received that there are three French Privateers which block up the mouth of the Gambia. . . ." Dundas, however, had his eye firmly fixed on money. The Government had spent all it was going to, he said, and anything more than that would have to be provided by the Association.

The African Association was not rich and, even if it had been, Banks was not the man to throw its money about. In 1800 Houghton's widow and children were still being at least partly supported by the Association; he scribbled sourly on an agenda, "I have always been anxious to preserve the funds of the Association intact and keep them free from the Canker worm of over anxious humanity." Now it seemed clear to him and his fellows that the Government was proposing to place a public burden upon private shoulders. "The Institution is supported entirely by the private Subscriptions of Individuals", the Committee pointed out to Dundas. The money was intended to finance "Travel into the unknown Regions of Africa"; to use it "in aid of the expence of Building a Fort at Fatatenda, of paying a Resident Consul, and maintaining a body of Troops" would make the withdrawal of many members very probable. They had recommended the appointment of a consul as a public measure "to enable the Merchants of Great Britain . . . to acquire to themselves, an immense Trade which at present is carried on between the empire of Morocco and the State of Tombuctoo with its Vicinities". War and privateers, however, made travel for both consul and merchants hazardous; perhaps it would be "better for the present to pause a little".

That innocuous little phrase put an end to Willis's ambitions. In February, Dundas annulled his appointment, postponed the voyage and asked for any outstanding money to be paid to the Association. Perhaps their stand had made them seem a deserving case for public charity. In the event, Willis was found to have spent rather more than Dundas had bargained for; the matter tails away into bureaucratic quagmires as miasmic and fatal as any on the Bight of Benin.

And what, meanwhile, of Mungo Park, who was to have sailed with Willis on the first stage of his own attempt on the interior? Long bored with the delays, he had left England in May of the previous year. By the time the Civil Service in London was beginning to set its terrier teeth in the affairs of quondam consul Willis, Park had left the coast three months behind him and was in ragged, desperate captivity in a place he called Benowm. The successor of Ledyard and Houghton was discovering, as they had, that Africa did not suffer strangers gladly.

This transformation from unemployed ship's doctor into African explorer had begun for Park on 23 July 1794. On that day a two-man committee of the African Association—Banks and Beaufoy, naturally—had met at the Thatched House Tavern and passed a resolution: "That Mr. Mungo Park having offered his Services to the Association as a Geographical Missionary to the interior countries of Africa; and appearing to the Committee to be well qualified for the Undertaking, his offer be accepted . . . ."

This choice of "geographical missionary" was by no means a random one, despite the fact that, after Houghton's death, the African Association was once more under all the pressures of being a sponsor without a protégé, an impresario without a virtuoso. Mungo Park had, after all, travelled halfway round the world. He had proved not only that he was able to observe, but also that he could collate and convey the results of his observation. Under Dickson's tutelage he had become no mean botanist. He was young, healthy and unencumbered. Above all, he was known to Sir Joseph Banks. He seemed in many respects the man to fulfil the Association's needs.

At that time, in the summer of 1794, Park's departure for Africa was still tied to the sending out of the unfortunate Willis as British consul in Senegambia, but he was asked "as soon as may be expedient" to travel on to the Niger, there to "ascertain the course, and, if possible, the rise and termination of that River". Park was to receive seven shillings and sixpence a day from 1 August until he set off from the banks of the Gambia, a sum that would then be doubled until "the day of his return to Europe, or to some European settlement, provided the day of his said return shall not exceed Two years from the day of his departure from the Gambia". In addition, £200 would be provided to buy trade goods and other necessities, a sum later increased by £55 when Park was forced to make his way to Africa alone, Willis having been becalmed on the listless oceans of governmental indecision.

Park knew, of course, that Houghton had almost certainly died while undertaking the journey that he himself was now proposing to make, "but this intelligence", he wrote, "instead of deterring me from my purpose, animated me to persist in the offer of my services with the greater solicitude". In order to place his enthusiasm in its right context, one has to realise what the word "Africa" meant during the last decades of the eighteenth century. C. T. Middleton in his *New and Complete System of Geography*, published in 1779, described the continent: "The barrenness in several places, the brutality and savageness of the natives and the ferocity of innumerable wild beasts in most of its countries evince that the rays of the sun are here so fervid and powerful as to dry and burn up the juices of the vegetable and overheat the blood of the animal creation, so that the first is rendered futile and the latter furious." Against this mixture of furnace and ferocity, Mungo Park pitted his scientific curiosity and his native strength. "I had a passionate desire to examine the productions of a country so little known, and to become experimentally acquainted with the modes of life and character of the natives. I knew that I was able to bear fatigue; and I relied on my youth and the strength of my constitution to preserve me from the effects of the climate."

He had been to see his mother, now widowed, during the second half of 1794, but in the months before he sailed he was too busy to return to Scotland. His brother John was in charge of the farm and he must have felt that affairs there were in good hands. In May he travelled down to Portsmouth, and on the 22nd he set sail aboard "the brig *Endeavour*, a small vessel trading to the Gambia for bees-wax and ivory". On 4 June he saw for the first time the reality of Africa, in the distant, floating blue of the mountains above Mogador. On 21 June, the *Endeavour* dropped anchor in the Gambia estuary. One sees Mungo Park at the rail, the bustling sailors about him. He stares across at the dun land, the dark-green trees. Alien cries float across the water. He peers into the distance, trying even now, perhaps, to discern his destiny. He is twenty-four years old and about to construct the meaning of his life.

Chapter Two

Venture into an Unknown World

When Mungo Park first set foot in Africa, on 21 June 1795, it was in sight of the guns—friendly to him—of Fort James Island. The fort had been set up in 1618, the year of George Thompson's expedition, in an attempt by the English to safeguard their traders and establish themselves upon the Gambia. The French, however, had placed a trading post of their own on the estuary's north bank; this, named Albreda, cannot have been far from the township Mungo Park calls Jillifree. (In the late 1950s Richard Owen tried to trace the precise course of Mungo Park's voyages and wrote a book about it, *Saga of the Niger*; he found the ruins of the settlement Park saw near a village named Juffure.) It was there, in the kingdom of Bara, that his ship, the *Endeavour*, first dropped anchor.

Did he, at that moment, give a thought to the skirmishing and cannonading, the forces of war and revolution, tearing at the fabric of the world he had left behind? Or had the sounds of that long violence sunk below the horizons of the Atlantic? It seems unlikely that they would have been easily forgotten, for all that he makes only the slightest reference to them; even here, on the African coast, the local opposition of Albreda and Fort James Island mirrored the major rivalry of the Western world. For over a hundred years (perhaps since the days of the Plantagenets, even of the Conquest), in Europe, India and North America, Britain and France had played out the bloody dramas of their confrontation.

France, of course, was undergoing extraordinary changes. It was only six years since, in his diary for 1789, Louis XVI had entered on 14 July the single, bored word "Nothing"—but that first Bastille Day had radically altered both his condition and that of the whole world. His execution had followed, and the Terror created by the absolutism of a group of virtuous paranoiacs. Now, however, it was eleven months since Robespierre himself had suffered on the guillotine his final political defeat. In another four months, the last of the riots that had since disrupted the country would be put down with a quick burst of artillery fire ordered by a twenty-six-year-old general named Napoleon Bonaparte. From the alliance formed to fight revolutionary France, Prussia had already withdrawn into a sullen neutrality; Austria was about to be crushed in a lightning campaign waged across Italy by this same extraordinary Bonaparte. Only Britain held tenaciously to its old rivalry, steadfast behind its implacable naval power.

It was a Britain that, even without the turmoil of revolution and quite apart from the pressures of war, was also undergoing profound changes. During the previous sixty years a spate of inventions had altered the nature of its industries, especially the manufacture of textiles, and, although in 1790 there were not a thousand Spinning Jennies quivering and clanking in its factories, had already begun to create new wealth, new confidence, new attitudes—wealth, confidence and attitudes that were the indirect causes of Mungo Park's own presence on the Gambia estuary. Meanwhile, some landowners were energetically developing novel methods of agriculture. Despite the protests of the dispossessed, the common lands of England, for centuries the peasants' guarantee of a minimal independence, were being enclosed; only hedges could give farmers anxious to try the new techniques the control they needed over herds and crops. New factories near the coalfields, common lands snatched for private use—under these influences there was beginning that slow movement of population that would end in the establishment of vast industrial cities, the scenes of so much misery and despair in the century to come. It was this disturbed world upon which Mungo Park now turned his back, to fix all his attention on the unknown kingdoms that awaited him, and on the mysterious river that flowed through those as yet unclassified domains.

Gathering information with that omnivorous unconcern for relevance which marks the true traveller, Mungo learned what he could of Bara—of this little state's wealth, its inhabitants' trade in salt, its king's insistence on the £20 duty that every ship, large or small, had to pay upon arrival. Already at this stage he was beginning to discover the energetic importunity of those in small authority, a kind of aggressive begging from which he was to suffer throughout much of his journey. So demanding were those in the train of the local *alqaid*, he tells us, "that traders, in order to get rid of them, are frequently obliged to grant their requests".

Bara, also known by its alternative name of Niumi, may have been established as early as the thirteenth century by Sire Birama Berete, one of the most powerful followers of the legendary Sundjata, founder of the Mali empire. Five centuries later, with its canoes carrying precious salt the 200 miles upriver to the Barraconda Falls and returning laden with, in Mungo Park's words, "Indian corn, cotton cloths, elephants' teeth, small quantities of gold dust, etc.", it was a tidily thriving little kingdom. Soon the *Endeavour*, however, had left behind the long mouth of the estuary and the busy settlements on its banks and was making its way up the slow, mud-brown stream of the Gambia itself. Convoluted mangrove thickets, bloated mudflats, swamps that seemed to stretch away towards the level horizons, heat, probing insects, all rendered almost unendurable by stoppages when the ship had to be towed—during these days Mungo Park must have begun to learn what miasmic portents of disease, what hazards of climate, what dreary monotony of terrain he had been asked to meet and overcome.

There is little that is truly inviting in the area that he was about to cross. Away from the coast, the land is flat, a place of low scrub, sparse grasslands, undistinguished hills, occasional streams, abrupt, inconsequential rocks—all this drying, grey, half desolate, in the months before the rains begin during July. From February onwards, the temperature and the humidity begin to rise, so that the coastal temperature of about 24°C (75°F) met with during December can rise on the inland plain and a few months later by over twenty degrees (i.e. to over 110°F). Between July and October, more than forty inches of rain can fall, and wide uncharted lagoons follow these downpours in many low-lying areas. To the north, however, beyond the river Senegal, the rains are less frequent, less rewarding; the land remains dry, the vegetation struggles, contorted, stunted, for survival. The dry Harmattan wind carries the dusty message of the desert southwards. Further north again, the Sahara brings all but the hardiest life to a stop.

The climate is demanding—even today, fewer than 100,000 Europeans have made a permanent home in West Africa. There are no inland refuges, no hill stations like those to which the sahibs of India could retreat. In the area that faced Mungo Park, there are occasional outcrops of rock, sudden escarpments; the main upland massif is the Futa Jallon, rising to over 4,000 feet, within which well to the surface the meagre beginnings of the region's great rivers. The Niger, like the others, rises here, beginning its enormous semi-circular sweep to the sea, 2,600 miles of islands, rapids, steady flow and near stagnation—all, in Mungo Park's day, mystery to Europeans. Along these rivers, crocodiles feign catalepsy and await their prey, hippopotami slide into the current to take on magisterial grace, birds—over 400 species—scream and scramble, cacophonous in voice and colour.

The *Endeavour* struggled on up the river to "a place of considerable trade" which Mungo Park calls Jonkakonda, but which must have been Joar, the main port of the kingdom of Salum. From there, a message was sent to Dr James Laidley, who was based in a trading post a little way upriver. Mungo Park had an introduction to him from Henry Beaufoy, and a letter of credit on him for £200. Laidley immediately invited Mungo to stay with him during his preparations for his journey, and on 5 July the young explorer arrived at Pisania, the trading post or "factory" where Laidley usually ruled in solitary state, his majestic loneliness now alleviated by "two gentlemen of the name of Ainslie, who were brothers". Mungo Park was now in the domains of the king of Niani (he writes "Yani"), about 100 miles from the coast, and able to establish his base, study the local *lingua franca*, Mandingo, and learn what he could about the lands and peoples that awaited him.

His information came largely from slatees, slave traders who made long journeys into the interior, returning with scuffling lines of slaves for sale on the coast, but what they told him was unreliable and frequently contradictory.

Then, at the end of July, he fell ill, having "imprudently exposed myself to the night dew"; Europeans who stayed in West Africa for any length of time invariably fell ill and often died. If the Black Vomit did not carry them off, the Ague might—both yellow fever and malaria being put down, as such sicknesses had been since before the Middle Ages, to foul air (a hypothesis to which *mal'aria* owes its Italian name). Authorities threw contempt on any idea that the ubiquitous mosquito had any part to play in the dissemination of disease. The land itself was sick, and released miasmatic vapours fatal to the passing stranger. The cures were hit-or-miss, patients recovering more through the body's inherent tendency to right itself than because of any remedies their doctors might suggest. Both blood-letting and the various purgatives pressed upon the suffering were often instruments in their destruction, for they weakened those who relied on them and allowed the fever an easy domination. Laxatives, emetics and Mungo Park's own favourite, liberal doses of calomel, caused more trouble than they cured. It was quinine that was to make the West African traveller at least reasonably secure, but it would be over half a century before Baikie, himself a naval surgeon, proved its value as cure and prophylactic during his arduous voyages along the lower Niger and its attendant streams.

Recovering slowly, Park was struck down again in September. He was young, however, and strong, and used to hardship, and had the companionship of Laidley, whose conversation, he records, "beguiled the tedious hours during that gloomy season, when the rain falls in torrents". Early in October the Gambia rose to its most impressive height, the rain-swollen river rolling past at a level Mungo Park estimates as fifteen feet higher than the normal high water. Then, slowly, this flood began to recede and the imprisoning humidity to diminish; the thunders rolled away southward and did not return. Invigorated, recovering more and more swiftly his earlier strength, he began to make preparations for his journey. On 1 December he wrote to the African Association from Pisania, "You need not be surprised at my long stay in Gambia for I assure you that this is the first opportunity that has presented itself since my arrival. . . ." He mentions his illness, and seems on the whole to be for a line or two a little defensive about not having begun his journey sooner. Because Willis had not arrived, he says, he might have lost the coming cool season as well, "had not Dr. Laidley, who has on every occasion seconded the laudable designs for the Association . . . provided me with two attendants, an horse, two asses, and every thing necessary for the journey."

He goes on to describe his attendants, one of whom "speaks good English, and goes as my interpreter. My terms with him are, ten bars per month [a bar was worth some two shillings in the English money of the period], from the time he leaves Pisania till his return; five bars per month to his wife during his absence; and if he accompanies me as far as Sego, he is to receive the price of two prime slaves on his return. The other is one of Dr. Laidley's own servants; he has always behaved in the most faithful manner, and the Doctor has offered him, as a reward for going with me, his freedom when he returns. A blacksmith and his son likewise accompany us; they have been employed by the Doctor for two years, and are now going to their native town, Jumbo, in the kingdom of Karta.

"With this small but select party, I shall take my departure to-morrow morning from Pisania. It is my intention to travel with as much expedition as possible, till I have crossed the Senegal and got into the kingdom of Casson. I shall then think the most troublesome part of the journey is over, and take the first opportunity of writing to the Association."

Because it was known that the Niger flowed past Timbuctu, away to the north-east, it seemed to Mungo Park and those who had advised him that his best route lay more or less due east from the Gambia. Eventually, he was bound to come across the river he sought. Moving parallel to the region's three great waterways, he would often find himself struggling against the grain of the land as the river-systems carved out their tributary valleys; but to the south lay the mountains of Futa Jallon and the Guinea uplands, to the north not only the dangers of the desert, but also the enmity of the Moors and even, perhaps, of the French. In the event, war would force him to make a detour, a course of action so disastrous in its outcome that it underlined the good sense of his original plan.

On 2 December 1795, then, Mungo Park, upright on his horse, flame-haired as any hero in a Border ballad, finally rode out at the head of his small party, intent on endeavour and success. He tells us nothing of his mood, nothing of fear or expectation. Yet he knew the dangers, having the long silence of Houghton as a warning before him, the memory of recent sickness within him. And he knew the rewards, the excitement and acclaim that awaited him if he should succeed, the patronage and support that he should have for life from the wealthy men who had sponsored him. Reaching for the Niger, he was stretching out into his own future, making perhaps the only effort he would ever be allowed to lay the foundations for an established respect. As a boy, he had dreamed and brooded over poetry—he cannot, still in his early twenties, have been unmoved by excitement, by curiosity, by a vision of himself at the very frontier of the known world, a noviciate to whom mysteries were about to be revealed, an adventurer setting forth upon the sworn quest that offered honour or death as its only alternative rewards. But of all this he says no word.

He had with him the interpreter, named Johnson, and Dr Laidley's servant, a boy named Demba. There was Tami, the blacksmith, returning home, like any other successful migrant craftsman, with the accumulated earnings of years of labour. There were two slave merchants on their way to Bondu and a traveller named Madibu bound for Bambara. "All these men travelled on foot, driving their asses before them", Mungo Park writes, adding with a touch of complacency that they had all "been taught to regard me with great respect, and to consider that their safe return hereafter, to the countries on the Gambia, would depend on my preservation."

A party travelled with them to see them off—Dr Laidley, the Ainsley brothers, various servants and domestics. They all passed the night "at the house of a black woman, who had formerly been the *chère amie* of a white trader named Hewett". She was known, in a respectful way, as Señora, perhaps because this kind of comfortable concubinage was more frequent among Portuguese settlers than among the less urgent English. Mungo Park, writing half a century before the Puritan gloom descended for its glum century over Britain, neither averts his eyes from this relationship nor waxes censorious, but presents it merely as one fact among others.

The next day, at one o'clock, there came the final parting. Laidley's party halted, Mungo Park's went on. Across nearly two centuries one can hear a determined cheerfulness, breezy farewells, perhaps a last joke or two called across a widening gap. Then even these sparse trees, these dusty woodlands, hid the two parties from each other. Stretching away to the east lay the rolling miles of Africa; facing them, still at their very edge, was Mungo Park, travelling with "provisions for two days; a small assortment of beads, amber and tobacco, for the purchase of a fresh supply as I proceeded; a few changes of linen, and other necessary apparel, an umbrella, a pocket sextant, a magnetic compass, and a thermometer; together with two fowling-pieces, two pairs of pistols, and some other small articles".

But what was this Africa that he was now about to penetrate? Its mysteriousness in European eyes was the very condition of his voyage. Yet the fact that so little was known, both within the continent and without, of its long history clearly does not mean that nothing could be known, that it had arrived uneventfully at that stage of development that Park was now about to examine. As a matter of fact, he was to travel into the West African interior at a period of great turmoil, in the aftermath of empire, invasion and collapse. But it is only over the last few decades that scholars have at last been able—or perhaps thought it worthwhile—to piece together the African story.

First in that enormous land-mass had appeared the precursors, the original men. Were they the ancestors of all humanity? Certainly one strain of mankind, if not all, had its genesis in Africa. Probably European Man derives from it; certainly African Man does, the negro, modified by and adapted to his world; the earliest inhabitant. Then, from further east, came (or returned) others, the Hamitic peoples, sweeping out of Asia, breaking further and further up that black shore, wave after wave falling and collapsing, leaving their deposits of culture, organisation and genes. When that storm subsided, negroes still dominated the banks of the Senegal, the Gambia, the upper reaches of the Niger, the banks of the Volta, the many-tongued mouth of the Niger where it drains painfully into the Bight of Benin. Further north, however, the Berber, the Tuareg, taller, narrow-nosed, had settled into domination. Some of these were very dark, but others were fair, straight-haired, almost Nordic—almost, in fact, "like us".

Small wonder, therefore, given the racial theories of the nineteenth century, and of the twentieth century until some fifteen years ago, that those new cultures deposited by the Hamitic invasions were thought by white historians to have been the only true ones in West Africa. (Indeed, the invasions themselves, still only theory, may never really have occurred; the blood-links between the two groupings may be closer than past experts have cared to imagine.) Today, our ideas are changing: we no longer need to postulate a lost or wandering Greek master-craftsman to explain the bronzes of Ife and Benin. Zimbabwe in all its grandeur is now acknowledged (reluctantly and with uneasiness, even in South Africa) as the work of black builders, the product of black culture and black social organisation. The economic roots of European domination have been, if not gnawed away, desiccated by a long and perhaps irreversible drought. The lush conditions of the past will never return, and vanished with them are the self-congratulatory simplicities of domination.

One other factor made a fundamental contribution to the societies and cultures of West Africa. In 639 the Arabs, their new belief in Mohammad stronger even than the swords with which they propagated it, burst out of their sandy peninsula. By 642, they had overrun Tripoli; by 711, despite tenacious Berber resistance, they had swept the length of Africa's northern coast and were beginning their invasion of Spain. For five centuries thereafter the southern parts of Spain were Arab and Muslim; behind them, on the African shore, the new religion took protected root.

Domination of the North African states gave the Arabs domination of the trade routes across the Sahara. Trade had always been a tradition between the people of the north and the negroes who lived south of the Sahara. What the northerners had to offer was salt, mined from the ancient Sahara deposits at Taghaza and Taodenni. The traders of the south brought as payment for it gold, dust taken from the long river banks, from sand spits and shallows: alluvial gold. And then, as for a thousand years to come, they had the people themselves as stock-in-trade—that is, their fellow blacks, negroes, the raw material of the traffic in slaves.

Thus, before the end of the eighth century, the Arabic writer al-Fazari was mentioning the existence of a "land of gold" beyond the desert, a kingdom named Ghana. A hundred years later, al-Yaqubi knew of other kingdoms, including what are most probably Mali (he called it "Mallel") and Kukyia (his "Kawkaw"), later the island capital of the great realm of Songhai. Another century on, and we have al-Mas'udi detailing the method of wordless bartering by which the salt and gold were exchanged, and a little later ibn-Hawqal could describe the trans-Sahara trade from his own experience of it. In the third quarter of the eleventh century, al-Bakri, a geographer who belonged to the intellectual élite that grew up among the Moors of Spain, described the kingdom that had been called Ghana by others, but seems, obscurely, to have had several other names: Akwar, Baghena, Hodh. Desert now covers with its bleak horizontals the pastures where cattle once grazed, but archaeologists have confirmed al-Bakri's description of the twin city where the king had his palace, a city of which one half was surrounded by the sacred groves of animism, and the other enriched by a dozen mosques, monuments to the southward spread of Islam.

Gold was the staple of this kingdom's trade with its northern neighbours, but its wealth also came from a system of import taxes—no small matter when one considers that incoming salt was sometimes exchanged for outgoing gold dust on a weight-for-weight basis. No wonder that the king could afford a standing army of 200,000 men, nor that the state should expand, demand tribute from its neighbours and even attempt to control the Sahara caravan routes by capturing Awdaghost (south of today's Tichitt), a trading centre belonging to the tribe most active in the trans-desert traffic, the Sanhaja.

That such an important kingdom could grow up so early suggests that the processes of civilisation had been continuing south of the Sahara for a long time. Certainly in northern Nigeria the Nok culture, a neolithic society, was working iron in the eighth century BC. It is likely that archaeology around Lake Chad and in the valleys of the Senegal and the Niger, where conditions for the development of agriculture were always good, will discover similar centres of early development. The working of iron, in its turn, suggests established contacts between the Mediterranean coast and these communities of the interior, contacts sufficiently developed to permit cultural diffusion—Carthage was an early African centre for the working of iron.

Contacts of this sort may give a clue to the importance of a kingdom like Ghana, a trading state straddling the north–south route, taxing the *entrepôt* trade and growing rich on the interchange between the products of the agricultural communities to the south of it and the artefact-bearing, salt-carrying merchants from the north. One import from the north that the Ghanaians may well, however, have kept to themselves, was the horse. Because of tsetse-fly and climatic problems, horses are not native to West Africa and even with modern veterinary science stand small chance of surviving there. A thousand years ago, only the repeated import of new stock allowed the rulers south of the Sahara to equip themselves and their soldiers with the horses (and camels), which gave them mobility. It was this mobility that in turn gave them the military edge over their neighbours and so allowed large kingdoms to rise, inflate and flourish.

Ghana's power, however, was to run into a force more powerful than mere self-interest—the ferocity of religious fundamentalism. A Muslim revival, strongly for puritanism and the virtue of the sword, united the Sanhaja. The tide of conquest swept away northwards to overwhelm first Morocco, then Spain, establishing the near-fanatical Almoravid empire in those countries; an early thrust had captured Awdaghost soon ater 1050, and, some thirty years later, one

of the original converts, Abu Bakr ibn 'Umar, ended his campaign by conquer-
ing Ghana itself and taking over its capital. His rule did not last long, but its
effects did. The western trade route to the northern littoral was disrupted,
Ghana itself became prey to slavers from the south, the conquerors' herds destroyed the inhabitants' grazing, the desert began to stretch and sigh and trickle
south, yard by yard, year by year, forcing back the people, shrinking the towns,
destroying the wells, driving out the flocks. The unity of the kingdom broke up;
the Muslim traders moved their headquarters to the north-east, to Walata.

According to Abu Abdullah Mohammad al-Idrisi, who was a grandson of the
emir of Malaga, became a world-famous geographer, and was perhaps an eyewitness of these changes, the capital of a somewhat shrunken Ghana had by the
early twelfth century been transferred to the banks of the Niger, a river that
commerce had turned into the kingdom's principal highway. One can see that
the state that controlled the Niger traffic controlled the flow of trade; with the
western Sahara route disused, shipments loaded or unloaded at Timbuctu and
Gao could be carried along the central and eastern desert routes connecting the
Niger with the Mediterranean countries, while the salt mines at Taghaza and
Taodenni became more immediately accessible. Domination of the Niger clearly
was worth fighting for, and, indeed, became the cause of many struggles; as a
result of these, there arose a new power—the empire of Mali.

There seem to have been states based on the upper Niger before this, strong
communities of the Mandingo (or Mande), still today the most numerous of the
negro peoples of the western savannahs. They are spread between the Senegal
basin and the headwaters of the Niger, a tall people, lean and long-eyed, merchants, traders, people of great commercial acumen. In the mid thirteenth century they forced their way to supremacy, building their middleman empire as
if to fill the vacuum, in the worlds of both commerce and political power,
caused by the collapse of ancient Ghana. Indeed, for the Islamic historians and
chroniclers, Mali and Ghana were continuous, the former following on from the
latter, but both of them Mandingo kingdoms, manifestations of the power
wielded by the black societies of western Africa south of the Sahara.

From the Niger, which Mali now controlled and which carried the trade
it either organised or taxed, the laden caravans passed to and fro, linking the new
empire with countries to the north and north-west, and with the more easterly
states, Tunisia and Egypt, whose prosperity attracted an increasing share of this
commerce. At the same time, the river gave the Mali traders access to the gold
deposits found among the headwaters of the Gambia, the Senegal and the Niger
itself, as well as those to the south, in the region of the upper Volta. Small
wonder that, as the thirteenth century passed, the trading towns on the banks of
the Niger grew greatly in importance: Gao, from which caravans set out in the
direction of Kano, of Bornu, of distant Nubia; Timbuctu, founded by the
Tuaregs as a staging post for their raids south, but now one end of the trading
route with Morocco, Tunis and Tripoli; and Jenne, further south, where the

Two illustrations from John Ogilby's *Africa*. Published at the time of Mungo Park, they give a notion of the state of botanical and zoological knowledge about Africa in the late-eighteenth century. The benign, fanciful animals (below) and the magnificent flowering tree (above) are an extension of European fantasy, as was much of the "knowledge" of Africa of the day.

Another of the illustrations of Mungo Park's travels from Aimé Olivier's *De L'Atlantique Au Niger*. The mysterious scene encapsulates the mystery which enshrouds Mungo Park's life and his death.

Volta gold was loaded on the boats that carried it to the waiting caravans of desert traders.

A hundred years later Mali stretched from the coastal lands between the mouths of the Gambia and the Senegal almost as far east as Sokoto, and from the borders of the Sahara, 150 miles north of Timbuctu, to the headwaters of the Niger. The whole Islamic world was very aware of this black kingdom, rich and powerful, which sent its gold north and east with a sort of canny prodigality. When its king, Mansa Musa, went on *hejaz* in 1324, he is said to have taken with him to Mecca 8,000 slaves, servants and guards. He carried so much gold to Cairo that the metal's value there dropped by over 10 per cent. Arab travellers wrote of his army of 100,000, of his wealth, luxury and power. The famous ibn-Battuta, one of the world's first genuine globetrotters, praised the strict justice of Mali's government and the widespread security enjoyed there by both inhabitants and strangers.

By the beginning of the fifteenth century, however, Mali was losing its power. Its size and the heterogeneous nature of its population not only created the conditions for dynastic struggles, but also enabled those engaged in them to find allies enough to turn their disagreements into civil war. At the same time there was conflict between the Muslims and those who had retained older beliefs; the homogeneity of religion could not therefore counter the disruptive effects of these tussles for the succession. The old, extended kingdom fell into parts. In the west, the non-Muslims inhabiting the Senegal valley claimed their independence. In the north, Timbuctu was again beset by its original founders, the Tuaregs. From the south, the Mossi of the upper Volta came swarming eagerly northwards, their raiding parties happy to tear at what remained of established wealth and order. More important, the Songhai now broke away, anxious to re-establish their own ancient kingdom.

These people, who still live in large numbers within the great northern arc of the Niger, had had a tradition of independence before their annexation to the Mali empire. Even during the reign of Mansa Musa II, who reigned some fifty years after his magnificent predecessor and namesake, armies were fighting to restore imperial authority east of Gao. By the turn of the fifteenth century, Mali power in the area was shadowy in the extreme—a blow to the empire's declining economy, for it was Songhai boatmen who carried its river trade. As the Tuaregs pushed south out of the desert and began to put that pressure on Timbuctu that would result at last in its capture, so the last vestiges of Mali strength were diverted. The Songhai kingdom was free to develop its own powerful autonomy.

By the middle of the fifteenth century, the Songhai were expanding; during the second half of the century, the expansion turned kingdom into empire as Ali the Great, who reigned until 1492, captured first Timbuctu and then Jenne. From then on Songhai pressed harder and harder upon the remnants of Mali greatness, forcing that state back to the south-east, until the concentration of its greatest power lay along the upper reaches of the Senegal and the Niger. But, for two centuries after it had been pushed out of the more northerly territories, it still retained its structure and its force. Indeed, its very defeat may have contributed to its survival, for in its new position it was cushioned from the dangers soon to threaten from the north.

Meanwhile it was a Mande, Askia Muhammad, who, after forcing the great Ali's son, Baro, off the throne, consolidated the Songhai dominions. The Mande rather than the Songhai provided the merchant and administrative classes, and it was natural that they should assume rulership. Gao, however, remained their centre and from it they drove back all threats from north and south, at the same time establishing dominance in some of the Hausa states to the east. The Songhai themselves, however, were less certain than the Mande of the latter's fitness to rule; in 1528 Muhammad was deposed, the beginning of a period of near-anarchy, of the rise and fall of rulers, claimants and usurpers, of a cacophony of rebellion and restoration, at each turn of which the dichotomy of the state, its division between Muslim Mande and animist Songhai, became deeper and more damaging.

Further to the east lay Bornu, recovering from a similar period of instability and civil strife; the smaller state of Katsina; and the southerly Kano, from which Katsina was struggling to be free. Succeeding too well, it briefly found itself paying tribute to Songhai instead, but a brisk cavalry action against a Songhai force late in the sixteenth century seems to have ended all talk of Katsina dependency. Meanwhile Kano itself, once a great centre of Islamic culture, was suffering in rather the same way as Songhai, with rulers tumbling into death or exile, until in 1528 Muhammad Zaki established dynastic stability.

All these states, so mysterious to European eyes, countries of dream and rumour inhabited by myths, were already well known in Islam. The Ottoman empire had contacts with their leaders; traders from as far away as Iraq found their profitable way to them; their scholars, holy men and kings made intermittent but noticeable appearances on the central stages of the Muslim world. The river Niger, the very existence of which was at times doubted by European geographers, had long been the creator of, the highway to, markets that drew merchants from all over northern Africa and the Near East. Its convenient course carried wealth, knowledge and the new religion across the width of western Africa; the towns and cities on its banks were interchange points between two worlds, marked by cartographers, noted by historians, exploited by merchants, in a commerce veiled from and almost totally ignored by a Europe busy about its very different voracity.

In 1591, the Songhai empire fell. Its boundaries had pushed northwards, over the edges of the Sahara, and had engulfed the salt-mines of Taghaza. But the foundations of trans-Sahara trade lay in the *exchange* of gold and salt; like Ghana earlier, Songhai, by controlling access to both, threatened that trade's continuance. Its mistake was to take up this posture of great power at a time when internal dissension had in reality weakened it. Like a giant who has out-grown his strength, it proved unable to withstand the first assault. To be fair, the 4,000-strong Moroccan army that crossed the desert to challenge the forces of Songhai had learned its tactics and its use of the new, fearsome firearms in sophisticated wars with Turks and Spaniards. Discipline and modern tactics, and the leadership of a young Spaniard known to the Moroccans as Jodar Pasha, kept the column in good heart during its two-month march to the Niger. Composed in part of Spanish mercenaries, it was professional and proficient. On 12 March 1591 it faced near Tondibi a Songhai army ten times its own size. Calmly it formed up with its back to the Niger, watching and waiting as the Songhai drove cattle like a living barricade before them, then suddenly unleash-ing the flash and stabbing flame, the roar, the coiling smoke and swift projectiles of modern war. Broken, the Songhai forces fled, the end of the battle so speedy and so decisive that comparatively few on either side were hurt.

There followed two decades of guerrilla warfare, two decades during which the Moroccans controlled the riverside cities and the Songhai fought them with ambush and sudden raid in the countryside. The Niger traffic dwindled. Gold no longer found its way to Jenne, Timbuctu and Gao. The caravan routes to the north, which the Moroccans had come all this way to defend, fell into disuse. As a result of defeat and the drying-up of wealth, the central power of the Songhai administration disappeared. The Tuaregs, pouncing on weakness like all nomad raiders, came whirling in from the desert to tear away what riches still remained. The story that had begun with Ghana and continued with Mali and then Songhai had effectively come to an end.

Parallel with this new condition of anarchy, in which the rise and fall of small kingdoms took the place of the growth and decline of large empires, there came a reduction in the importance of the trans-Sahara trade. Europe, Portugal in the van, had for two centuries been establishing its forts and trading posts on the West African coast. As these gained in importance during the seventeenth and eighteenth centuries, so the current of trade began to run in a wholly new direction. It was from the coast in the south and not from the desert in the north that desirable artefacts now made their way to the rich communities spread east and west of the Niger curve; it was to that coast that gold and, increasingly, slaves were sent to pay for these artefacts. Thus the economic base upon which the previous powers had been able to build was crumbling; no empire the size of Mali would ever again be able to sustain itself on wealth derived from trade between the Sahara and the Niger.

The dominion established by the Moroccans, overcome by the difficulties of communication posed by such distances and such terrain—it took six months for a local governor on the Niger to have his most elementary orders confirmed from Marrakesh—began to collapse within thirty years of its establishment. Local rulers vied with each other, struggled for power, for some semblance of permanence, then were overwhelmed, discarded. Some called in the Tuaregs to aid them, which often proved a self-defeating device. Office was usurped, taken back by force or treachery, usurped a second time. The administration's wealth depended upon trade, yet the rivalries of rulership weakened resolution and diverted force. In the vacuum left, brigands, robbers and river-pirates went merrily about their work, the turmoil they caused compounded by rebellion and political upheaval. Spasmodic expeditions to restore order only increased the general confusion. Such expeditions, like the internecine and dynastic battles, often brought employment to Arab, Berber, Tuareg and Bambaran mercenaries, who then, in their turn, released from contract, turned to pillage and rapine as a simple solution to their economic problems. By the middle of the eighteenth century, administrative structure had almost wholly collapsed; after 1737, when the forces of what was left of government were defeated by the Tadmakkat Tuaregs, the whole area of the middle Niger lay open and defenceless to these marauders, a people who since the beginning of memory, it seemed, had supplemented the bleakness of a desert living by the rich pickings of trade-route robbery.

Meanwhile, further south, a largely Bambaran state was coming into existence around Segu. The Bambara were a pastoral people, cultivators; Mande traders gave their community a commercial stiffening; a ruling dynasty in part Fulani—those strange, long-headed people of Hamitic physique and negro language—presided over a close-knit society, based on clan-clusters joined into village communities. During the eighteenth century, however, the unity of this small state was threatened by religious differences, Muslim traders beginning to feel themselves somewhat superior to the animist farmers and peasants.

The rise of a Bambaran ruler named Mamari, a man of both power and perception, led to the establishment of a personal tyranny that considerably altered the political situation on the upper reaches of the Niger. Mamari established suzerainty over the neighbouring Somono, a people who lived along the river banks. As a result, the Bambara were able to exploit and tax the continuing Niger trade. It seemed as if a small nucleus of power had been established that would drag the political centre of gravity south from the middle reaches of the river.

In 1755, however, Mamari died. As so often before, in Africa as in every other corner of the world, the passing of a great leader exposed those who followed him to the dangers of power wielded without understanding. Leaders came and went in turbulent succession for over a decade. In 1766, though, Ngolo Diara took power, and with a grimness one may imagine held on to it. Unlike his three predecessors, he avoided assassination; by the time of his death twenty-four years later, Segu was a settled entity with an established dynasty to rule it. His son, Mansong, ruled it for eighteen years, despite early internal struggles and an apparently endless war against his western neighbours of Dedugu, Kaarta, Beledugu and Fuladugu.

The peoples to the west, mainly the Massassi, had long been enemies of Segu, for they had been among those defeated and driven away by the great Mamari. After Ngolo died in 1790, they took the opportunity to destroy the riverside town of Nyamina, careering through its lanes with fire and spearpoint in 1792 and razing it to the ground. Mansong of Segu took four years of warfare to achieve his retaliation—the destruction of Guemu, the capital of Kaarta. That year, 1796, was the first of Mansong's real power, the year in which Segu began really to impose its rule on its neighbours. It was also the year of Mungo Park's struggle to reach the banks of the Niger. For it was this landscape of war and rivalry, varied by the sudden thrusts of Moorish raiders from the north, that Park was entering. These were the dangers and distractions that, unknown to him—unknown to any European—lay across his path as, in that warm African December of 1795, he set out with nervous determination into the woodlands of the Gambia valley.

The violence he was to suffer, the banditry, the insecurity—about all of which he would later write in hard-edged detail—would help to fix Africa in the European mind as a place of savagery and danger, inhabited by the warlike, the bigoted, the simple-minded and the untrustworthy. He himself never saw it in these terms and always paid tribute to the sophistication and generosity of many of the people he met; it was simply that he had arrived at a moment of transition and upheaval. To understand the world he was now entering he would have had to have access to a different literature, a different history, a different tradition. As it was, those vast states, Ghana, Mali and Songhai, with which the Mediterranean countries of Africa had dealt in turn for a thousand years, were hardly even names to him. As far as Mungo Park was concerned, he was engaged on a venture into a hitherto almost impenetrable darkness.

As he rode, he reported later, his thoughts were full of gloom and trepidation. "I had now before me a boundless forest, and a country, the inhabitants of which were strangers to civilised life, and to most of whom a white man was the object of curiosity or plunder." He might have cheered himself with the thought that the forest was not, after all, boundless, nor particularly heavy; as to curiosity, one may point out that few of those he was to meet would regard with anything but astonishment the sight of a man going through so much hardship and travelling such huge distances for nothing more than a glimpse of a river. "I reflected", he goes on with a determined sobriety, "that I had parted from the last European I might probably behold, and perhaps quitted for ever the comforts of Christian society." I fancy there is some glancing over the shoulder at an expectant readership in these sentences, the attitudinising of a man putting on a necessary public face. In any case, whatever melancholy he may have felt was soon dispelled when, three miles later, he was, for the first time of many, waylaid by men purporting to be emissaries of the local chief and demanding that he pay the tax that local law imposed on wayfarers. Four bars of tobacco satisfied them; later encounters of the same sort would not pass off so cheaply.

The next day Park crossed into the neighbouring kingdom of Wuli, another of the former dependencies of Mali founded, according to tradition, by Sire Birama Berete. Indeed, it is Wuli in particular of which this was said, and perhaps it is significant that Mungo Park tells us that the king's name was Jatta, for the fourteenth-century historian ibn-Khaldun begins his chronicle of the kings of Mali with that line's overwhelming founder, the hero who first carved out the Mali empire, Mari-Djata. A supplementary oral tradition gives his name as Sundjata. Wuli's Jatta, therefore, may have claimed this illustrious descent, either by blood (he belonged to the same people, the Malinke) or by the long percolation of a diminishing power. Whether he did or not, he seems to have been friendly and concerned, warning Mungo Park against his proposed journey and pointing, as an awful example, to the fate of Major Houghton. People further east, he thought—since, unlike the sophisticates of Wuli, they had never seen a white man—would murder him as soon as he appeared. Park, of course, was obdurate; no merely local assessment of the risks could now, one supposes, alter the one he had made nor undermine his determination to succeed. Finally, Jatta agreed to appoint a guide who would lead him as far as his country's borders.

That night Mungo Park rested in a small village some three hours' journey from Jatta's small capital, Medina. That had been a place of some thousand houses, protected by a high clay wall, somewhat neglected, and a decrepit wooden fence that the housewives of the town used as a reserve store of firewood. The village, by contrast, was probably no more than a small huddle of low-roofed dwellings set about the beaten earth of a central space. It brought the young Mungo, however, to a curious moment of authority and judgement; a sheep had been killed for his party's evening meal, and now Johnson and one of the slave traders were arguing over which of them should have the horns. The *ad hoc* judge, an instant Solomon, saw division as the answer and awarded the disputants one horn each. Such objects were prized as holders for scraps of paper on which a verse from the Koran had been written; these were believed (as, indeed, they still are) to have great power to protect those who carried them. Mungo Park notes that they were sought after and considered valuable by everyone, irrespective of religion—Muslims and animists both had great faith in their efficacy.

Next day, he noticed another aspect of the local beliefs, and in describing it gave the language a new phrase. For as he writes, he saw "hanging upon a tree, a sort of masquerade habit, made of the bark of trees, which I was told on inquiry belonged to MUMBO JUMBO". This half-embodied spirit apparently was called in to reinforce the husband's authority when his wives, in this polygamous society, disagreed among themselves. He or his nominee dressed up in the robes at nightfall, summoned everyone to the *bentaba*, the place set aside for public meetings (often under a great silk-cotton tree), and after several hours of singing and dancing, pointed out the offender, had her stripped and then beat her with the prescribed rod of this punitive office. With a proper censoriousness, Mungo notes "that the rest of the women are the loudest in their exclamations on this occasion against their unhappy sister. Daylight puts an end to this indecent and unmanly revel." Only until the next time, however—the practice still lingers on today.

Three days later, having exchanged his Wuli guide for two elephant hunters —there had been three, but one absconded with his three bars advance payment —Park marched his companions into the dusty near-desert that lay between Wuli and the neighbouring kingdom of Bundu. This state had been, according to tradition, founded by one of that holy Muslim clan the marabouts. Despite these origins and the strong Muslim influence still to be found among both the people and their laws, by Mungo Park's day the king had reverted to animism— though he retained his Islamic title of Almami. Belief in nature spirits was wide-spread among followers of all religions, however. The men leading Park's party across these borders provide a good example—they were nervous of bandits, but also of other, less concrete dangers, though, despite a night spent in the open air, nothing came ranting out of the bush to threaten them. And per-haps it was the charms these guides repeated, "muttering a few sentences, and spitting upon a stone" at various points along the way, and the strip of cloth they added to the devotional rags that fluttered like inconsequential bunting on a holy tree they passed, that kept them safe.

By now, apparently, Park was beginning to settle into the mood of accept-ance necessary to a traveller in places where his own conventions do not reach. He writes that, "although the African mode of living was at first unpleasant to me, yet I found at length that custom surmounted trifling inconveniences and, made everything palatable and easy". He seems to have set out with few preju-dices about the status of the European as against the African, although under-standably enough he had his own feelings about the absolute nature of Christian truth. The kind of patronising conviction some later travellers laboured under, that they and their kind were representatives and exemplars of the only civilisa-tion worth the name, seems absent from everything he wrote about the people he met. When they were good to him, he records it with gratitude; when they were unpleasant, with an indignation not unmixed with understanding. He makes no blanket judgements, nor allows his feelings on one occasion to carry over to another. It is likely that this freshness of approach, this openness to the actual and not the prejudged value of everyone he met, later helped to save his life. Any man carrying pride—especially unfounded pride—like a banner before him is unlikely to survive long in a world so ferocious as the one that he was about to meet.

Chapter Three

The Almami, the Tunka, Demba Sego and Others

By mid-December, he was on his way to the capital of Bundu. This is said to have been, turn and turn about, in either Boulebané or Koussan, both placed between the Nieriko and Falémé rivers; Mungo Park, however, describes his crossing of the mimosa-flanked, mussel-rich Nieriko and his four-day journey across Bundu to the banks of the Falémé, which he tells us he crossed in order to reach the capital. This, in his account, was called Fattaconda. On the way, he spent one night miserably in a hut with only a little straw for his bedding; he had some compensation the next day, however, when with his eighteenth-century eye he was able to regard with guiltless approbation the women of that country "dressed in a thin French gauze . . . this being a light airy dress, and well calculated to display the shape of their persons, is much esteemed by the ladies". However, these ladies proved so eager and so importunate in demanding the presents that perhaps they felt their beauty deserved—"they tore my cloak, cut the buttons from my boy's clothes, and were proceeding to other outrages"—that he was forced to flee.

On 20 December he reached the Falémé, noticing there lusty fields of a grain that he identifies, with an erudition perhaps borrowed from his brother-in-law (though natural history was, as we have seen, an interest of his), as *Holcus cernuus*. More importantly, he met an old man, *sherif* in a riverside village, who had seen Houghton in the nearby kingdom of Kaarta. In return for this information, which showed that he was still, without really intending it, following his predecessor's route, Mungo Park gave the old man a few sheets of paper, valuable because upon them would be written those potent and comforting verses from the Koran. On the 21st, there came the crossing, west to east, of the clear-watered Falémé; by noon, Mungo was riding into Fattaconda. There, as so often elsewhere, he found shelter in a private house, this the dwelling "of a respectable Slatee"; there was an element of chance about these invitations, for strangers were expected to put themselves on view at the *bentaba* until taken in by someone sufficiently wealthy and hospitable.

He was taken to visit the king, whom to his surprise he found sitting alone under a distant tree. Mungo, no doubt with set ideas about royalty, was a little suspicious about this meeting, but the interpreter guiding him assured him that, to avoid crowds, the king often gave audience in such seclusion. The king listened to his visitor's story; "he asked if I wished to purchase any slaves, or gold: being answered in the negative, he seemed rather surprised". The king, the Almami, asked to see Mungo again that evening; knowing that Houghton had been rather cavalierly treated, the young Scot retained all his original doubts. He was, after all, more than 250 miles from the coast now, and totally in the power of those who ruled the lands he was crossing.

The Almami lived in a complex, labyrinthine palace, a place of corridors and sudden courtyards, of high walls and narrow entrances. He received Mungo Park seated on his mat, and took from him with evident pleasure the presents he had brought—gunpowder, amber, tobacco and, especially, an umbrella. He then became pointedly polite about the fine blue coat his visitor was wearing, finally asking for it outright, and Mungo, remembering that such a "request of an African prince, in his own domains . . . comes little short of a command", reluctantly took it off and laid it at the delighted monarch's feet.

The next morning, the Almami asked Mungo to let a little of his blood, a practice that Africans of the time, like Europeans, considered healthy in itself and efficacious for a vast variety of ailments; the sight of the bared lancet, however, caused him to have second thoughts. Instead, he was led away to meet the dozen or so royal wives, whose banishment to the palace harem had done nothing to diminish their curiosity about such exotic strangers. The young Mungo seems to have had an interesting time as they crowded round him, staring at his pale skin, his clearly defined features, the flame of his hair. His colour, they declared, "was produced when I was an infant, by dipping me in milk; and they insisted that my nose had been pinched every day till it acquired its present unsightly and unnatural conformation". He returned their doubts about his appearance with compliments about theirs; they shooed these away, calling him, in a term that might have floated out of New Orleans, "honey mouth"—but happily giving him presents of honey and of fish before he left. Thus, despite his early suspicions, Mungo Park's stay in Bundu's capital proved pleasant and not too demanding personally or diplomatically; when he left, the Almami presented him with five drachms (just over a quarter of an ounce) of gold.

He now set off in a more or less northerly direction, crossing out of Bundu into the neighbouring kingdom of Kajaaga by night, in order to avoid robbery. Silence, moonlight, the heavy immobility of the forest, the sudden, swiftly moving blacknesses that were jackals or hyenas, all made this march a deeply impressive experience. The party walked in silence, or spoke, when they had to, in whispers; as they progressed, the dawn criss-crossed the sky with light, but they halted for only a short while at a little village, then pressed on through this ominous no-man's-land. It was afternoon before they finally rested, in a town called Joag, well within the frontiers of the new domain.

Kajaaga was a small kingdom lying at the junction of the Falémé with the great Senegal river; historians know it as Goye or Galam. It had since ancient days been one of the primary suppliers of alluvial gold; at the turn of the sixteenth century it had been, with Kaarta, one of the disputed territories between the fading Mali and the ascendant Songhai empires, but may, around that period and because of the general turmoil in western Sudan, have achieved its own independence. The dynasty on the throne there when Mungo Park arrived was of the Soninke people, a branch of the widespread Mandingoes, and had been founded in the seventeenth century by a man named Silman Khassa. His line was known as the Bathily dynasty and he and his successors took their title of Tunka from the Soninke language. It was therefore a country long-established and well rooted at the time when, just before Christmas 1795, Mungo Park crossed its border.

His Christmas Eve entertainment was the revelry his appearance had induced among the inhabitants of a town he names as Dramanet. Great fires were lit, the drums were brought out, the crowds came pouring out of their houses; soon the darkness boomed and crackled with the complex rhythms of African music, the firelight snapped, in sudden, reflected orange, red and yellow, off the glistening skin of dancers, in the glitter of appraising eyes, in the wide gleam of hospitable smiles. Young Mungo, however, professes himself shocked; as always, one knows nothing of his feelings except from his own record of largely conventional reactions, although one remembers that he was young and had been many months alone. (Despite the fact that nothing scandalous about them has percolated down the decades, it may be just possible that Dr Laidley and the Ainsley brothers, like others on that coast, had made arrangements for their own comfort and so provided an example for any passing voyager to copy; certainly the eighteenth century was less squeamish in these matters than the age of Victoria, and West Africa not noted for its high sexual morality; but there is of course not the slightest support for any such speculation.) Thus Mungo writes, with Edinburgh primness, that the dances "consisted more in wanton gestures than in muscular exertion or graceful attitudes. The ladies vied with each other in displaying the most voluptuous movements imaginable." Is there a hint that his disapproval was not completely wholehearted? It does not matter—he was soon to have other matters on his mind.

Men came into town in the small hours, riders, sent from the king, bearing messages of royal irritation. Strangers to Galam were expected to pay tribute to the ruler, to offer presents or pay a tax; Mungo Park had not done so, and as a result he and his and all their baggage were forfeit. He stared at the circle that had formed around him, silent men, each with his musket in his hand. One of these, laden with amulets, was spokesman; they had orders, he said, to take the strangers to the capital, Maana, and the waiting, outraged king. Mungo appeared to agree; the blacksmith, Tami, was in despair, for he was a native of the neighbouring state, Khasson, and the king of Galam, it was said, was on the point of going to war with that country. If the king's men once took him prisoner, therefore, he could see no future for himself but one of poverty and slavery. Mungo now began to temporise, to argue, to apologise, to explain—finally, to pay. He gave away the Almami of Bundu's five drachms of gold, and they were gratefully received; more was wanted, however. Bags were opened, packages broken into, goods and clothing scattered. When the men of Galam at last rode away with the onset of daylight, they carried with them half of what Mungo had brought into the kingdom.

Moneyless, Mungo and his party now faced hunger—and the blacksmith, worse, if he should be discovered as a native of Khasson. In the evening—dinner time on Christmas Day—Park records, there was an instance of that benevolence from an anonymous African which was so often to save him and which he always noticed with a meticulous gratitude. An old woman, a slave with a basket on her head, took pity on his dejection and gave him a few handfuls of the groundnuts she was carrying. "I reflected with pleasure on the conduct of this poor untutored slave. . . . Experience had taught her that hunger was painful, and her own distresses made her commiserate those of others."

He was soon to find himself assistance of a more powerful kind. A dispute of the ruling dynasty, the Bathilys, with their neighbours had brought the nephew of Khasson's king on a soothing embassy to Galam. Curiosity now led him to visit Mungo Park; compassion perhaps, but much more certainly greed and the desire to score a diplomatic point, made him offer the forlorn Scot his protection. By daylight on the morning of 27 December, the prince, named Demba Sego, his retinue, Mungo Park and his companions, thirty people in all, were riding east out of Joag on their way, they hoped, to safety. To make this more certain, the interpreter, Johnson, tied a white chicken as sacrifice to the branches of a sacred tree. Mungo Park is scornful of this, pointing to it as evidence of ineradicable superstition in even such negroes as Johnson, who had spent years of his life in the West Indies and in England. Perhaps this attitude was based on Park's own dour Lowland convictions—had he been a Highlander, full of superstitions of his own, he might have regarded such beliefs with a more tolerant eye. But now, when Johnson described the wood spirits he wanted to propitiate—"powerful . . . beings of a white colour, with long flowing hair"—he laughed at him, "but could not condemn the piety of his motives". No, indeed: the satisfied spirits would, after all, keep him safe too.

The next day they were at Kayes, on the Senegal, where a century later the French would anchor one end of the railway line intended to link this river with the Niger at Bamoko, over 300 miles away. In Mungo Park's day it was a large village divided by the river, here looking "remarkably black and deep". It took two hours to take the attendant horses and asses across to the Khasson side of the river; then Park and Demba Sego embarked in a canoe. It was perhaps an omen of what was to come that on the way the prince's curiosity and, it may be, greed, caused him to stretch out for a tin box belonging to Park; in his eagerness he over-balanced, the canoe capsized, all had to be hauled back to the bank and, soaking wet, begin the crossing a second time.

It is an oddity, which an accident of this sort brings to the attention, that Mungo Park never willingly relinquished his Western clothing. Houghton had worn the flowing robes of the Moors, cool, practical and inconspicuous; many other European explorers were to adopt local costumes in their travels. Not so this young man, who appears never even to have considered it. This seems to demonstrate a somewhat stiff-necked sense of himself—but one so firm, so un-questioned, that it may well have preserved him in the weeks ahead. Clothes may not make the man, but they express him, and it may be that the very lack of pliability, the nice sense of who and what he was, demonstrated by his choice —or his refusal to make a choice—of clothing, prevented later any possibility of self-betrayal, any hint that he might succumb to the overwhelming and dangerous *otherness* of the alien continent into which he had ventured.

No sooner safe than sorry. Within his own borders, Demba Sego relinquished the appearance of a pure compassion and demanded recompense for what he had done. Mungo Park records, "I made no observation upon his conduct, and gave him seven bars of amber, and some tobacco, with which he seemed to be content". And the prince's father, waiting for them, regarded Park with curiosity and not a little suspicion, asking him the reason for his voyage. "I related to him . . . the motives that induced me to explore the country. But he seemed to doubt the truth of what I asserted . . . ." Curiosity about the world is not every-where considered the self-evident virtue it seems to Europeans, conditioned as they are to believe the close observation of externals the only method for approaching truth. The old man had seen only one white man before—from his description it soon became clear that Park was still following on Houghton's trail.

Park was now halted in the little frontier town of Tisi (Teesee in his spelling), living in the high-walled citadel of Demba Sego and his father, the king's brother. He had covered nearly 500 miles since leaving Jillifree. As always, he was observant, interested, picking out the excitements that local life provided— like the trial and public whipping of a priest who had seduced a young wife. The lash "made him roar until the woods resounded with his screams. The sur-rounding multitude, by their hooting and laughing, manifested how much they enjoyed the punishment of the old gallant . . . ." But the times were uneasy, war and predation were in the offing. Demba Sego had borrowed his horse and ridden away to adjust a dispute with a settlement of Moors. Across the river, the men of Galam prepared for war; to the north, the Moors were poised for further raids. Unrecorded by Mungo Park, who mentions few such anniversaries, the year turned; it was now 1796.

From the surrounding countryside, hundreds abruptly descended on the little town; Demba Sego's father had organised supplies to last the people there for a whole year, in case the Moors destroyed the growing crops, and now all that had been sold or given him was being brought within his walls. Everywhere there was singing and the low throbbing of drums, and in the evening these streams of merriment and music coalesced around the *bentaba* into one lake of noise. All night the fires blazed, the dancers swung and shuffled and stamped; the drums held the populace in thrall. And then, for days thereafter, parties of these yokels, not yet returned to their villages, would cluster around their new and monstrous attraction—the white-skinned stranger. Park records "one party giving way to another, as soon as curiosity was gratified".

On 5 January 1796, he found himself on the edge of another historical phenomenon, one that had had the whole of that part of West Africa stirring for some years. Park records an embassy arriving from "Almami Abdulkader, king of Foota Torra", and demanding the conversion of the people of Khasson to Islam; otherwise his country would ally itself with Galam in the coming struggle. Abdul Kader was a marabout (Muslim hermit) who had been handed the kingship of Futa-Toro after a revolution against the previous dynasty, which had ruled since the beginning of the sixteenth century. This had occurred some twenty years before; in the intervening period, Abdul Kader had replaced the old aristocracy with his own friends, helpers and clansmen, so providing himself with a power-base from which to help along the conversion of his neighbours to Islam. Since Futa-Toro was a relatively large state, stretching along the Senegal from the borders of Galam some 300 miles to the sea, people took seriously the requests of its king. When they did not he attacked them, and several of the little countries through which Mungo Park passed had felt, or would feel, the weight of his inspired displeasure. It is no surprise that when he finally died, in 1804, at the age of eighty-four, it should have been in mysterious but violent circumstances. Since another eight years were still to pass before this deliverance, the people of Tisi became somewhat anxious at his embassy's announcement. "Accordingly, one and all publicly offered up eleven prayers, which were considered a sufficient testimony of their having renounced paganism, and embraced the doctrines of the Prophet."

A few days later, Demba Sego returned with Park's horse and all seemed set for the little expedition's departure towards the capital and the king. But the prince's father now demanded travellers' dues from Park, "besides which he expected, he said, some acknowledgement for his kindess towards me". Seven bars of amber and five of tobacco were coldly received by the old man's son and emissary; they were not, he pointed out, what a person in his father's position expected to receive from strangers. His men leaped upon Park's bundles and cases, once again goods and clothes were strewn all about—and once again half of what he owned was taken. The next day, his belongings thus swiftly diminished by three-quarters, he set off again, and that afternoon, with a jubilation of gunfire and a garland of songs, Tami the blacksmith at last reached his native place. Park was moved by the joy with which the family received their kinsman, especially with the delight of his blind mother, who caressed his face and arms with a constant, careful intensity. Watching the two of them, he was filled with the conviction "that whatever difference there is between the Negro and European in the conformation of the nose and the colour of the skin, there is none in the genuine sympathies and characteristic feelings of our common nature".

For twenty-four hours Park remained in that place and among the continuing revelry—he gives no details, merely mentions "feasting and merriment"—and then set off for the capital, Koniakori, which lies some fifty miles east northeast of Kayes. The blacksmith, proving himself a faithful friend, decided to go with him, and together they stopped in a little village, Sulu, just south of Koniakori. Here he called on a trader, Salim Dacauri, a wealthy man who owed Dr Laidley money in the ordinary way of trade, a sum that, in a letter, Laidley asked him to place at Mungo Park's disposal. But there was little time for friendship; news in such countries moves more swiftly than those it tattles of. Within a few hours a party of men had arrived from the king—he was, they said, impatient to see the stranger. There was nothing for it, therefore, but to climb back into the saddle and do as bidden.

The next day, 15 January, the king received his visitor; he was a man of about sixty, seated as always on a ceremonial mat. His name Park gives as Demba Sego Jalla (the Diallo were a Fulani clan powerful further south, which might explain the name), and he was an old man who had gained the affection and respect of his people by keeping his ferocity for the battlefield, where it gained him some success, and by displaying in peacetime a mildness not always characteristic of monarchs in that area at that period (or any monarchs in any period, perhaps). He had given Houghton a white horse, he said, but the unfortunate man had perished at the hands of the Moors, somewhere beyond the land of Kaarta, to the south-east. Park put together a present for the king from the few possessions he had been left, the modesty of the gift not diminishing the royal pleasure at receiving it; Demba Sego Jalla sent him in return a bullock so milk-white that it was considered a particular mark of his esteem.

The whole area, however, was in turmoil, the power battles spreading like the resonance of some explosion as the Moroccan hold on what had been Songhai weakened, loosened, fell away. Not only were Khasson and Galam at loggerheads, the issue complicated by the incursions of Moors on the look-out for small conquests and large loot, but in addition Kaarta, further south, and above all Segu, the land of the Bambara, on the Niger itself, were involved. As we have seen, it was Segu that was the immediate cause of the disturbances in the upper Niger region. In the middle of the eighteenth century, Mamari Kulubali had established its power; his successors, however, proved unable to control the *ton dyon*, a sort of Praetorian Guard he had created. These became the king makers and breakers, one unfortunate monarch surviving in rulership only fifteen days before being assassinated. It was in 1776 that the powerful Ngolo Diara came to the throne and at last stabilised the political and dynastic situations; when he died in 1790, his son, Mansong, succeeded him after a short struggle.

Kaarta lies to the north of Segu, and was then dominated by a sub-clan of the Mande, the Diaware. Between Segu and their lands was the enclave of a different clan, the Massassi, but around the middle of the eighteenth century they fell foul of the great Mamari and were almost wiped out. The remnants of this people then moved away from Segu, for a while lived amicably with the Diaware, then slowly gained ascendancy over them. The king of Kaarta when Mungo Park was in the region, Desse Koro, who had come to that throne almost ten years before, was a Massassi. When, after the death of Ngolo Diara, there was rivalry for the throne of Segu between his two sons, Mansong and his brother, Desse Koro supported the wrong claimant; it was just five years before Park's arrival that Kaarta forces had, during the succession struggles, destroyed the Segu town Nyamina. Now the time was approaching when Mansong, securely enthroned, would take revenge for that ill-judged invasion.

North of Kaarta lay Khasson, and there, at this moment, preparing to begin his journey into this unsuspected maelstrom, waited Mungo Park with his servants, his beasts and his ambition. The king, in his friendly way, sent messengers into Kaarta to discover what the exact situation there was, while Park remained in Sulu and completed his business with Salim Dacauri. His delay brought in its train the usual hazard—a rapacious royal demand made by a peremptory, sharp-eyed prince—but Salim's diplomacy prevented any great loss on this occasion. Until 3 February, Park waited in the merchant's house, observing the wealth and cultivation of this thickly-populated country. He points out that, although the king of Khasson's domains were only small, the royal war drum could mobilise a force of 4,000 fighting men with its insistent, booming demand.

It was on 2 February that the king's messengers returned with the news that the Kaarta–Segu war had not yet broken out, and the next day Mungo Park set out, striking now more directly for the Niger. By the 8th, however, he was meeting ominous crowds of refugees fleeing with what they could carry from the threatened lands further south. A profiteering landlord almost brought him to the point of altercation, but his companions' firm grasp on the reality of their situation persuaded him to compliance. Indeed, the reluctant handing over of his favourite blanket converted the landlord into guide—and not only on the physical plane. In a particularly shadowy place along the road this amulet-hung holy man went through a little ritual—blasts on a whistle, a precisely placed spear on the roadway, a mutter of prayers—and so learned from the ubiquitous spirits that no danger awaited them on their journey. Nightfall on the 11th found them in the deserted, ruined town of Karankalla, a place plundered and destroyed by the Bambarans of Segu some four years earlier.

The next day Park's party, led by the holy landlord, and by the son of a provincial governor who had earlier offered to help them, arrived at the capital, a town named Guemu (or "Kemmoo" in Park's spelling), which was situated south-west of Nioro. It had been established by the present king's father, Sira Bo, some twenty-five years earlier, and Mungo Park describes it as "situated in the middle of an open plain, the country for two miles round being cleared of wood, by great consumption of that article for building and fuel". He was given a hut, large and spacious, for his lodging—and seems to have needed all its size, for he immediately became one of the sights of the capital, something no one should miss. Very soon "I was surrounded by as many as the hut could contain. When the first party, however, had seen me, and asked a few questions, they retired to make room for another company; and in this manner the hut was filled and emptied thirteen different times." Park gives no hint of how he received all this attention, though it is my experience that the ceaseless staring of hordes of people, in a place where one appears an exotic stranger to them but friendless and lonely to oneself, moves one through acquiescence and self-pity to feverish and illogical irritation in a very short time indeed. The young Scot, however, seems to have been both amiable and equable in temperament, and to have made no attempt—doomed in any case—to drive away the curious or to hide himself away.

That evening he was summoned to see the king, whose name he renders, pleasantly, as Daisy Koorabarri. This was that Desse Koro whose ambitions had led him into an erroneous intervention in Segu's dynastic struggles and whose people as a result were now awaiting Bambaran retribution. Park writes that the number of the king's attendants surprised him, as did "the good order that seemed to prevail among them". Men sat on the king's right, women and children on the left; between them passed this lanky emissary of the European spirit, his weather-reddened face and flaming hair doubtless a sensation to those who had not yet bothered to see him in his hut. "The king . . . was not to be distinguished from his subjects by any superiority in point of dress; a bank of earth about two feet high, upon which was spread a leopard's skin, constituted the only mark of royal dignity." Park, seated on the ground before him, explained who he was and what he was doing in that part of the world; Desse Koro said that he wished he could be more helpful, but there was no doubt that, if the young Scot continued on his way, the Bambarans would kill him as a spy, while if he remained in Kaarta he was at risk, might be killed in some accident, and the king would then be blamed for his murder. The best thing, therefore, would be if he returned to Khasson and waited out the war there.

But the rains were coming, and the expedition had so far seen and done nothing of note; Timbuctu was still far away, and even the banks of the Niger had not been reached. Park had no intention of turning back now. Faced with this determination, Desse Koro suggested that he take a different route, roundabout but safer, by way of the frontier town of Jarra and the kingdom of Ludamar beyond. If "Jarra" is Dyara, which lay not far from Nioro, it meant Park's leaving in a north-easterly direction, then swinging round to approach Segu from the north. Dyara had been an independent kingdom for about a century and a half, but in 1754 it fell under the suzerainty of the kings of Kaarta. Beyond it lay the wide horizons of the western Sudan, the many principalities and chief-doms of which were dominated by Moors, Tuaregs and Berbers. One of these was the little state of Ludamar.

Chapter Four

Imprisonment in Ludamar

It was on 13 February 1796—Park not being a man for omens—that the young Scot left Guemu, escorted by three of the king's sons and a party of 200 horsemen. Thus protected, he may have been secure from attack, but robbery was another matter: it was probably some of the escort themselves who broke into his cases on the first night. However, on the 15th all except two of these somewhat dubious helpers turned back, and, guided by the two remaining, Park's company continued. The following night they halted in a town from which, the following day, a large, nervous party were due to ride to Jarra, a much bigger town, to see what refuge they could provide for their vulnerable property and families. The whole region, threatened by the Bambarans from the south and constantly raided by the "Moors"—the Berbers or Tuaregs—from the north, was in a state of anxiety and fear. It was decided that Park and his companions would travel with the larger party the following day, seeking in numbers some protection against the disasters that threatened.

That such disasters were not the mere figments of anxious imaginations Mungo Park learned at two o'clock the following morning. He awoke, startled from comfort by the screams of women, the confused yelling of men, the distant whooping of an unseen enemy, a muffled rolling of hoof beats, the sharp cough of musket fire. Was it the war, the Bambaran army in military array descending upon Kaarta from this unexpected direction? He clambered to the roof of his hut. Beyond the mud walls of the town, dark in the moonlight, white dust rising, a herd of cattle came stampeding towards the nearby wells. Behind them, carolling and shooting, rode five white-robed raiders. The townsfolk, in their hundreds, were running for the ramparts, but once there they stood, staring, pointing, watching with the feverish intensity of the helpless, as the Moors cut out sixteen of their best bullocks. Satisfied, the five brought these stolen beasts round under the very noses of the people—within pistol shot, Park estimates. Four vain shots did blast across the night, the people's only reply to those who had robbed them. Then raiders and cattle were gone, the night closing about them, the dust subsiding above the remaining herd, while all around, doubtless, could be heard the chattering of those who had witnessed this calm brigandage.

Then, suddenly, there came the loud calling of grief; one of the herdsmen had been shot below the knee and was now being brought in, to the lamentation of his mother. To hers, more and more spectators added their own; at last, however, some of them came to Park and asked him to look at the wound. The young man had lost a great deal of blood, the bones of his leg were shattered, he had in Park's opinion only a small chance of surviving. Amputation, Park felt, would give him that chance (though shock killed most of those whom gangrene spared in those days of unsophisticated surgery). The lad's family were horrified—no one had ever heard of such a way of dealing with wounds and accidents. With incredulity Park records that "indeed they evidently considered me as a sort of cannibal for proposing so cruel and unheard of an operation, which in their opinion would be attended with more pain and danger than the wound itself". This is a view that, with hindsight, many of today's experts would endorse. Instead, in his throes the youth was taught Islam's great primary statement, "There is no god but God, and Mahomed is his Prophet", and so died assured of Paradise.

The dangers that beset these borders now necessitated another night march; it was at dawn on 18 February that Park and his companions finally crossed the border into Ludamar. The frontier village was named Simbing—a name that Park had seen on Houghton's final note; and at this point he gives some details of how that unfortunate Irish soldier came to disappear. At Jarra he fell in with some Moorish merchants who persuaded him in some way that his best route lay through Tichitt, ten days' travelling to the north. At some point he became suspicious and asked to return to Jarra, whereupon his guides did what they had probably intended from the beginning, robbed him of all he owned and left him in the desert to perish. He made his way to an oasis named Tarra, and after a while died there—whether murdered or through poverty and hunger, no one seemed certain.

Jarra, Park tells us, was "of considerable extent". Its houses were of stone bound with clay, and those who lived in them were for the most part black Africans paying tribute to their Moorish overlords. It is not clear who these "Moors" actually were, though Park's description of them as "a mixed race between the Moors (properly so called) of the north, and the Negroes of the south" suggests that, if they were not what he thought them, of mixed blood, they were perhaps partly of the Fulani people. What is certain is that the negroes of the area were in fear of them, that they demanded and were paid extortionate tribute, and that what did not come to them in the normal way of oppressive taxation they took by force, like robbers.

Park lodged at the house of a slatee who, like Salim Dacauri, owed money to Laidley. This man, Daman Jumma, willingly paid what he could of the outstanding sum to Park, but the wildness of the times had not been conducive to

trade and the five slaves' worth that Park had been told to expect had dwindled
to two. Park's servants, meanwhile, had come to the end of the road. They stood
in daily danger of being taken and sold into slavery; Park does not mention,
though doubtless he understood, that while they remained in his entourage they
would be both conspicuous and objects of curiosity and suspicion.

It took fourteen days to get the permission of Ali, the local overlord, to
travel across his domains to Segu; five cotton robes may have helped this petty
monarch to make up his mind. Park handed his assembled notes and papers to
Johnson to carry back with him to Pisania, then shed all but essential baggage,
leaving what he did not need in the care of his slatee host. At the last moment,
the boy, Demba, decided to travel on with him after all, a decision he was
doubtless to regret later; on the other hand, he did admit that his expressed desire
to go back had been intended only to put pressure on Park. To those who travelled with him, at any rate, it seemed clear that they had gone as far as normal
circumstances permitted. Further on, they knew, the extraordinary awaited
them, and they had no great ambition to meet it. They had not, of course, come
so far to make this journey as Park had, nor had they anything to gain by making
their stumbling and dangerous way to the banks of yet another water-course.
If they understood Park's eagerness, they certainly did not share it—and whether
they understood it is doubtful. The hope of reward and the tug of loyalty kept
them going, their involvement personal; his inexplicable ambitions, his strange
European passion to see something *for the first time*, must have seemed to them
oddities to be put up with rather than feelings that one should either emulate or
envy.

Three days brought him to a town named Dina, a large place, the houses on
its dusty streets stone-built, as in Jarra. But here there was no longer to be
found the straightforward and fundamentally friendly curiosity displayed by the
people further west. No questions here, a polite examination, a departure to let
in yet another relay of the studious. These now were Muslim lands, there was a
smell of desert in the air, a wind that came wafting from the pious countries to
north and east. The people of this part of the world had felt the edge of fanaticism and revival, they had been Muslim for eight centuries and they knew that
they did not like unbelievers and that they hated Christians. "They assembled
round the hut . . . where I lodged, and treated me with the greatest insolence.
They hissed, they shouted, they abused me; they even spat in my face . . . ."
With a patience almost unnatural in a man so young, Park gave them no pro-
vocation to attack him and ransack his baggage; for the latter, as it turned out,
greed and religion provided their own—the fact that he was a Christian was
enough to justify robbery. "They accordingly opened my bundles, and robbed
me of everything they fancied."

To Park it was clearly time to move on; to those with him, it was as clearly
time to retreat. Without frills he tells us that "I resolved to proceed alone". At
two o'clock the next morning, he did so, marching away across the moonlit

plain, the howling of distant beasts making it, as he puts it, "necessary to proceed with caution".

This avoidance of drama in the narrative, the refusal to give us a hint of his
actual feelings, the matter-of-factness of it all, almost persuades us past this
moment, the first sign of the hard core of his dedication. Yet here he was,
surrounded by hostility, in an unfamiliar environment, hundreds of miles from
anyone he knew, Houghton's death his immediate warning, nevertheless striking out on his own if no one would go with him, taking on the whole continent
single-handed, determined to outface distance, heat, carnivores and the accumulated fanaticism of all Islam.

As it happened, Demba followed him and, after the lad's persuasion, so did
the guide lent him by his host in Jarra. They moved on across the sandy soil as
dawn overtook them, and the day's heat. Around noon Demba investigated a
water-hole, but was driven off by the growling of a lion. They stayed the night
peaceably enough in a small town, then travelled on, eastwards, their path
crossing that of a vast, clattering army of locusts. On that day, 4 March, they
arrived in Sampaka, a town that had been much fought over in the battles between the Bambara and the Moors driving down from the north. The next
night they stopped at a little village, happening on a feast day; led by the
musicians, the people of the place came to where Park was staying, their curiosity this time, however oppressive, remaining good-tempered. The immediate
destination Park now had in mind was the town of Gumba (Kumbi, perhaps,
one-time capital of the ancient empire of Ghana) and, since a party was due
to go there from Sampaka on the following day, he decided to wait the extra
day and leave with them. To avoid the crowds, however, he moved out of the
town itself, to the nearby village of Sami.

Now sheep were killed, the corn liquor was brought out, there was friendship in the air. A few days' march, and the Niger would be before him, its flow
majestic, doubtless, and carrying with it all his hopes and ambitions into a future
of assured success. Abruptly, circumstance ambushed him—"a party of Moors
unexpectedly entered the hut, and dispelled the golden dream". Ali, after all,
had not forgotten him, had sent men after him, had demanded his presence.
If he would not come freely, he would be taken. Park was terror-stricken, perhaps precisely because he had believed himself so safe. The Moors were reassur-
ing, though adamant—it was Ali's wife Fatima who wanted to see him, they
said; once she had satisfied her curiosity, Ali would doubtless set him free. There
was nothing for Park to do but turn his back on hope and the purpose of his
march, and do as the Moorish king had ordered. By 11 March, he was back in
Dina.

There, almost at once, he experienced the half-mad capriciousness of the
seedy aristocrats into whose hands he had now fallen. One of Ali's sons, imagining him a craftsman, perhaps, or an expert simply because he was European,
handed him a double-barrelled gun, told him to dye the stock and mend the lock.

Park said he could not do it, did not know how. With an autocratic illogicality, the prince said, "If you cannot repair a gun, give me some knives and scissors at once!"

Demba, interpreting, pointed out that Park carried none with him. Giving insanity another hitch, the prince grabbed a musket, cocked it, rammed it against the side of Demba's head. Attendants fell on him, wrested aside the barrel, pinioned his arms. At the same time, they signalled frantically at Park and the boy to leave.

That night, Demba tried to escape, but was caught and brought back; they were in truth Ali's prisoners. They travelled the next day through an increasing heat. It was near-desert that now stretched about them, the southern scrubland fringe of the Sahara. Their water ran out; to allay their thirst, they sucked a vegetable gum. At five in the afternoon, they saw the stretched, haphazard tents of Ali's camp, the herds of cattle, goats and camels, the people drawing water in leather buckets from the wells. When, just before sunset, they finally reached it, the people crowded with a sort of furious curiosity about them, pulling at Park's clothing, grabbing his buttons, reaching for his hat.

From all this the king's tent may have seemed a sort of refuge. "Ali was sitting upon a black leather cushion, clipping a few hairs from his upper lip; a female attendant holding up a looking-glass before him. He appeared to be an old man, of the Arab cast, with a long white beard; and he had a sullen and in-dignant aspect." Perhaps because he could not speak Arabic, Ali said little to him; the women, however, peered at him, rattled off questions by the dozen, "inspected every part of my apparel, searched my pockets, and obliged me to unbutton my waistcoat, and display the whiteness of my skin; they even counted my toes and fingers . . . ."

But if this seems pleasantry, more serious trials were soon to begin. There came a snorting, a snuffling, perhaps some laughter; dragged in on ropes by busy boys came a wild hog, evil-eyed, high-smelling. They tied it to a tent-rope and Ali, in sign-language, asked Park to kill and dress it; prudently, he refused. Suddenly, they released the boar, scampered expectantly out of the way, hoping perhaps to see the infidel destroyed. But the untutored hog proved unable to tell Muslim from Christian—humans were all the same to him, and he hated them indiscriminately. Under his unselective attack, the crowd scattered and the brute, sides heaving, crawled at last into what seemed a haven dark enough for safety—the shadowy cave under Ali's low couch.

Probably disappointed in this entertainment, Ali had Park sent to the tent of the chief slave; in the morning, he was housed again, this time in a straw hut that he found both cool and comfortable, but that was made less than desirable by the companion with whom he had to share it—the same furious hog with which he had been faced the night before. Despite its evil temper, it was Park who remained the centre of attention, and not all its attempts to bite those who came close enough could prevent crowds from staring at him, making him show them the white skin of his body and demonstrating the nature and fastenings of his clothes. Not even night brought much relief—Park was awoken by an intruder touching his shoulder. He leaped out of sleep, the man swung about, tripped, fell across the tethered boar. There was a grunt, the ripping of teeth, a high scream cutting across the night; outside, the camp, alarmed, came abruptly to life. Men raced for their camels, thinking Park escaped; among them Ali himself, running from the unexpected, distant tent in which he had been sleeping. (Park observes that "the tyrannical and cruel behaviour of this man made him so jealous of every person around him, that even his own slaves and domestics knew not where he slept".)

The next day followed the same pattern as the one before: "the boys assembled to beat the hog, and the men and women to plague the Christian". And here in the narrative feeling intrudes, a detestation for the people who were so maltreating him. This, one suspects, had its consequences in the preparations that Park made for his second expedition; but that was still years away. Here he confines himself to recording the Moors' "rudeness, ferocity and fanaticism". They could show him no compassion—"I was a *stranger*, I was *unprotected*, and I was a *Christian*"— and their treatment of him had its political justification, for it seemed quite possible that he was a spy. But he called again on a quality that one would have thought was now beginning to run a little dry—his patience. He remained compliant, conciliatory, obedient, in the hope of thus toning down their ferocity; but "from sunrise to sunset was I obliged to suffer, with an unruffled countenance, the insults of the rudest savages on earth".

After a very brief and unsuccessful period as a barber—he was asked to shave the head of a young prince, but "unfortunately made a slight incision in the boy's head"—his captors on the whole left Mungo Park to stew in his captivity. This suited him, "for I had laid it down as a rule, to make myself as useless and insignificant as possible, as the only means of recovering my liberty". In this passive policy of last resort he must have been unhappily confirmed by the unexpected arrival of his interpreter, Johnson, who had been intercepted and brought to Ali's encampment. With him the Moors brought the clothes and other effects that Park had left in the merchant's house in Jarra; Ali searched these and, his greed stimulated and thwarted at the same time by his discovering neither amber nor gold, stacked them away, keeping from his prisoner even a change of clothing. He went further, and now had Park himself forcibly searched, taking from him all he carried; to Ali's doubtless satisfaction, this included the small store of gold and amber that Park had hidden on him. All the Scot now owned were the clothes he wore, and a spare compass, which he had prudently buried in the sand. A corollary of this robbery was Ali's wonder at the needle of Park's pocket compass, which seemed to point unwaveringly towards the Sahara. Park explained—to disguise his own ignorance about the nature of magnetic north—that the needle pointed the way to his mother; if she died, it would direct him to her grave. Concerned at its powerful magical properties, Ali handed the compass back.

All decisions as to what should be done with the prisoner—ideas wavered between cutting off his right hand, putting out his eyes and executing him—were now deferred until the return of Fatima, Ali's wife, who was travelling somewhere far to the north. Fever descended on Park once again, and he became more and more oppressed by the journey that awaited him even if he should get away unscathed from Ali's camp, for the rainy months were almost on him; within weeks, the plains between the desert and the Niger would have become soggy levels of mud under a booming sky and unrelenting downpours. Meanwhile the endless petty demands, the mean-minded, tiny tortures, the half-teasing bullying that he had been exposed to from the beginning continued, rising sometimes to peaks of bored exasperation in his captors, that fury with the helpless that characterises the cruel, during which it seemed that they might kill him out of mere weariness, the mere desperation of a vacant mind.

One evening, however, he found himself faced with an aggressive curiosity of a different kind, a sort of teasing perhaps pleasanter than what he had been used to. A party of women appeared in his hut, determined, it seemed, to discover whether Christians, like Muslims, were circumcised. Astonished, Mungo Park decided to treat the matter as a joke—indeed, it is hard to see what alternatives he had. To resist forcibly might have proved more dangerous than embarrassing; to comply too readily would have risked the jealous intervention of the men. He told them, therefore, "that it was not customary in my country to give ocular demonstration in such cases, before so many beautiful women". Instead, selecting the youngest and prettiest, he agreed to take her, as the representative of the rest, if the others would leave the two of them alone. In the mood that prevailed, this caused no outrage; the women laughed and left. Later, the girl he had selected sent him meal and milk, a gentler supper than he was used to and sign, perhaps, that his tall figure, his clear-cut features and the blue of his eyes had retained their effect despite the miseries of his condition.

He was not finished with female curiosity, however, for a few days later, wrapped in a cloak to disguise the indecency of his tight breeches, he was taken on a round of Ali's consorts, four ladies all "remarkably corpulent, which is considered here the highest mark of beauty". These visits reduced Park to the status of a kind of dancing bear, with the Moors galloping around him, laughing and waving their muskets, "seemingly to display their superior prowess over a miserable captive".

Days passed, long days of depression, of heat so great that bare skin could not feel the breeze without pain, of sudden whirlwinds, lashing the tents, dragging them down at times, flinging the fine sand like smoke into the sky. Early in April, however, with a south-westerly wind, heavy rain fell, portent of the months that lay ahead. In faraway Italy, Napoleon was winning a victory a week against the Austrian armies. Park, with a perhaps Scottish zeal for learning, began to study the Arabic alphabet, asking whoever came to see him to help him as he wrote the characters in the sand—"I discovered that, by engaging their attention in this way, they were not so troublesome as otherwise they would have been". And, around the middle of the month, he found himself with a companion in his hut, a *sherif* who had come to visit Ali. That tyrant, however, had left to seek his Fatima, still lingering in the north, and, while waiting for Ali's return, the *sherif* shared Park's sleeping quarters. With explorer's zeal, the young Scot picked the well-stocked brain of this old man, who spoke both Bambara and Arabic, who had lived in Timbuctu and had travelled in the Hausa lands further east, and who knew the southern Sahara, since he himself came from Oulata. A few days later another *sherif* arrived, Sidi Mahomed Mura Abdalla, bringing salt and coming from even further afield, for his travels had begun in Morocco.

With Ali gone, his servants had no great incentive to look after the prisoners, so all three of them, Demba, Johnson and Park himself, suffered severely from hunger and malnutrition. The fact is that they were not eating enough even when food was being regularly prepared; now, when sometimes forty-eight hours went by between meals, they had no resources left to combat their debility. It must have seemed to them—and to the two servants in particular, with little interest in their surroundings and few resources of education—as though time itself had ended. Lethargy, heat, weakness, monotony, day after day passing in unalterable sequence, one impossible to distinguish from another, the whole blurring into a monstrous, directionless present from which all purpose had been drained: it was a lunatic conundrum to which only death, perhaps, would prove a solution.

The world outside, however, had after all continued to exist throughout these weeks, and now its pressures brought an alteration in their circumstances. The causes lay in the very war that had forced Park to the detour now ending in this captivity. In his own narrative, he attributes the causes of the war to a dispute over cattle, although as we have seen its roots went further back and wound in fairly complex patterns; he is probably more accurate in some of the detail he gives: the embassy sent by Mansong of Segu to Desse Koro telling him that his slaves had better begin to prepare accommodation for the 9,000 Bambarans about to descend on his capital; Mansong's messenger then presenting the king of Kaarta with a pair of iron sandals, and warning him that he would never be safe from Bambaran arrows until he had worn these sandals out in flight. Desse's response was the mobilisation of his army, though it was weakened by the departure of several powerful clans, in Park's account permitted to leave for Khasson and other neighbouring territories by the king, but probably determined to move whatever Desse might command.

Mansong advanced on 22 February; Desse Koro retreated to the hills, taking refuge in a fortified town. His sons refused this cautious method of prosecuting the war, and were properly punished for their vanity by comprehensive defeat. Mansong then began plundering Kaarta, ransacking its villages and destroying

its crops, while at the same time besieging Desse's forces in their upland stronghold. Two months went by in stalemate, at the end of which time it was
Mansong and not the wily and well-prepared Desse who faced the starvation of
his forces. At this point, he sent to Ali to supply him 200 horsemen, with whose
support he felt he could overpower the garrison guarding the fortified town's
northern gate; Ali, although he had earlier agreed to help Mansong, now refused to send these reinforcements. Furious, the Bambaran monarch raised the
siege and marched towards Ali's encampment. On 30 April, therefore, Park
writes, "At daybreak the whole camp was in motion. The baggage was carried
upon bullocks . . . and upon this was commonly placed one or two women, for
the Moorish women are very bad walkers. The king's favourite concubines
rode upon camels, with . . . a canopy to shelter them from the sun." With this
concern for the priorities, Ali and his people scrambled northwards, terrified of
the consequences that their shortsighted diplomacy might bring on them.

As it happened, Desse Koro was the only one to reap any benefit from all
this manoeuvring—disgusted with the turn events had taken, Mansong retired
grumbling to his own capital at Segu. For Mungo Park, Ali's flight brought new
torments. There in the north, at Bu Baker, the heat was greater and the water
scarcer. He at last met the elusive Fatima—"a woman of the Arab cast, with
long black hair, and remarkably corpulent"—and after many questions she
presented him with a bowl of milk; but those about him were rarely to prove
so generous. Ali had allowed him a water-skin, and Fatima from time to time
even allowed him a little water to go in it, but the wells were inadequate, and
at this time of year were doubtless beginning to run dry. Ali's people had no
intention of sharing what water was left with a captive, and a Christian at that.
When the boy Demba went to fill the skin, they treated him so badly that he
refused to go again. Thirst makes its own rules—Demba went begging for water
among the Moors and negroes of the camp, and very soon Park was doing the
same. The rewards were meagre; his nights were now filled with dreams of
glittering brooks, of tumbling springs, of clear rivulets at the edges of which he
could sprawl and drink his fill.

At the height of his distress he set out himself one midnight to walk to the
wells, about half a mile from the camp. He followed the sound of the herds and
soon found the water, people everywhere busily drawing it up, cattle drinking
from troughs, everywhere the moonlight glinting and glittering on scattered
spray, people calling, perhaps laughing, the whole like a mirage to a thirsty man
—a mirage swiftly transformed into nightmare. He wandered from well to well,
he asked for a drink, a mouthful, and everywhere received abuse. At last an old
man poured some for him, but to avoid contaminating any vessel of his own,
into the trough the cattle were using. Park was beyond caring and, "kneeling
down, thrust my head between two of the cows, and drank with great pleasure".

Chapter Five

"Look at the Water!"

May passed; in the distance, thunder over the southern plains rumbled out messages of imminent inundation. The Moors began to prepare for the migration they made during the rainy season, northwards into the desert. This caused a minor political upheaval, for those erstwhile subjects of Desse Koro who had taken refuge with Ali rather than fight in their king's cause would be left without protection once the Moors left. Considering attack their best means of defence, they asked Ali for 200 of his horsemen to help them fling Desse off his throne. To discuss what terms they would offer for the use of this vital cavalry, Ali sent his son to Jarra, and Park, seeing his opportunity, asked to go with him. It was Fatima to whom he made the request, and it was she whose intercession with her husband—decisive in this as in most other matters—brought Park the permission he wanted.

In the end, Ali proved less rapacious than his behaviour might have suggested. Most of Park's clothing was returned to him, as was his horse, before he left the camp on 26 May. Johnson and Demba travelled with him, and so did a number of Moorish cavalrymen. Around noon they overtook Ali and another fifty riders, and camped that night in cramped and overcrowded conditions, hardly improved by a violent sandstorm that began around dawn and blasted for hour after hour from the north-east. The cattle stampeded, desperate for shelter, and Park, sleeping in the open, found himself not only in great discomfort, but also in considerable danger.

Perhaps it was the sandstorm that twisted Ali's temper one notch further towards intemperate lunacy. In any case, that morning one of his servants came to Park and ordered him to get ready to leave. A moment later he had taken Demba by the shoulders: "Ali will be his master in future!" Park was dumbfounded, but the man turned to him and went on, "This business is settled at last. The boy and everything except your horse goes back to Bu Baker. But you may take the old fool back with you to Jarra." Bu Baker was the camp that they had left; the "old fool" was Johnson. Furiously, Park marched into Ali's tent. He argued—as he says, "perhaps in too passionate a strain"—that he had been punished enough for his imprudence in entering Ali's kingdom, that the boy Demba was free and no slave, had followed him by his own decision and looked to him for protection. "Ali made no reply, but with a haughty air and malignant smile, told his interpreter, that if I did not mount my horse immediately, he would send me back likewise. There is something in the frown of a tyrant which rouses the most secret emotions of the heart; I could not suppress my feelings, and for once entertained an indignant wish to rid the world of such a monster."

It was clear that Park could do nothing to alter Demba's new condition. There were farewells, therefore, and tears; then three men led the boy away and, heavy-hearted, Park rode onward with the main party. He had promised Demba that he would redeem him somehow, yet he was not a free man himself, and many hundreds of miles from the resources that might help him. One may imagine that he felt oppressed by his helplessness and all the fury of his frustration. In Jarra he asked his friend, once more his host, the slatee Daman Jumma, to intercede with Ali; these negotiations proved that there was more than tyranny behind Ali's actions, for he considered that Park, without Demba's knowledge of Bambaran to assist him, had no chance of escape. On the other hand, he was quite willing to sell the boy, at the usual fee, as a personal slave to Daman.

The price Ali fixed for his friendly assistance in the rebellion against Desse Koro was 400 head of cattle, 200 garments and quantities of beads and other ornaments. This proved high for the rebels, but they knew it was a matter of their skins or the king's, so, looking about them for those more helpless than themselves, their eyes lit upon the population of Jarra itself. Why not, they suggested to Ali, take from them half the required cattle—they would undertake to replace them later. Ali was not a man overperplexed by the niceties of justice; he seized the cattle and prepared to depart. To Mungo Park's joy, his plans included a swift return to Jarra, so swift, indeed, that he himself suggested that his captive might await his return in Daman Jumma's house. This naturally delighted Park, "but I had experienced so many disappointments that I was unwilling to indulge the hope of its being true, until Johnson came and told me that Ali . . . was actually gone from the town".

Beyond the town, however, matters were stirring, and the delight the people there felt at Ali's departure was soon tempered by news of Desse Koro's distant —but approaching—movements. He had attacked Khasson and massacred the population of three towns; then, having heard of the preparations being made by those who had based themselves on Jarra, he had turned in that direction. Frantically, the threatened clans asked Ali to send the horsemen he had promised. They might have learned Mansong's lesson more easily by observation, without going to the bitter lengths of experience—Ali's cavalry was busy, elsewhere engaged, unavailable. Desperately, they gathered their force together and, on 18 June, 800 of them marched away into the land of Kaarta.

Their record on this expedition proved fairly ignominious, however. Avoiding Desse's main force, which they realized was too large for them to handle, they ravaged a little town and, carrying off all its inhabitants, scurried with these slaves and captured herds back to Jarra, moving at night to avoid the king of Kaarta's retribution. By 26 June, Desse Koro was on the move. He took the little frontier village of Simbing and marched swiftly on Jarra. There, all was panic, a desperate packing, a swift preparation of food for the flight to come; by mid-morning the following day, a new line of refugees was straggling south on the roads leading to Segu, half the population of Jarra anxiously on the move. "Their departure was very affecting", Park notes, "the women and children crying; the men sullen and dejected; and all of them looking back with regret on their native town, beyond which their ambition had never tempted them to stray . . . ."

Very soon thereafter, news reached the town that the army, briefly deployed to halt Desse's advance, had scattered without fight. "The terror of the towns-people . . . is not easily to be described. Indeed, the screams of the women and children, and the great hurry and confusion that everywhere prevailed, made me suspect that the Kaartans had already entered the town." Not afraid of Desse, but determined not to be killed by mistake, Park too rode out of town, until on the summit of a nearby hill he paused to look back. Everywhere, he could see "the poor inhabitants who were thronging after me, driving their sheep, cows, goats, etc., and carrying a scanty portion of provisions, and a few clothes. There was a great noise and crying everywhere upon the road; for many aged people and children were unable to walk, and these, with the sick, were obliged to be carried; otherwise they must have been left to certain destruction." It was a situation over which, he said, he could not help lamenting, and certainly by now he must have seen his fill of human cruelty and suffered enough by it himself to feel a strong, sympathetic involvement with any of its victims. Nor had his own troubles come to an end.

By the beginning of July, he had made his way to the town of Queira. That day, however, into what he must have thought might become a haven and a base for his further travels, there arrived Ali's chief slave, with four riders, come to fetch him to Bu Baker again. "All this was like a stroke of thunder to me", Park tells us, "for I dreaded nothing so much as confinement again among the Moors." He felt he could not return to that condition, that if he did the out-come would be death, and that his only hope lay to the south, on the road to Segu. Johnson agreed—it was the right course for Park to take. But he himself had come to the end of his travels; he would not have been there then had the Moors not brought him back from Jarra and into captivity. Daman had offered him a fair price—that of half a slave—for taking a *coffle* (a slave caravan) to the coast and he was going to accept the offer. He had, after all, a wife and children waiting for him on the banks of the Gambia estuary.

Park now revived his earlier resolution: he would travel on alone. Again, the tone is matter of fact—"I resolved to proceed by myself". It is as though no other course was open to him. But of course there was, although he does not mention it. There was nothing to prevent his slipping away and circumspectly linking up later with Johnson and his train of fettered slaves. No one would have blamed him. He had been nearly three months a prisoner, had lost almost all his possessions, had suffered fever and maltreatment and was now caught up in the turmoils of a war. Ali's minions were searching for him, somewhere to the north-west Desse Koro's army was still on the rampage, ahead of him lay roads and tracks made cacophonous by endless lines of refugees. The rains were almost upon him. The lands all around were unknown and troubled. Everywhere he went he was likely to meet with suspicion and worse, to be treated as a hated infidel, as a spy, at best as a curiosity of little worth. He does not discuss these matters with us; if they were present in his mind, if it took any effort of will to dismiss them, if he had to persuade himself back to his task, he does not mention it. "I resolved to proceed by myself"—the words carry a burden of heroism, traditionally understated in a way that almost lets it slip by unnoticed. Perhaps he did not really notice it himself.

"About midnight I got my clothes in readiness, which consisted of two shirts, two pairs of trousers, two pocket-handkerchiefs, an upper and under waistcoat, a hat, and a pair of half boots; these, with a cloak, constituted my whole wardrobe. And I had not one single bead, nor any other article of value in my possession, to purchase victuals for myself, or corn for my horse." Alone, then, moneyless, there he was, standing upright in the night, grabbing at his chance of life, facing south, towards where the Niger flowed. "A cold sweat moistened my forehead as I thought on the dreadful alternative, and reflected that, one way or the other, my fate must be decided in the course of the following day." He took up his bundle, thrusting speculation aside, picked his way delicately between sleepers, swung into the saddle of his sad but willing nag, asked Johnson to take care of his notes and papers, murmured his farewells, his thanks, his messages for the friends who would be fretting, who were in fact giving up hope, at Pisania, then rode slowly off into the soft, unquiet darkness.

Shepherds stoned him; then time passed and he felt himself safe. But yells behind him alerted him and all his optimism curdled. Three riders were behind him, muskets in hand, shouting that he must halt. He had no alternatives left. He waited for them, turned at their command, rode back the way he had come. But in shadow, unexpectedly, they stopped; his bundle opened, they searched what belongings he had left, displaying for them the same rueful contempt that he had himself. They took the only article that pleased them—his cloak, his protection against rain and insects, his covering at night. He argued, hurried after them, begged, until a presented musket stopped him where he stood. Disconsolately, he watched these robbers ride away, yet had the comfort of his freedom to console him. He turned his horse into the dark safety of the woods;

soon landmarks led him to the eastward route he had already travelled, so many weeks before.

"It is impossible to describe the joy that arose in my mind when I looked around and concluded that I was out of danger. I felt like one recovered from sickness; I breathed freer; I found unusual lightness in my limbs; even the desert looked pleasant . . . ." Yet he was only provisionally free, for any party of marauding Moors might rob him, or kill him, or drag him back to Ali's tents. And even if no Moors discovered him, a greater problem loomed—"I had no means of procuring food, nor prospect of finding water". Yet he travelled on, his compass-bearing east south-east, while above him the unrelenting sun clambered to its savage noon. The world turned insubstantial, his own dazed vision and the vibrations of the heat blurring all outline. He met goatherds—the flocks were Ali's—who seemed as thirsty and were as waterless as he. The afternoon dragged, metal-heavy; it burdened him. He swayed in his saddle, his eyes blurred, the thirst drummed and writhed within him. With cracked lips he chewed at the leaves of shrubs, then, dry-mouthed, spat out their bitterness. Desperately, just before sunset, he climbed a tree, but in every direction the plain stretched away to ill-defined horizons, "as level and uninterrupted as that of the sea". He took off his horse's bridle, to let it find its own sustenance from the few dry shrubs and grasses that grew there, then tumbled, strength fled, upon the sand.

The sinking sun brought him back from his expectations of death—"Here then . . . terminate all my hopes of being useful in my day and generation"—and the evening's cool regenerated him to some extent. Beside his horse, therefore, he stumbled on into the gathering darkness. Suddenly light speared across the sky, there was the distant call of thunder; a long wind grabbed at the stiff branches of the shrubs, and piling clouds darkened even the night. Park trembled with the expectation of rain; he tilted back his head, he opened his cracked lips to receive that succour. Instead, a sudden harshness, a tearing at his skin—it was sand the wind had brought him, turning hope in all truth to dust in his mouth. This storm then for an hour, he in imminent danger, he felt, of suffocation; then the sand cleared away, the lightning, as though released, struck again and again—and finally the rain, falling in great drops, a fat, wonderful torrent, to catch which he spread his clothes wide on the ground and let them soak in that marvellous moisture, so that he could wring them out and suck them, and drink, and drink.

An encampment was the next hazard, one that, despite his hunger, was to be avoided. For all his care, however, a woman saw him and screamed, her fear sending out men to search for him. Hiding, he let that hunt die down, then moved cautiously further. Frogs called him to water, and at last he could drink his fill, despite the muddiness of the small springs he found; his head lowered beside that of his horse, both of them greedy for that relief. More happily, he climbed into a nearby tree, saw smoke a dozen miles away, a target for his next march. It was late in the morning that he reached it, a small village still in Ali's domain. The headman refused him all assistance, but, as Park points out, "in Africa, as in Europe, hospitality does not always prefer the highest dwellings". He appealed to "an old, motherly-looking woman" who sat spinning cotton at the door of her hut. Soon he was within, seated on the earthen floor, eating a warmed-up dish of *kous-kous*. He gave her one of his two remaining handkerchiefs; she fed corn to his horse.

At this point, Mungo Park, less free with piety than some, does permit himself a paragraph of gratitude "to that gracious and bountiful Being, whose power had supported me under so many dangers". Another threatened, however: the men, assembling by the old lady's hut, began, it seemed to him, to murmur that it might be wise to carry this stranger to Ali—perhaps they would earn themselves a reward. His calm simulated, his movements deliberate, but sweat doubtless dampening his palms, Mungo Park thanked the old lady, gathered up the remaining corn and led his horse from the village. He took the northern path, attempting to persuade the villagers that from that direction he had nothing to fear; nevertheless, a couple of miles went by before the following children, eager to gaze their fill, at last turned back to their homes. Then, free of anxiety, thirst and hunger allayed, he turned away into the woods and, in the shade of a large tree, went peacefully to sleep.

He travelled the whole of that afternoon, then slept, despite prowling beasts and blood-hungry mosquitoes. The next day he moved on, almost directly to the south now, the country dry, open, rolling and filled with racing antelopes, families of wild pig and long-legged, gawky ostriches. He was given food by a shepherd, a Fulani who brought him into his low tent "in which the family, the furniture, etc., seem huddled together like so many articles in a chest". He crawled in on hands and knees; the shepherd, his wife, his three children and his six-foot guest filled the tent almost to danger-point, but the cramped conditions did not prevent Park from eating the dish of boiled corn and dates that he was offered. He records that the wife and children, however, the moment they learned he was a Christian, leaped terrified from the tent. Buying corn for his horse in exchange for three or four brass buttons, he travelled on into the evening.

At sunset, he came across one of the main routes into the land of the Bambara, but the noise of others on it drove him into the undergrowth. "As these thickets are generally full of wild beasts, I found my situation rather unpleasant; sitting in the dark, holding my horse by the nose with both hands to prevent him from neighing, and equally afraid of the natives without, and the wild beasts within." But the locals passed chattering on their way and Park travelled on through the night, until frogs again led him to drinking water; satisfied, he slept in a large tree, only to be wakened by, he tells us, wolves—jackals, more probably, scavenging and snuffling through the undergrowth near the path. Later that day, at about ten in the morning, he stopped in a town he calls Wawra. The date was

5 July 1796. He had reached a place that, though still technically within the borders of Kaarta, now paid tribute to Mansong, leader of the Bambara, king of Segu. For the moment, perhaps, he was safe—provided the Bambara did not prove as hostile as had the Moors.

The chief man of the place offered him a welcome the warmth of which augured well, and safe behind the high town walls, surrounded by Fulani and Mandingo people, but no Moors, Park was at last able to relax. Not for the first time, however, the curiosity he stirred up prevented his resting. Two hours of sleep, and then the debate about his origins, carried on with eloquence by a growing crowd, woke him. Was he a Moor? Was he an Arab? Where was he from? The head man had, as was perhaps his right, the final word; he had been to Gambia and "assured them that I was certainly a white man; but he was convinced from my appearance that I was a very poor one".

Once word spread of his destination, Park soon discovered the aftermath of war. Mansong and his warriors had passed that way three years before; now bereaved women came to him, begging him when in Segu to try and discover what had happened to their children, carried off as prizes in victory. The headman examined his baggage, meanwhile, but took nothing—there was, after all, little enough to take. And, after a night of rain, Park was on the move again, travelling in the open now, his companion a Mandingo on his way to what he gives as Dingyee to buy corn. Here too people treated him hospitably—although in the morning he had to pay forfeit. A lock of white man's hair, the old Fulani with whom he had lodged told him, would give the person who owned it all the knowledge white men possessed. Would Park, as a charm of great practical value, permit his host to cut such a lock from his head? Of course Mungo Park agreed—"and my landlord's thirst for learning was such that, with cutting and pulling, he cropped one side of my head pretty closely". Only by clapping on his hat could Park persuade him to leave the rest; it was thus a little lopsidedly that he rode on towards Segu.

A day's march further on, however, in Ouossebou, he was held up for want of a guide, the road ahead passing through bush country and hard to follow. For four days he waited, and then a party of Kaartans, fleeing from Moorish tyranny and on their way to offer allegiance to Mansong, agreed to take him with them. They left at daybreak, travelled all day with only two stops, and were wearily approaching their destination, a town named Satilé, when they saw that their arrival had produced flight, shouts of warning and of fear, the pointless scurrying of panic. Before they reached them, the gates had been slammed shut—the townsfolk had taken them for marauding Moors, and it took long argument before they were persuaded to let them in.

Rain in the night, and the morning's road slippery with mud; beside it, the signs of war—a village ruined, its wells filled in, its great central tree burned down. At day's end, however, there was a fertile valley fringed by rocky cliffs, a wealthy town set in it and hospitality to be found there matching its wealth.

Fine mutton to eat that night, therefore, and plentiful corn for the horses, and
the next day they were on the move again, arriving in mid-afternoon at the
great market-town of Mourdhia. It was an important interchange point in the
salt trade, a Muslim town much visited by Moorish traders, but one far more
hospitable than had been the towns and camps of the Muslim fanatics in the
north.

On 16 July, now accompanying a train of fourteen asses laden with salt, on
a road winding between rocky hills (from which romantic ambush Moorish
robbers sometimes sprang), Park and his companions set out once more. The
salt was bound for Sansanding—and Sansanding was on the river Niger. Now
all he had to do to arrive at the centre of the mystery that he had been pursuing
through all these months of hardship was to keep going. The days now passed
monotonously, and their weariness was less well supported by the hospitality
of the people. Strangers passed here too often for these countryfolk to be free
with food and shelter. They were sometimes refused all assistance, and were
usually short of food. Park's horse especially now began to fail. He fell further
and further behind the others. When on the 18th Park stopped for the night, he
was given water to drink, and nothing else, not even shelter on a night of wind
and driving rain.

In the morning, long argument and—as so often—female compassion combined to give him at least a breakfast: a handful of meal mixed with water. Then,
wearily enough, onward, travelling alone now, the others half a day or more
ahead. At a watering place, however, he fell in with two men who were on their
way to Segu. This and a drink of milk altered his mood and he rode happily
into the afternoon. A festival of sorts, a round of drinks in a wayside village,
everyone pleasantly intoxicated, then onward past the derision of these Bambaran sophisticates to one more stopping place. And he must indeed have
seemed extraordinary, a tall, gaunt man, russet from the weather, his eyes bright
against the sunburn, that flame of hair topping all, though damped a little by
the hat he wore, his clothes unfamiliar, travel-stained, torn, plodding beside an
emaciated horse, its sharp-contoured bones and hanging head making it seem
on the very point of collapse.

It is unlikely that he cared about the laughter with which he was received,
the staring faces, the calling boys. The talk now was of the Joliba—"The Great
Water"—the Niger, that mysterious river that had provided the reason for all
his courage, all his stubbornness. "You will see it tomorrow", his guides told
him, and all that night, safe from lions behind the mud walls of the village where
he lay—though not from the manoeuvres of mosquitoes crazed with greed—he
thought about the journey he had made, the eight long months it had taken,
the difficulties he had overcome, the fulfilment of his hopes which awaited him.

He was ready before daylight, dressed and his horse saddled, but had to wait
impatiently until the gates were opened. Soon however he was travelling down
the well-marked road, everywhere groups of people, asses, women with baskets,

moving in the same direction. For this was market-day in Segu and all the countryside was making its way there. Just before he reached the town he again met the Kaartans with whom he had been travelling earlier. The ground lay flat, level, marshy—there was water close by. Against the dappled blue and white of the sky, a smoke haze wavered, sign of urban activity, a sort of flag marking the position of Segu. Park began to look around, anxiously, now keyed up for his first glimpse of the river.

"Look ahead!" called his companions. "Look at the water!" One can hear them, laughing a little, perhaps, indulging him, pointing the direction. And Park looked ahead: "I saw with infinite pleasure the great object of my mission —the long sought for majestic Niger, glittering to the morning sun, as broad as the Thames at Westminster, and flowing slowly *to the eastward*. I hastened to the brink, and, having drank of the water, lifted up my fervent thanks in prayer to the Great Ruler of all things, for having thus far crowned my endeavours with success."

Chapter Six

A Necessary Reappraisal

Segu was a city of great importance to the commerce of West Africa. It lay—it lies—some 750 miles from the coast, though Mungo Park had travelled nearer 1,000 to reach it. The French slavers, though they were never as active as the English, nevertheless took many thousands of unfortunates off the coasts of Senegal and Gambia. Most of these seem to have passed through the slave markets of Segu, before marching, chained and despondent, westward to the waiting ships. It was a centre for the grain trade also, and a point of interchange for the products of both Futa Jallon to the west and the upland area of the Kong further south. It had, as we have seen, achieved under Mansong and his father a widespread power, for a while taking precedence even over Timbuctu and Jenne, both of which it had over the previous decades been attempting to dominate. The rivalry between Segu itself and Kaarta to the north, however, had led to a diminution of Bambara power, Timbuctu fell to the Tuaregs and, as Mungo Park discovered, peace and safety departed from the area.

He discovered the city to be divided into four, each with its own defensive wall, two sections on one side of the river, two on the other. They were places of flat-roofed, white-washed houses, clay-built and sometimes of two storeys. He estimated that about 30,000 people lived there. One of the main sources of the city's revenue was the many ferries that plied across the Niger, each a long, narrow canoe made of two hollowed tree-trunks laid end to end. There was a press of people waiting to cross at each of the three embarkation points and it was with something of a sense of wonder that Park sat and waited, staring around at the multiplicity of those who stood near him—robed Moors, Arabic in feature; Bambara peasants with their produce or their beasts; tall, pale-skinned Fulanis—and beyond them the gleaming, clustered houses, bright under the hazy July sky. "The view of this extensive city; the numerous canoes upon the river; the crowded population, and the cultivated state of the surrounding country, formed altogether a prospect of civilisation and magnificence, which I little expected to find in the bosom of Africa."

This pleasant prospect was never to be translated into comfortable experience. Word of his presence, which must have been exciting enough to have started a torrent of rumours, had reached the brooding Mansong, king of Segu. An envoy was sent across the river—Park was banned from the royal presence, at least until all suspicions about him had been cleared up. Meanwhile, he would find lodging—the envoy pointed—over there, in that village, only a few miles away, on the river bank. Park trudged despondently on, only to find that suspicion seemed to have spread from the king to his subjects. All doors were closed to him. Hungry and at the end of patience, with nowhere to stay and yet unable to move on, he sat under a tree, while the day passed and, in the evening skies, the clouds built up, harbingers of that night's rain.

It was a woman once again who took pity on him, seeing him as she returned from her work in the fields and taking him back to her hut. A mat on the floor was his bed, a broiled fish his supper. Then she and the other women settled to their evening work, the spinning of cotton, and as they span they sang, and the songs they sang were sometimes traditional and sometimes extemporised, and one of the subjects they picked to sing about was Mungo Park. "The air was sweet and plaintive, and the words, literally translated, were these: 'The winds roared, and the rains fell. The poor white man, faint and weary, came and sat under our tree. He has no mother to bring him milk; no wife to grind his corn. . . . Let us pity the white man; no mother has he . . . .'

Having paid the women of the house with his only available coin—four of the brass buttons from his waistcoat—he waited on in the village for word from the king. Instead, there came rumours, stories that "Mansong had received some very unfavourable accounts of me from the Moors and Slatees"—it was believed he was a spy, or at least had come all this way for no good purpose. It took two whole days of waiting, during which the king sent a demand for presents and Park had to reply that he had nothing left to give, before Mansong made up his mind. If this ragged white man was really intent on nothing more than examining a river already well known to everyone, if he was really intent on moving on to Jenne and Timbuctu, the sooner he started the better Segu's monarch would like it. So eager was the king to get rid of him, that he gave him 5,000 cowrie shells to help him on his way. These shells were currency throughout West Africa (and as far afield as the coast of India), their value based, certainly in the upper and middle Niger regions and the western Sudan, on that of the *mithqal*, the gold coin that was used in all major transactions. They were thus the small change of the area, the money one used when shopping in the market or buying a goat; during normal times, when drought and disaster had not distorted the exchange rate, one gold *mithqal* was worth some 3,000 cowrie shells. In a note Mungo Park tells us that 100 of these shells would buy a day's necessities for himself and his horse; he reckons that 250 cowrie shells were worth one of his British (late eighteenth-century) shillings.

Mansong also offered a guide to lead Park as far as Sansanding, and from him more information was forthcoming about the king's attitude. On the one hand, there were the natural suspicions of a monarch at war. "He argued probably as my guide argued: who, when he was told that I had come from a great distance, and through many dangers, to behold the Joliba river, naturally inquired if there were no rivers in my own country . . . ." But on the other there was, apparently, a desire to save Park, at least in his domains, from the malice of Muslim fanatics. Therefore the gift of money, the guide, the helpfulness; therefore, too, the closed gates, the haughty messengers, the refusal to be involved.

That evening, however, Park learned that to the east lay a vast ambush for any Christian, with Jenne only nominally under the king of Segu and Timbuctu already totally under Muslim domination. These reports seemed to him too vague and unsubstantiated to force him to turn back yet and he "determined to proceed". Therefore on 24 July he was on the move again, his route down-river, his direction to the north of east. The country was fertile—Park describes the harvesting of the shea nut, there very plentiful—and all along the river banks fishing villages testified to the wealth of those waters. At five in the after-noon, he and his guide arrived at the large town of Sansanding, another of the great trading centres of the upper Niger. Although it is situated not much more than thirty miles from Segu, the fact that it stands just above the great north-ward bend in the Niger makes it a point of convergence for the various routes crossing the river from the Sahara and the countries beyond. Berbers travelling south from the Hodh and Oulata to trade found it the most convenient point to make for; for them as for the Moorish and Arabic caravans, the place's reputa-tion as a vast storehouse of the local millet was its especial attraction. It was also a religious centre of some importance, a fact that would increase in importance as Bambaran influence—which wrapped Islam into its animist traditions without much sense of conflict—began to wane during the early decades of the nine-teenth century.

Park was quite impressed with the town, which he estimated held some 10,000 citizens; eight years later, when he came there a second time, he des-cribed it more fully, writing of the market, crowded day and night, its stalls selling balls of indigo or wood-ash, others offering beads, others again cloth brought from Jenne or the Hausa lands. "I observed one stall with nothing but antimony in small bits; another with sulphur, and a third with copper and silver rings and bracelets. In the houses fronting the square is sold scarlet, amber, silks from Morocco, and tobacco. . . . Adjoining this is the salt market. . . . A slab of salt is sold commonly for eight thousand cowries; a large butcher's stall . . . is in the centre of the square, and as good and fat meat sold every day as any in England. The beer market is at a little distance . . . and there are often exposed for sale from eighty to one hundred calabashes of beer, each containing about two gallons. Near the beer market is the place where red and yellow leather is sold." Apart from all this there was a huge market once a week—on Tuesdays—

where traders from the surrounding countryside came in to buy their goods wholesale, taking them back to their own villages to retail them.

Into this clatter, this activity, this endless commercial clamour, Park now made his way—quietly, he hoped, unnoticed, but seen soon enough; too soon for him. Soon hundreds were about him, some claiming indeed that they knew him. He thinks that, since they pointed south when asked where they had seen him, they had come across white men on the Cape Coast, but south of Sansanding lie the Ivory Coast and the Gold Coast, and east of them the Slave Coast, on all of which white men had been familiar for centuries. In any case, it was not friendship that this crowd now exuded, but religious fanaticism and the desire for, if not a forced conversion, at least a public demonstration of respect for Islam. The king's representative, however, promised that he would see to it that Park left first thing in the morning and this to some extent allayed their fervour. A night shared with an infidel could, it seems, be borne. As a matter of fact, even outward adherence to Islamic precepts and a repetition of verses from the Koran would not necessarily have gained these Muslims' respect; Jews, who travelled the same route and had adapted to these requirements, were nevertheless despised and often badly treated: "even the Moors themselves allowed", Park notes, "that though I was a Christian, I was a better man than a Jew". For all their detestation of his religion, and for all the assurances given them by Mamadi, the head man, he was forcibly placed on display, seated in a high place at the door of the mosque so that everyone could see him.

Nightfall brought no real respite, for even when he had been given a hut to sleep in, crowds came pouring over the little mud wall protecting it "in order, they said, to see me *perform my evening devotions, and eat eggs*". His italics emphasise his consternation, perhaps his amusement—the people of Sansanding seemed to be under the impression that Europeans ate raw eggs and "subsist almost entirely on this diet". Persuasion, however, brought him a meal of mutton, so that it was after all not unrefreshed that he was able to leave early the next day. By 25 July he was in the town of Niari, and there he stayed for two days, washing his clothes and resting his long-suffering horse. (In a world that must have seemed to him by now like the memory of a dream, Napoleon besieged Mantua, the people of France were beginning to gather that year's good harvest, their contentment keeping in power for a little while the corrupt Directory, while in distant Russia death capsized great Catherine.)

On 28 July Mungo Park was in Niami, inhabited largely by Fulani from the Massina area, on the borders of which he now was. This had for many centuries been territory where the Fulani, usually a minority people, were the most numerous grouping, so much so, indeed, that it had over the previous two centuries become one of the centres of their emigrations. The Fulani are one of the abiding mysteries of Africa, for no one is certain of their origins; one of the likeliest explanations for the mixture they represent—negro language and skin colour, non-negro features and bone structure—is that they are in fact mixed, the product of Berber forays into the middle Senegal regions from the tenth century on. Others say, however, that they have migrated westward from ancient homelands in upper Egypt. They were pastoral people, cattle-tending, intelligent. They took early to urban life, to political activity, to the sophistication of Islam. Often it was through them that the Muslim religion spread; certainly it was through them that in the western Sudan it was fanatically revived and maintained, several times through the proclamation of *jehad* or holy war. In many places where they were a minority, they became by these methods and qualities nevertheless the dominant force.

They reached this area on the Niger, the kingdom of Massina, around the beginning of the fifteenth century, becoming from then on one of the groupings most loyal to the Mali empire. Having for two centuries been under the suzerainty of its rulers, they had since its fall been subjects of the Songhai, then of the Ruma people of Timbuctu (these the offspring of Moroccan invaders and their Songhai wives) and, now, of the king of Segu to the south-west of them and, to the north-east, of the recent Tuareg conquerors of Timbuctu. It was because of these pressures that Massina had become a centre of emigration, and Futa Jallon, in Mungo Park's time a fount of religious aggression, a force for chastising the ungodly, had been largely peopled from there .Yet the Massina Fulani survived, retained their dominance, and were, in fact, on the verge of codifying their local identity in the structures and institutions of a state; their leader, named Seku Ahmadu, was about to step out on the stage of their confused and complicated history.

Mungo Park, that lone Christian, was thus on his way deeper and deeper into lands steeped for centuries in a profound Muslim absolutism, a fanatical fundamentalism compounded not only by the paranoia of a small people, but also by the proven political effectiveness of such convictions. On this day, however, 28 July, his main concern was with lions. He saw what he called "a large animal of a cameleopard kind"—from his description almost certainly a giraffe, though just possibly perhaps a displaced okapi from the Congo regions—but this trotted quietly away, as well it might. Soon, however, there was genuine alarm, his guide declaring a lion's presence, but Park was too concerned about his horse's weariness to swing it about and persuade it into a gallop. He should not therefore have been as astonished as he tells us he was to see "a large red lion a short distance from the bush, with his head couched between his forepaws". He was about to fling himself to the ground, leaving his horse to be eaten—the impulse an insight into his swift practicality—when he realised that the lion had no intention of displaying the kind of energy needed to pull down either man or horse. Not unnaturally, Park records that he could not take his eyes off this immobile predator: "My eyes were so rivetted upon this sovereign of the beasts, that I found it impossible to remove them until we were at a considerable distance . . . ."

That evening he and his guide halted in a riverside village, the water wide there, its flow visible from the high bank for miles in both directions, the cattle-dotted islands of Fulani herdsmen calm and green among the easy waves. There were crocodiles there and in the nearby swamps, but Park, quite rightly, found them "of little account to the traveller when compared with the amazing swarms of mosquitoes, which rise from the swamps and creeks in such numbers as to harass even the most torpid of the natives; and as my clothes were now almost worn to rags, I was but ill-prepared to resist their attacks". Sleepless, his legs and arms covered in angry marks, he became, he says, "very feverish and un-easy". He had no inkling, of course, of the diseases these bites might have brought or aggravated.

"Early in the morning my landlord, observing that I was sickly, hurried me away . . . ." Park was now very weak; his horse, scrawny, sagging, was on the threshold of collapse. Six miles from their starting-point, the beast passed that threshold, falling in slow mid-stride, lying by the wayside, unwilling or un-able to stand again. Park removed saddle and bridle, gathered grass for it, then watched its sufferings with concern and foreboding, "for I could not suppress the sad apprehension that I should myself in a short time lie down and perish in the same manner of fatigue and hunger". But as yet he would not accept the retreat that the logic of his situation seemed to demand; doggedly, on foot, he made his way to the next village, Ke. The headman there had no interest in his plight and would give him no help. Instead, he called a fisherman to carry him further and it was thus by water that he arrived at a town named Murzan. From there he crossed to the other bank and a large town he calls Silla.

There he sat alone under a tree. The Bambaran that he knew was now of little use to him, and would be, he was told, of no use at all once he reached Jenne and other places to the east. Night fell, and with it came the rain. He begged for shelter and was at last allowed entry to the one damp room set aside for the lodging of strangers. There, as the rain roared outside, he lay in the swift shudderings of his fever. "Worn down by sickness, exhausted with hunger and fatigue, half naked, and without any article of value by which I might pro-cure provisions, clothes or lodging, I began to reflect seriously on my situation." The understatement of the last phrase, almost ludicrous in view of the facts, disguises, one imagines, his despair. He was totally isolated, dependent on charity in a country where he and his kind were hated. Nature had turned against him, for the land was now under the lash of the seasonal rains—"the rice grounds and swamps were everywhere overflowed; and in a few days more, travelling of every kind, unless by water, would be completely obstructed". But he had no money to buy or hire a canoe, and, even if he had, he realised that every mile he travelled eastward down the Niger would bring him "more and more within the power of . . . merciless fanatics". And if he died, what would he have achieved? What he had learned would not survive him.

Not that the prospect to the west of him was much easier. Hundreds of miles lay between him and safety, miles that his weakness would double and treble.

He was alone, moneyless and on foot. And there, too, the land was not empty of Muslim fanatics happy to maltreat a Christian. Nevertheless, at the end of that journey, should he reach it, lay security, a passage to England, success and acclamation. Eastward, there lay only death. "Had there been the most distant prospect of a successful termination, neither the unavoidable hardships of the journey, or the dangers of a second captivity, should have forced me to desist." Given his record, one need not doubt it; he had already gone further and for longer and through greater difficulties than the gentlemen in London, his "honourable employers", as he calls them, had any right to expect. Even in the extremity of his despondency and exhaustion, he tried to do what seemed to him his duty to them before turning back by gathering what information he could about Jenne, Timbuctu and the Hausa states, all those fabulous regions whose mysteries he had so desperately hoped to solve. But at eight o'clock on the morning of 30 July, he stepped down into the narrow length of a canoe, that step the first of his long-delayed retreat.

But consider him at this moment, the gaunt stranger, busy about his errand, afloat now on the river that he had come so far to find, everything about him utterly meaningless to the inhabitants of those lands so far from his home. Those watching from the bank, seeing his canoe long, dark, bobbing on the slow waves, he in his curious clothes conspicuous, laughable; those with him, sitting impassively before and behind, perhaps with bundles, with grain or a trussed fowl; those waiting at the town, busy about their day's beginning, half-stopping as they carried cloth or drove a flock, the goats turning their heads, their busy mouths scrabbling at dust, at wisps of ancient vegetation, as unconcerned as those who herded them at this approaching oddity, this meaningless traveller immersed in his imcomprehensible pursuits: all would have been equally baffled to explain the purposes of this apparently deranged voyager.

Vary the picture. At Dover, say, there lands, energetically, a tall man, broad-shouldered, black, from Africa. He wears a long, white robe, speaks a strange language, worships gods whom those around him mistrust. He begins to trudge inland, looking about him as though the world had become an exhibition. Assume the year the same, 1797, wars overseas, Bonaparte rising across the Channel, though not known by many yet, the revolution based in Paris threateningly defending itself, England on the alert. This man, this tall, black stranger, begins to penetrate deeper into the country; in remote villages, boys jeer at him, dogs bark at his fluttering—now sadly travel-stained—clothing. Asked where he is going, he replies in his inadequate English that he is searching for a river— he believes it is named the Humber—in order to verify its existence and discover the direction of its flow. Churchmen preach against his idolatry and somewhere just east of Northampton, say, he is stoned by zealous Christians. Something like this analogy was to occur to Park, for in his own book he wrote, "Let us suppose a black merchant of Hindostan to have found his way into the centre of England with a box of jewels at his back, and that the law of the country afforded him no security; in such a case, the wonder would be, not that the stranger was robbed of any part of his riches, but that any part was left for a second predator.''

Being unfamiliar, this version of exploration seems amusing. One can imagine what the pamphleteers, the cartoonists, what *Punch* would have made of it. Yet was what Mungo Park was doing so very different? To say that it was not does not lessen his courage, his determination, his almost superhuman tenacity. Perhaps precisely because of the self-evident romance of the project, the attractive nature of the adventurer at its centre, its implications should be looked at a little more closely.

First, it seems to me that the story of European exploration, particularly in Africa and Asia, was based on a single monstrous assumption: that reality is limited by the powers of Western observation. What the black man or the brown man may have seen, the native of the country and perfectly clear in his witness, was taken to have no validity. An "explorer" was needed, a white man, a stranger—by no means always trained in the skills and technology of scientific observation—whose verification *alone* could bring this or that natural phenomenon into the orbit of what truly existed. (The same has been true in the discovery of new species of animals, which are not taken to exist, are not even believed to be probable, are often not even searched for, until the reliable eye of a white traveller happens upon them.)

The assumption behind all this is clear in its turn: that the inhabitants of these countries, of whole continents together, have a hold on reality much weaker than the Westerners'. They are, as it were, erratic, their observations dubious, their claims indiscriminate and arbitrary. No allowance in such a view for the fact that they have survived—a minimum requirement, but one not always easy to achieve. Certainly no allowance for the fact they they have developed complex social organisations, institutions, economies, religious rituals and profound mythologies, variegated art forms—sculpture, poetry, music, dance—and, at times, far-flung empires of great power and wealth. No understanding at all for the fact that people in other lands have often evolved a reality parallel to that of the West, with its own quite different sets of customs, morals and priorities, but but one quite capable of sorting out the various levels of existence and distinguishing an orang-utan from a ghost.

Of course, the local populations excited European curiosity, just as the local flora and fauna did. Nor was it an unsympathetic curiosity—it is just that it was nothing more. It did not allow the investigated a reality that could in any way challenge that of the investigators. The former were passive, the later active; if one was to learn from the other, there would never be any question about who was the teacher, who the taught. But certainly the scientific inquiries the explorer was charged with included the observation of the customs and beliefs by which those he came across lived out their lives. For him, indeed, such a study was often a necessity of survival, and in any case was always fleshed out by his direct experience of those whose social priorities he was examining. It was rarely the explorers (Burton was a major exception, as was Stanley, and the unspeakable Speke) who found the men and women among whom they travelled negligible, certainly not until the senseless patriotisms and racial self-satisfaction that afflicted whites in the second half of the nineteenth century.

But for most of those to whom the explorer reported, his sponsors in Europe, what he had to say about people never rose above the interesting. Rousseau's pleasant fiction of the Noble Savage, which might have reinforced this interest with a respect that must have modified European arrogance, had had its inadequacies revealed not only in the human failures of the French Revolution, but also by the actual experience of travellers in distant parts. The world was proving, on the whole, to be fairly short of nobility. In Britain, meanwhile, Bentham's doctrine of Utilitarianism, with its strong preference for a social order assuring each individual an equable and contented life, was beginning to dominate the intellectual scene. It was not on the whole a doctrine that enabled these fathers of anthropology (some of them members of the African Association) to view with true understanding the realities of African life, especially as witnessed during this turbulent period. Another conception of order and contentment might have led them to a different view, but that leap of the imagination was beyond them.

What is cause, what consequence? The fact is that vast areas of Africa were, so to speak, depopulated by this selective European eye. Those who lived in them had a lessened reality—they were of as little account as was what they claimed to have seen and experienced. They had existence, but no significance, just as some natural feature might have: a mountain, or a stand of trees. What is cause, what consequence? In West Africa particularly, slavery had already dehumanised the people in the eyes of many Europeans. Was that a cause or a consequence? Were Europeans able to trade in slaves because they thought blacks lesser, or did they think blacks lesser because they were able to enslave them? Whichever way round the truth ran, it was certainly a fact: those active in the slave traffic and those who passively acquiesced in it agreed, openly or tacitly, on the natural dominance of those who traded in slaves over the slaves so traded. Had they admitted these black people into that full "reality" they themselves inhabited, they must have found slavery, the buying and selling of people, as abhorrent as did those who, waking to the truth, became abolitionists.

But in some ways the passion for "exploration", for "opening up Africa", in which the abolitionists shared, was another aspect of the same mental quirk. The process turned the people who already lived in Africa into things, passive objects waiting to be found, existing in an unreal landscape the mountains of which did not rise into the sky, the rivers of which did not truly flow, until "exploration" had marked them on a map—the white man's map. The fact that many of the earlier explorers were either missionaries or, what is worse, zealous Christians who behaved as if they were, did not improve matters. Those who waited for their enlivening message were not only less "real" than these courageous strangers comes to pummel their souls into some shape acceptable to heaven; they were also in a state of hellish and dangerous ignorance. Fully human they could not be, by their very natures, under the fierce scrutiny of the religious eye. To reinforce their certainties, missionaries and others tended to dwell upon the "savagery" and "superstition" they found in those they came across. Such people, then, were in every way to be disregarded; they were negligible, mere raw material that had to be worked on—educated, converted—before achieving even a relative humanity.

There was thus no psychological bar to the economic exploitation of these territories, so recently "undiscovered", and these people, so far below the proper standards of "civilisation". It is true that the full force of imperial greed was not felt in West Africa until the last quarter of the nineteenth century, but it does not follow from this that some abrupt alteration occurred in the European mind at some time around 1875. Whatever the declared intentions of those who in increasing numbers made their way into the difficult lands that lay between the coast, the Congo basin and the northern deserts, their underlying assumptions, and even more so those of their sponsors in Europe, prepared the way for the imperialism to come. These were lying ready to hand when the time arrived to justify the scrabbling after possessions which the new phase of capitalism made so essential. Indeed, so widespread, so apparently self-evident, were these assumptions, that they rarely needed to be mentioned. It was not the simple morality of fire-power that persuaded the Western nations of their right to colonise: it was their collective conviction of racial superiority. Even when the explorers, and especially the early explorers like Mungo Park, emphasised the humanity they held in common with those among whom they made their way, the very fact of their presence in those countries, the very fact that they were *explorers* and not simple travellers, undermined the liberalism of their evidence. When the time came, therefore, Western man could move in and make his killing with an easy conscience.

Today's Africa, of course, is not the same as the one that the first explorers entered in hope and trepidation nearly two centuries ago. One great factor that has stimulated change has been a Western culture that, for 150 years convinced of its universal value, necessarily altered everything it touched. Indeed, many in Africa begged to be changed—the successes of the West are obvious, rewarding and infinitely seductive. The culture of the powerful has attractions greater than its intrinsic value: its trappings may serve to camouflage the weak. Nor is that all. It is clear that contact with the West has brought benefits: in medicine, in transport, in irrigation and the consequent agriculture, more dubiously in education, in political structures, in urbanisation, industrialisation and defence. The onslaught of Europe, therefore, was sustained by a complex logic and had

its own attractions for those ostensibly oppressed. In succumbing to these attractions, however, some paid a price—occasionally, indeed, becoming precisely the
negligible shadow-people that the mythology of exploitation and exploration
had implied they already were. It was this process of diminution, this general
disruption, this overturning of an ancient order and an ancient self-respect, that
the early explorers unknowingly dragged in their wake. Their own certainty,
sustaining them, drawing from them the uttermost resources of courage, would
in time infect with uncertainty the descendants of those who now attacked,
jeered at or succoured them.

Thus we come back to Mungo Park. For in the great body of Africa he was
the first, the earliest of those magnificent travellers who, criss-crossing the continent, put on it the stamp of European ownership. In their wake came the men
with Bibles and the men with guns, the traders, the educators, the administrators, the whole gallery of exploiters intent on shaping what they found either in
their own image of for their own needs. And, of them all, Mungo Park was the
first. Not that he realised it; his task had been given him and he had undertaken
it for various reasons, but mainly for ambition's sake. He would succeed at it if
he could. If it had not been Park, it would certainly have been another. But still,
it was Park and not another. It is he, weary, sun-darkened, leaning a little sideways in that canoe, his eyes on the long flow of the river as it moves north and
east towards those lands and cities that he had so desperately wanted to see, it is
he, solitary, hungry, dejected, who has come all this way to give a new reality
to the well-fed, busy people all about, to the banks and islands of this stream, to
the states and plants and beasts and cluttered villages past which his route has
wound. It is he who carries with him, who represents, that overwhelming
Western passion—*the desire to know*.

There is nothing ignoble in it, this restless curiosity that has pushed and
plucked and carved at the structures and distances of the universe. But it is an
oddity in the world, and not the universal quality, the passion shared by all the
human race, that Western man has believed it. In its development, in the over-
riding importance it was finally given, it is unique to Western civilisation. It is
quite recent, too—the original tale of Dr Faustus was a sixteenth-century Catholic
tract warning us where our curiosity might lead us, showing us that it was an
aspect of that most dangerous sin, Pride. We ignored the warning, altered our
sense of the universe, our understanding of time, the scale of human beings. In
the scramble after fact, we sacrificed a certain sense of human dignity, of human
worth—perhaps a sort of truth, too, was flung aside. We search for these today,
but nothing answers. About us, the stars stretch away in looped infinity; we
have lost our stage, our right to eternity's special attention. Instead, we have
Faustus as hero.

Other societies have solved their problems differently. What is humanity?
Where is the earth? Was there a beginning? Is there to be an end? Who shapes
our destiny? Such questions have been asked everywhere; only in the West have

we tried to answer them factually. People elsewhere have been less afraid of the truths of myth. With magic—that hit-or-miss science of the unscientific—they have tried to control the arbitrariness of the natural world. They have been less obsessed by what they could merely see, by what the light could show them. For them, an invisible world extended into a most important elsewhere, and ambassadors, special but by no means unique, could be sent into it, just as messengers from time to time came from it. The world was a continuing story with a vast array of characters, some eternal, others long-dead yet active still, others again living now, a small part of the interwoven plot. What happened in that story had to be accepted; magic and ritual might persuade this or that force to show a momentary benevolence, but final decisions were not to be questioned. Good harvest, earthquake, nets heavy with fish, the coming of white men, a drought—all were part of an unalterable fabric.

Only Western man thought it necessary, with a Promethean nobility, to attempt an alteration. He alone refused acceptance as an adequate response—instead, he became a coloniser. Everything had to be dragged into his grasp, had to be controlled, altered, at the very least dissected and understood. Micro-organisms, quasars, the South Pole, Linear-B, all was dragged into his maw in a desperate attempt to release himself from humanity's traditional role—that of victim. He would not accept his fate in mystical passivity, he would not beg from the divine the moments of compassion that made his fate bearable. He would swallow the universe, he would stretch for and chew and digest every-thing; once he had done so, he need no longer claim to have displaced the gods, for gods would have become unnecessary.

One skirmish in this continuing struggle was the exploration of Africa. For those who lived there, who knew where they lived and did not care to learn those matters that did not concern them, this "exploration" was itself a mystery. In the end, for many of them it was to be a disaster. So, then, here is long-legged Mungo Park, his skin drum-tight over his prominent bones, his body all lean-ness, trembling still with the aftermath of fever, his muscles aching: what was he to those people, on that day at the end of July 1797, but a tramp? He was a laughing stock, a person of no account, a man perhaps insane and certainly worth no more than the charity and often the contempt that was due to the poverty-stricken. In any assembly that might have gathered on the banks of the Niger, he would have been the most negligible individual—curious, certainly, to be examined and laughed at, but not to be taken seriously. And these are the terms of the paradox that we, looking back some eighteen decades, can see so clearly, and that no one there had the slightest chance of perceiving.

Consider what this tramp, this pauper of no account, this laughable stranger, was bringing in his wake. With his coming, their whole manner of life had suddenly come under threat. Because he had made that journey, harbinger of armies to come, the very river he was now crossing, the swamps and plains, the villages and towns, the crops and markets, the very people who lived there, would all be altered and, in many cases, swept away for ever. Less than 150 years later, the French, administrators—"owners"—of these lands, began an enormous irrigation scheme. Dams were built, canals, ditches. By 1962, 120,000 acres were under cultivation there. Rice and cotton were grown, and sugar; in the careful fields, cattle grazed. It is at the centre of this system that Sansanding remains.

And the people? Why, the French moved the Mossi, 5,000 of them, mostly young, many of them forcibly, from their kingdom, Yatenga, on the upper Volta. They resettled them on this Niger Irrigation Project. But the Mossi had a religion bound up with their need to ensure that the gods gave them a plentiful water supply. Now, without effort, they had one, guaranteed not by their "earth custodian", in whom much power resided, but by technicians—ultimately, by European engineers. Thus undermined, and surrounded by Muslims, the Mossi accepted the dominant religion. Their complex kinship structures were upset; families were divided, individuals housed under the roofs of strangers. Extended families broke up. The ancient authority vested in the elders was undermined, for in this new place, where new techniques had to be learned, where they were given no formal role to play by the administrators, their wisdom seemed irrelevant; meanwhile, those who remained behind were, quite simply, too far away to sway a new and distant generation. The young men were nevertheless expected by them to identify with their old homeland, to keep their bonds with their families, to marry as their elders commanded. When they returned to Yatenga, however, they discovered that the religion they had adopted—though usually only formally—and the skills they had learned, had no place in their old communities, with their very different conditions and demands. Disruption, therefore, a clash of cultures, conflict both individual and collective.

Such stories were to be repeated elsewhere in Africa. Some areas would prove resistant to the whites and the superficial culture-grafts they brought with them. Some tribes and peoples would take from the newcomers what they needed, and reject the rest. Others would stand almost wholly aloof, clinging to their ancient ways even when alterations in the world around them made this self-destructive. Others again would be destroyed by accepting, or being forced to accept, in their totality new economic systems, agricultural methods, religious practices, political institutions. Of course, this is not a matter for reproach or unalloyed gloom. Often it has enriched African life. Peanuts, maize and tobacco were almost certainly brought into Africa by the early Portuguese. New methods of communication have altered the scale of community in many areas. By a selective acceptance of exotic innovation, many groups have been able to live fuller lives.

Nevertheless, the changes occurred. Africa was altered. Parts of it were destroyed; weakened cultures, their rituals and institutions rendered irrelevant, rarely recover without fundamental differences in their structure, and many of Africa's ancient cultures were weakened, are being weakened further today.

These changes were brought about by the white man's intervention, and the whites could intervene because they believed Africa, despite the evidence of their senses, to be *tabula rasa*. It was a place that had to be brought into existence; it had people who had to be dragged into humanity. The whites knew nothing of African history, cared nothing for Africa's ritual art. Mungo Park, travelling through West Africa, witnessing everywhere he went music and dancing, never once mentions masks. Nowhere has the cunning of the mask-maker developed to as high a level of skill as in West Africa, yet no one would realise this from the chronicle of his travels.

Mungo Park himself was no racist. He detested slavery, he liked the black people he travelled among—it was the Tuaregs and the Berbers from further north whom he hated and feared. His quarrel with them was not a racial one either, but religious. Had they treated him well, he would have responded. Yet he had no idea of the empires once controlling the banks of this sluggish river on which he now bobbed in the first stage of his retreat. He did not realise that he had stumbled into the region of the Niger at a time of great political up-heaval—rather as a stranger might have trudged into the turmoil of the Balkans after the Ottoman empire had begun to wither, the Hapsburgs to lose their grip: his reports would have made Europe seem a wilderness of savagery. So with Park, caught up in the consequences of imperial collapse, but understanding little of the reasons for the general insecurity. What he wrote must have helped to form the picture that Europeans were to have of Africa as an untamed place where no one was safe, an area of deserts and forests full of wild beasts and savage men.

Park would not, perhaps, have recognised the picture, although it was one well established by mid-century. His own death would have helped establish it. Thus he tightened by a further notch the resolution of Europe to intervene in Africa. He too helped in painting that picture of an unknown continent inhabited by negligible people who had to be educated, trained, humanised. But it was not that that made him unique: it was that he was the first. He had no inkling of his own significance, any more than might a virus first entering the body that it would help to modify. Yet this is what he was: out-rider of a force working a social alteration no less complete, no less far-reaching, for being so slow to act. He was like one of the micro-organisms now in his own bloodstream, the effects he was to cause ineradicable and often disastrous, despite his own neutrality. Bacteria feel no malice: their actions are self-evident, inevitable. So too the whites of the nineteenth century in their breach of Africa's social and cultural integrity, in their indifference to any view that Africa might take of itself. As the body seems to bacteria, it was something good to eat and they ate it. In the end, the anti-bodies rallied and the bacteria were, little by little, ejected; by then, though, much damage had been done.

Regard this young Scotsman, therefore, at the end of his resources, his face turned towards safety, watching pensively the approaching bank, the town of

D

Murzan upon it. In the watery morning sun, the little houses gleam, their whitewash bright. The mud walls are pocked with slanting shadows. Boys are running, pointing; from somewhere a shout goes up, women set down bales and stare. The white man has come back. He gets to his feet in the rocking canoe, gathers his poor belongings. His clothes gape where they have been torn, where buttons have been ripped away or stolen. His hair seems brilliant, here in a world of dark people, his eyes glitter like those of the mad. His cheekbones bite through the skin in the high contours of poverty. He steps ashore and the crowd parts .Wondering boys stare up at him, elbow each other, giggle. One bends and throws a stone, is reproved by a passing elder. Park stands below the grey skies of rain-sodden Africa and two girls glance at each other and smile. He is bringing their world to an end, but they do not know it. And neither does he.

Chapter Seven

The Long Retreat

Mungo Park had turned back only some 250 miles upriver from Timbuctu. Now he was faced with the much longer journey to the coast: Jillifree lay 750 miles due west of the lowest point on the Niger that he had been able to reach. And it was as nearly as possible along that direct east–west route that he would make his bid for safety. It began by simply following the river; when it branched out across country, it would be as the well-worn slave trail that led eventually to the Gambia estuary.

For sixty cowries, Park hired a canoe to take him on to Ke, where he was allowed, for forty cowries more, to share a slave's hut. "This poor Negro, perceiving that I was sickly, and that my clothes were very ragged, humanely lent me a large cloth to cover me for the night." The next day Park with the headman's brother walked on upstream to Modibu; on the way, his guide, having failed to persuade him to walk in front through a dangerous thicket, threw down the saddle he was carrying, sad relic of the abandoned horse, and left. Park, overburdened, flung the saddle into the river, whereupon the other reappeared, fished it out and made off with it. In Modibu, however, there was reunion: the man was there and the saddle with him, his conscience having troubled him. All this became more than a diversionary anecdote when, from a nearby hut, Park heard the neighing of a horse. It was his own, recovered from its fatigue and kept and cared for by the headman of Modibu. It was therefore a reconstituted pairing of man and horse that made its way onward to Niami.

It was August now, the rain flailing down like punishment, the streams and lakes and swamplands filling, overflowing, the plains turning to mud, this then liquefying into wide, brown floods. After three days, Park nevertheless started out again, his way now hard to follow, often knee-deep in water, his horse stumbling often, twice being held completely by the mud. By 7 August he was struggling in water that was sometimes chest-high, and that evening, spent in a village west of Niari, not even the offer of 200 cowries could persuade anyone to become his guide. Nevertheless he managed to make his way to a village

named Sibiti, where he spent the night in a damp hut, listening to sudden slide
and tumble as outside, one after another, three huts collapsed under the unremitting rain. In the morning he saw that fourteen huts had been destroyed in
this way since the rains had begun. After another day spent waiting, the headman
of the village forced him to move on; he took the road to Sansanding with some
foreboding. Word about him had gone out; it seemed clear that rumours he
had heard of Mansong's having decided he was a spy were true.

It was no surprise that Mamari, in Sansanding, proved as cool as the rest—
though late that evening the headman came to him privately to warn him to
move swiftly in the morning and not to linger anywhere near Segu. Mansong,
he said, had already sent a canoe downriver to try and bring him back. The
next day, 12 August, Mamari's caution was confirmed when Park was refused
entry into the small town of Kabba, but merely led about the walls and shown
the road west. This apparent surliness was, however, kindly meant, he thought
—Mansong's men were probably about and searching for him. Park cautiously
left the main road, where everyone seemed to be expecting him and no one
was prepared to help, and in a small village on a side road found shelter for the
night.

Next day he travelled on in the same atmosphere of hostility and imminent
danger. He wondered whether he should strike out to the south, swimming his
horse across the Niger and making for the coast in that direction, "but reflecting
that I had ten days to travel before I should reach Kong, and afterwards an extensive country to traverse, inhabited by various nations, with whose language
and manners I was totally unacquainted, I relinquished this scheme". He still
had in mind the purpose for which he had been sent to Africa, and felt he would
best answer that "by proceeding westward along the Niger, endeavouring to
ascertain how far the river was navigable". It was also his most direct route, in
many ways, and the easiest to follow; in any case, having made a decision, he
must have felt a little more in control of his destiny.

He now rode on, not stopping at the towns and villages he passed—most
people, in any case, taking him for a Moor, their most probable explanation for
any unfamiliar traveller. On the 15th he tried to buy corn, but found no one
willing to sell it to him, since it was in short supply. A villager, however,
offered him some in return for a blessing, which Park gave him "in plain
English, and he received it with a thousand acknowledgements". This was, he
writes, "the third successive day that I had subsisted entirely upon raw corn".
The next day he struggled on, slipping in the mud, the horse once almost
drowning, the rain still falling, the mud clinging, drying in layers, both steed
and rider caked with it, so that "in passing the village of Callimana, the people
compared us to two dirty elephants". He rode through a town he names as
Yamina, ravaged a few years before by Desse Koro of Kaarta; the next day he saw
further ruins, small towns emptied and destroyed in that same campaign. This
was, of course, that Nyamina and its attendant villages the destruction of which,

during Segu's dynastic troubles, had brought Mansong's recent vengeance upon Kaarta.

The route now turned against him. He writes that "the high grass and bushes seemed completely to obstruct the road, and the low lands were all so flooded by the river, that the Niger had the appearance of an extensive lake". The next day, not surprisingly, he lost his way entirely. He was about to swim a stream barring his way when a passing stranger warned him, with some force, of waiting crocodiles, and helped him find the ferry that carried vulnerable travellers across that dangerous water. That night he spent in a town where "the language of the natives was improved, from the corrupted dialect of Bambarra, to the pure Mandingo". He was, it seemed, moving out of the lands controlled by the baleful Mansong, king of Segu. This linguistic improvement, however, was not matched by any in the people's attitude to him—he explains their in-hospitality by pointing out that their headman had recently died—and he was forced to spend another night of wind and rain lying in wet grass, without a roof. He himself was fed only through the charity of the stranger who had earlier helped him across that dangerous stream; his horse was left miserably hungry.

At sunset on 20 August, Park arrived at the large town of Koulikoro, a settlement with a very long history indeed, for it is the site of one of the earliest iron-smelting operations in Africa, the workings going back to centuries before the Europeans arrived even on the distant coast. In Park's day it was another of the riverside centres for the interchange of salt from the north with local pro-duce, and for the sale of slaves. Here he found lodging in the house of a one-time slave, now a Muslim and a merchant. Anxious to add to his amulets and charms, and thus presumably to his good fortune, this man now asked his lodger to write him out something efficacious to protect him from the wicked—in return, he offered a supper of rice. "The proposal was of too great conse-quence to me to be refused; I therefore wrote the board (a sort of slate) full from top to botton on both sides; and my landlord, to be certain of having the whole force of the charm, washed the writing from the board into a calabash with a little water, and having said a few prayers over it, drank this powerful draught: after which, lest a single word should escape, he licked the board until it was quite dry." Such powers bring their own rewards: soon the headman's son had appeared with half a sheet of writing paper and a request for a charm that would make him wealthy. That night, for the first time in many days, Mungo Park slept in comfort and with a full belly.

Soon he was on his way again, struggling on through the mud and rain, swimming the streams that now with greater frequency barred his way; his precious papers he kept in his hat. He was always soaked in any case, and these strenuous dips helped to wash away the accumulated mud that covered him. At five o'clock on the afternoon of 23 August, he arrived in Bamako, a town that he had heard much talked of as a market centre, but the size of which

disappointed him. It is another very ancient site of human activity, being one
centre for the manufacture of tools by a widespread grouping of Stone Age
people known as the Sangoans, whose activities began some 50,000 years ago.
It had become one of the great market towns on the Niger, the river still being
easily navigable at this point. Ninety years after Park's arrival, French troops
under a Captain Gallieni were to occupy it, and, twenty years after that, it
would become one terminus of the railway linking the Niger to the Senegal
at Kayes (visited by Park eight months before, on his outward journey).

At Bamako, although well and courteously treated, Park received the dis-
couraging information that the direct road to the west was impassable. The
only ferry on his route was too small to take his horse and could not, apparently,
be by-passed; elsewhere, floods covered the land. If he was to continue on the
straightest way to safety, along the river, he would have to wait out the rainy
months until the summer heat once more hardened the pathways. But of course
he could not wait, having neither money nor supplies—"I resolved to push on".
Again that quiet phrase, a summary of all the force and dogged vigour with
which he drove himself forward against the intransigence of man and nature.
He was not a person easily stopped.

In the morning his landlord fortunately suggested a quite different, upland
route and, from the local headman, Park learned of a travelling minstrel about
to go that way. As a result, he determined to leave the bank of the Niger, and
to make his way to the coast directly across country from a point a little further
north. As usual, he tells us nothing of his feelings at the moment when he
turned from the river that he had struggled through so much hardship to
investigate. He had been defeated in his main purpose, had been forced to
retreat—it might have been forgiven him had he looked out for a last time
across the waters of the Niger in a mood of bitterness or regret, full of resolves
for the future. But he is Mungo Park, a Border Scot, and one almost at the end
of his resources; he has no time for such sentimental fripperies. He simply turns
away and, with his musical guide to lead him, rides off into the hills.

Erratic as artists are supposed to be, this singer soon led him along the wrong
road, told him the horse-route lay the far side of a ridge, "and throwing his
drum upon his back, mounted up the rocks, leaving me to admire his agility,
and trace out a road for myself". This Park managed to do, then spent a night,
like those he had experienced earlier in his travels, surrounded by the persistent,
but gentle, and again hospitable, curiosity of villagers; the next day he travelled
on in the company of two shepherds. But a country in turmoil sets up its endless
ambushes. The shepherds, unhampered by weakness or a failing horse, hurried
ahead; suddenly there came a screaming, a scrambling of panic, a yell of anger
and intimidation. Bandits had struck; one shepherd had been hit and taken, the
other cowered, head low, awaiting an unlikely deliverance. Park, as always,
continued, but such resolution was here out of place. Soon he was the centre of
a sullen group, a prisoner again, his destination "the king of the Foulahs". This,

he must have realised, was an unlikely outcome to the adventure; sure enough, in the first dark and overgrown place the party stopped.

"This will do", one of them said. Elsewhere, daylight glittered; here in the thicket all was gloom. A hand snatched off his hat. Park drew himself up—without it, he said, he would go no further. Did those around him laugh? A knife gleamed, struck—it was not his life they wanted yet, however, and this wound was only to his clothes—another button stolen! Park was now an old hand at playing this sort of victim. He sat still, he made no protest, he offered them only his passive acquiescence. There was, after all, nothing else to prevent them taking the short step from robbery to murder. They searched him, then made him strip. They examined everything—his second waistcoat, his broken boots. They led away his horse, then debated how they should leave him. Naked, however, he would not survive, and it seemed they did not intend to kill him. They gave him back his torn shirt, a pair of trousers; just before they left, one of them flung back the first article they had taken, his hat, in some ways the most valuable thing he possessed, for it was in its crown that he kept his papers.

"After they were gone, I sat for some time looking around me with amazement and terror. Whichever way I turned, nothing appeared but danger and difficulty. I saw myself in the midst of a vast wilderness in the depth of the rainy season, naked and alone; surrounded by savage animals, and men still more savage. I was five hundred miles from the nearest European settlement. . . . I confess that my spirits began to fail me." But, curiously, the sight of a small moss suddenly transfixed him with the realisation of an unexpected beauty. "Can that Being (thought I) who planted, watered, and brought to perfection, in this obscure part of the world, a thing which appears of so small importance, look with unconcern upon the situation and sufferings of creatures formed after His own image?—surely not!" Thus heartened, Park marched resolutely on, soon catching up the two shepherds, these not surprisingly overcome with astonishment at his survival. So he came to Sibidulu and another frontier.

Mungo Park calls the state he was now entering Manding, the name still given to the area west of Bamako. Clearly the word comes from the people who, tall and slender, inhabited it, the Mandingo, the dominant linguistic grouping in this part of Africa; the Bambara, for example, are themselves a Mandingo sub-group. It was near here that the great Mandingo empire of Mali had its beginnings; by the time Park reached this part of the world, however, the territory had split into innumerable little nodules of local power, each presided over by a chief and only very loosely, if at all, organised into large political structures.

Sibidulu, "situated in a fertile valley, surrounded with high rocky hills", proved hospitable. The local chief treated him with concern and, told of the robbery, despatched a message to Bamako in an effort to clear the matter up. Park himself waited two days for a reply to this small embassy, then was granted permission to travel on as far as a town he calls Wonda. There he was lodged in the open-sided schoolhouse and waited for news to reach him of his horse and, in particular, his clothes. "The little raiment upon me could neither protect me from the sun by day, nor the dews and mosquitoes by night; indeed, my shirt was not only worn thin, like a piece of muslin, but withal was ... very dirty...." Meanwhile, fever struck him, the more viciously for his long weakness; he had bouts of trembling, of successive heat and cold, every day during the nine that he remained in this town.

On 6 September, messengers arrived from Sibidulu, bringing with them— witness to the region's continuing law and order—Park's horse and clothes. He has nothing to say of surprise or gratitude, but mentions with alarm that his pocket compass had been broken. He may have regretted now the one he buried, perhaps too prudently, at Ali's camp in Bu Baker. His horse, too, though returned, proved less than serviceable, tumbling the next day into a deep well from which it had to be hurriedly dragged. This mishap decided him finally to abandon the unfortunate beast—it was only a cluster of bones and misery by now—and he made a gift of it to his landlord, presenting his bridle and saddle to the efficient chief at Sibidulu who had brought them back. His boots converted into sandals, a leather bag (his landlord's present to him) over his shoulder, but the fever still pressing on him, he marched off to the west on the 8th.

He moved now through an area suffering from great shortages of food, even from starvation. Regretfully, chieftains and headmen had to limit what they could grant him, as they did what they gave to their own people. At some point, he hurt his ankle, and it began to swell and throb, until he could hardly bear to put his foot on the ground. If he regretted his horse, he does not mention it. On 11 September he arrived in a town named Kinyeto, and was able to remain three days in order partially to recover; then he pressed onward again, through sticky heat and high humidity and rainfall. He suffered high fevers again, and was sometimes delirious at night.

In a place called Mansia he was in danger of being robbed and perhaps killed by the local chieftain. This was a man at least prepared to do his own dirty work, for he came himself in the darkness to try and enter Park's hut. Thwarted, he presumably retired towards morning in order to sleep off his exertions, for Park reports that he was able to leave that town before "this inhospitable chief should devise means to detain me". That afternoon he reached a rich little township named Kamalia, still over 500 miles from the coast, and there came to the house of a man named Karfa Taura. It was his brother with whom he had stayed in Kinyeto. And this man proved that Samaritan whom Park, in his condition, most desperately needed.

Karfa was slowly gathering a *coffle* of slaves to take to the coast, and though his fellow entrepreneurs proved doubtful of Park's being white, so weatherbeaten was he, so yellowed by sickness, he said he would be glad to have this wandering European accompany his caravan. The only difficulty was, however, that it would be some time yet before it set off, for the eight rivers that lay across its way would have to dwindle until they were fordable before anyone could make that journey and hope to arrive. If Park could eat the food that ordinary people ate, he himself would see him lodged and fed until the rains were over, "and that after he had conducted me in safety to the Gambia, I might then make him what return I thought proper".

A deal was struck—this apparently penniless wanderer guaranteed him the full price of a slave and Karfa Taura accepted. A great gloom lifted from Mungo Park, who had stared forward into a waiting wilderness, a five days' journey through land where no one lived, crossed by rivers that, during these months, no one could ford. "I had almost marked out the place where I was doomed, I thought, to perish, when this friendly Negro stretched out his hospitable hand for my relief."

Two meals a day, a hut for himself, enough to eat: it seemed luxury. But fever plagued him, day by day weakened him. On the third day, out walking, his muscles gave way and he fell. After that, he remained often in his hut, in the shadowed solitude that matched his mood. At times he managed to crawl into daylight, to sit half-dozing in the air, under a sky still drooping with incipient rain. At night he shivered in the tremors or blazed with the incandescence of his sickness; he murmured out the incoherent monologues of delirium. No one came near him, except for Karfa Taura himself, who visited him every day to see how he was.

The rains dwindled, the clouds thinned; as if it was these that had weighed it down and kept it in place, his fever lifted as the season turned. He was still weak, but on the edge, at least, of convalescence. He could drag his sleeping-mat out to a tamarind tree nearby and sniff up the scents of the renewed countryside. As always, those envious even of the food he ate, as well as those who hated his religion, began to spread stories about him. A slatee arrived from Segu, bringing with him the suspicions held of Park in that place. Karfa refused to be swayed from his kindness (and the hope, to be sure, of payment to come) and continued to treat Park according to their agreement, as well as with the courtesy that appears to have been natural to him.

One encounter shamed and disturbed Park. The slatee from Segu had brought with him five slaves. Park was speaking with these when one of them asked him for a little food. "I'm a stranger," Park told him. "I have none to give you."

The slave looked at him for a moment, sadness in his expression. "I gave *you* victuals when you was hungry", he said. "Have you forgotten the man who brought you milk at Karankalla?" He looked down, sighed deeply. "But the irons were not then upon my legs!"

Park begged a few handfuls of groundnuts from Karfa and passed these to the slave. The man had been captured by Mansong's forces and sent for sale to the slave-market of Segu. His four companions too were prisoners of war. So the gentlemen planters of Virginia, or Jamaica, or Alabama, would profit from wars unknown to them, from the rivalry of kings the very existence of whom they would not credit.

In the middle of December, Karfa left to collect the rest of the slaves he needed from the slave-market of Kangaba, to which Mansong sent his prisoners, as he did to all the centres of the slave trade which clustered along the Niger. For a month, therefore, Park was left on his own, to recover slowly from his weakness, to take endless notes about the life about him, and to prepare for the final drive westward to the coast and safety. He had now been travelling for over a year, so it seemed time to take stock of what had happened to him, what he had seen and suffered; he tried, both then and when he was home again, to set this into the kind of order that would make sense to his "honourable employers" and the great public beyond. He speaks of those he had travelled among, speaks of the gentleness and cheerfulness of the Mandingo peoples, does not skate around their "insurmountable propensity . . . to steal from me the few effects I was possessed of", but points out that "it were well to consider whether the lower order of people in any part of Europe would have acted . . . with greater honesty towards a stranger". And he then praises the strength of affection that he found between parents and children, remembering the many instances of this that he had come across. He talks of their cosmology, of their musical instruments and their skill with weapons, of their burial customs and their industries— a catalogue detailing so complex a social organisation, so complete a life, that it is a wonder that its publication did not bring to an abrupt end European support for slavery.

Mungo Park, as a matter of fact, who knew very well the intense interest of the British in the disputed institution of slavery (his own opinions on the subject were later to cause much controversy), gave a great deal of his attention to the place held by slaves in Mandingo society. Since he estimated that there were three slaves to every free man, this place was by no means a negligible one. Domestic slaves working in the household were the best treated—there were rules that limited their masters' authority. Worst off were those unfortunates, like the ones Park met, who had been taken prisoner during a war and dragged across a dozen borders to increase their value—the further from home they were, the less their chances of escape and thus the more they were worth. Most of those taken to the waiting Europeans on the coast were slaves of this description —but had also been born into slavery. It was slaves who made up the bulk of the fighting force; those captured in battle became, as it were, slaves twice over— though, from another point of view, they merely changed owners. Their condition, however, then became deplorable, for they were parted from their families, from the countries and languages they knew, and often found themselves packed into those ghastly shackle-loud holds in which the slavers, their ships racing death on favourable winds, carried them across the Atlantic before sickness destroyed them.

It was near the end of January before Karfa returned, bringing with him thirteen slaves he had bought and a young girl he had married, she his fourth wife. The bride was welcomed by the three whose condition she now shared; the slaves, war captives, settled dourly to their fate. About this they had wild and terrifying ideas—embarkation, after all, was usually as final as death, for as few came back from it as returned from the grave. They believed, above all, that they were destined to be eaten, either by whites or by the clients of whites; their terror of the journey ahead of them was not excessive when measured against these expectations. Park points out that they were not, on the whole, badly treated, despite the shackles that fastened them into clumsy, shuffling groups—such indifferent benevolence existing, of course, within the monstrous context of the trade itself. But only when they rebelled, or looked as if they might rebel, did they suffer the bite and crack of the lash; at other times, since their condition was the slavers' profit, they were allowed enough to eat and drink and such small comforts as shade and song. On the march to the coast, however, they often did begin to suffer from the inhumanity of their owners, the need for speed and a deliberate shortage of supplies resulting in appalling cruelties.

Now there passed weeks of delay, as those about to leave for the coast made journeys of farewell to their relations, collected debts or simply waited for favourable omens or a lucky date. Then Ramadan overtook them, and the month-long fast. Eventually, 19 April 1797 was fixed as the departure date, one Park met with a heart lightened not only by the prospect of his return to the coast, but also by the sudden flight, a dozen hours before the appearance of their principal creditor, of those over-orthodox Moors who had been most stridently his opponents. His remaining enemies thus undermined, his worn clothing at last replaced by local garments, his security assured by the patronage of Karfa and the road clear ahead of him, Park set out happily on the final stages of his journey.

They were a large party, seventy-three in all: thirty-five slaves when all had been gathered, plus fourteen free men (six of them singers, minstrels) and all their wives and attendants. So they wound their way out of the Manding territory and towards more depopulated regions. On the night of the 21st they halted in a small town—two of their minstrels declaimed their history for the delectation and information of the townsfolk—and on 23 April at last straggled their way into the wilderness of the Dialonka. This, like Manding, was presumably named after the tribe once associated with the area—in this case the Dialonke, who had ruled here and in regions to the west, but who had fallen foul of Islam and its local propagators, the Fulani. Religion mingled with the ownership of land as a cause for strife; war had curdled the erstwhile tranquillity of Futa Jallon, south-west of the route Park was now following, and Fulani columns had ever since been causing panic and destruction throughout the region. These, spreading outwards, raided their deadly rivals, the once-supreme Dialonke, and their allies. On the edge of the true wilderness Park saw the ruins of two small towns, said to have been destroyed by Fulani raiders from Fuladugu, the most westerly of the territories under Mansong's suzerainty. Thus in the whole region there seemed to be rivalry and bloodshed between these two of Africa's peoples.

A river-crossing followed, then a reorganisation of the caravan: fighting men and guides ahead, the rest of the free men at the rear, and in the centre the women (to be protected) and the slaves (to be prevented from escaping). The country may have been uninhabited, but it was remarkably well suited to settlement, its low hills and frequent rounded valleys, wooded, but not oppressive with forest, were rich in game, while its rivers were made sluggish by fish.

Next day one of the women slaves, called Niali, began to give trouble—she was, as Park puts it, "very sulky". She refused to eat, then began to hang behind the rest; her load removed, she was forced to walk in front to make sure she kept moving. Later in the morning, however, honey was found in a tree-trunk— and a little later, the desperate bees who had made it found them. Then there was a shouting, a running to and fro, a scattering of all order. Nearly everyone was stung and it took a smoke screen to drive away these rightly furious insects; Niali, unable to run far, had taken cover in a stream, but had been appallingly stung nevertheless. She was washed, leaves were rubbed into her stings, and she was requested to walk on. She refused. Thereupon she was whipped "and after bearing patiently a few strokes, she started up, and walked with tolerable expedition for four or five hours longer". When, at a halt, she tried to escape, she was too weak to run even from slavery. She fell, and once more did not get up. She was whipped a second time, no doubt to a slaver the best encouragement for an exhausted girl. If she hoped that collapse was the necessary gateway to freedom, she discovered her mistake; she was carried further in an improvised bamboo litter. Her discontent spread; the march had been long and hot, food scanty. The slaves that evening were put in irons, for "some of them *snapt their fingers*, which among Negroes is a sure sign of desperation". It is hard to tell whether Park's italics mark a moment of irony.

The next day, after debating whether the now stiff and pain-racked Niali should have her throat cut, the *coffle* simply went on without her. She was left without food or protection, in a land where no one lived. At night, the predators called aloud their bloody intentions—it is unlikely that she survived another twenty-four hours. No wonder that the caravan marched on that day in perturbed silence. The road was monotonous now: occasionally a river to cross, scrub, sandy stretches, the heat striking at them, the land forlorn in its loneliness. Recent tracks caused them to disperse, for few travelled here who were not intent on robbery, and the sign of a *coffle*'s passing would draw them like a loving summons. It was mid-afternoon on 27 April before they saw a village to mark the end of their exhausting traverse. That they were not safe yet was proved by the kidnapping of a boy in their party, one of a group in the care of a schoolmaster. He was returned, only his clothes stolen, probably because the schoolmaster lived no more than a few days' journey from this village. That was too close for the kidnapper to feel safe with a young slave who might be identified. The incident shows, however, how vulnerable travellers were in an area where they were unknown, how insecure were those unable to call on the concern of the respected or the protection of the powerful. The social consequences of institutionalised slavery ran deep and wide, bringing uncertainty into everyone's life.

On 28 April the *coffle* crossed the Bafing river; a few days later the schoolmaster arrived home, amid the delighted welcome of his family, and in his small, hospitable town the caravan remained three days. They were now at the rim of the Djoloff country, last remnants of a powerful state that once flourished north of the Gambia. Landlocked itself, it had taken tribute from each of the coastal kingdoms—200 loin cloths, two horses, a groom and a cook, four times a year— until the arrival of the Portuguese had given its one-time vassals the wealth and power to rebel. Park speaks of "Damel, king of Djoloff", a monarch who stood up to and tamed the proselytising Abdul Kader of Futa Toro; the dynasty whose title was the Damel-Tègne, however, ruled the twin kingdoms of Cayor and Baol, coastal lands that lay between the Senegal and the Gambia and had in fact been among those rebelling against Djoloff suzerainty. According to history, it was the king of Cayor, the Damel Ngoné Ndella Coumba, who defeated Abdul Kader—and, as Park was told, released him after capture, because of the pleadings of his subjects (or, it has been held, because of his powerfully religious personality, too threatening for him to be killed in a land where men live so close to their gods).

On 7 May the *coffle* set out again, towards the river Falémé. By the 11th it had reached a town Park calls "Satadoo"—certainly Satadougou, a chiefdom at the edge of the Bambuk region, governed by a continuing dynasty of the Dyula. These were Muslim families, who three centuries earlier had settled there, as in many other places, to protect the interests of the Mali empire, both in the nearby goldfields and on the trade routes that carried their product. The empire had long collapsed, but they remained, often in positions of power; the gold, too, was still to be found, and Park himself was shown some collected in the hills not far away. Despite this, Satadougou seemed a forlorn place, for constand raids by the Fulani of Futa Jallon had driven many people to safer regions. That same afternoon, the caravan crossed the Falémé, sign to Park that he was once more in familiar territory, for he had crossed the same stream, west to east, during his outward journey through Bundu, so many months before.

Four days in Tambacunda to sort out a marital tangle: one of the traders with the caravan had lived there, but had been away so long that his wife had remarried. Now she was given her choice of husbands—and then the *coffle* was on the road again. There were ruined villages on its path, and tales of Fulani raiders, but the caravan's own progress was uneventful. There were nevertheless the constant tragedies of the slave trade: in one town, a slave was found too weak to continue and was consequently exchanged for a young girl belonging to a local citizen. No one told the girl, however, and she came as happily and curiously as anyone to see the caravan depart. "Never was a face of serenity more suddenly changed into one of the deepest distress", Park writes; "the terror she manifested on having the load put upon her head, and the rope fastened round her neck . . . were truly affecting."

By 2 June they had reached Barraconda, where the Gambia tumbles white with virulent spray about the rocks and sudden edges of the rapids; they were again in the kingdom of Wuli and almost at their destination. On 5 June, Park stood once more at the spot where, eighteen months earlier, Laidley had waved his optimistic farewells; there must now have been a gathering excitement within him, a sense that he had after all achieved something. Though he had not reached Timbuctu or the Hausa lands, which remained like fables just beyond reality, he had stood on the banks of the Niger, had sailed upon its slow, brown waters, had spoken with those who travelled its course and sold their produce in the markets that sprawled at its sides. He had gone further than others, and he had survived.

As the trade in slaves was then sluggish—a consequence of far-off, European wars—it was decided that the *coffle* should stop there in Wuli and temporary accommodation be found for the slaves, while Park went on to the coast. Karfa travelled with him, for he said he would not leave him until he finally departed from Africa. First, however, Park said his farewells to the slaves, who, "amidst their own infinitely greater sufferings, would commiserate mine; and frequently of their own accord, bring water to quench my thirst, and at night collect branches and leaves to prepare me a bed in the wilderness". Park was a rare man in his ability to see the constant humanity of humans. Every person he met seems to have achieved particularity in his eyes; he had a simple respect for people, and this may have been as significant as his doggedness and courage in his struggles to survive. No condition or race of human beings seem ever to have been prejudged by him, so that his reactions to them were always open and fair; "slave" was a description of a person's situation, not an implicit condemnation, certainly not an indication of a natural inferiority. Indeed, status does not appear to have concerned him over-much, and in his universe was never distributed on racial grounds. A monarch was a monarch, an aristocrat an aristocrat, whatever the colour of his skin or the poverty of his people's circumstances—just as scoundrels and tyrants proclaimed themselves by their actions and not their antecedents.

This trait of character allowed any generosity or nobility in those he met to register with him, and it suggests a lack of cant, more typical of the eighteenth century than the nineteenth, which must have made him an easy man to befriend and help. Wherever it was possible to find helpfulness, charity and an amicable hospitality, he seems to have found it, a tribute as much to the complementary qualities in him as it is to those who displayed them for his benefit. When it came to slavery, he was not, of course, free of the guilt that drove—and properly drove—all the abolitionists, but he understood the limits of what was possible.

"My good wishes and prayers were all I could bestow upon them, and it afforded me some consolation to be told, that they were sensible I had no more to give."

Thus partially absolved, he now hurried down the course of the Gambia. He spent the night at the house of a "Seniora Camilla", an "aged black female", presumably the same—although he does not mention it—as the lady he had met on his outward journey, the one-time consort of the long-departed Hewett. From her he learned that the coast had given him up for dead. He had become, it was firmly believed, another victim of the Moors' religious fervour, murdered by them as Houghton had been before him. Park, for his part, asked after Johnson and Demba; to his distress, neither had reappeared.

Now, however, there came a time of greetings, of questions and cries of bewilderment and admiration, as first Robert Ainsley came to see him and then, on 12 June, once more at Pisania, Dr Laidley himself. He "received me with great joy and satisfaction, as one risen from the dead". Now Park became again the European gentleman, dressing in clothes he had left on the coast and shaving off his russet beard. Karfa was not impressed by his new neatness: shaving, he said, had turned Park from a man into a boy.

No ship had visited the coast for months and it seemed as though even now Park would find it impossible to leave West Africa. Karfa returned to his slaves expecting to see Park once more before he left. But unexpectedly, a day after the trader's departure, an American ship dropped anchor in the Gambia. It was on this that Park embarked, though pestilence and a lack of provisions held the vessel on that coast until the beginning of October. The ship's surgeon died, and Park stood in for him, a peripatetic locum. After a month's voyage, the ship plagued by leaks and the slaves by sickness, they arrived in a desperate condition in the West Indies. It was therefore from St John's in Antigua that Park at last set sail for London.

During that journey across the Atlantic, from the humid African coast to those West Indian islands where the men and women they carried would be deployed for a lifetime's labour—for some, a lifetime's torture—did Mungo Park reflect on what he had achieved? And in what terms? He records that the ship carried 130 Africans; he discusses how they came to be there; he tells us that many of them had heard of him before they were captured, and two of them had actually seen him. He was a humane man and by no means a slaver: "My conversation with them in their native language gave them great comfort", he writes. His awareness of their humanity and his abhorrence of their fate never led him to question his own role. It would of course be foolish to expect him to have become anachronistically aware of economic and social forces not to be charted for half a century or more. Yet, for all his own humility and openness, he was the unknowing agent of corruption. We have a witness for it, as unaware as Mungo Park himself: his friend and benefactor Karfa Taura, a man of substance, a kindly man, a leader in his community. His experience on the coast turned him into a child, into a self-denigrating apologist for what he was, for the place he lived in and the people who lived there. Faced with the material clutter, the machinery and wealth, of the white settlements, what was his response? A bemused wonder and the repeated cry, "Black men are nothing!" He would ask Mungo Park, "Why have you, who are no trader, come to explore so miserable a country as Africa?" Park adds, "He meant by this to signify that, after what I must have witnessed in my own country, nothing in Africa could, in his opinion, deserve a moment's attention. I have preserved these little traits of character in this worthy Negro, not only from regard to the man, but also because they appear to me to demonstrate that he possessed a mind *above his condition*. . . ." With italics Park emphasises this good opinion. He meant it, too, for he doubled the sum he had promised Karfa.

It was, of course, precisely those who were most intelligent and imaginative who were struck hardest by the superiority in arms, technology and social organisation of the whites. In the decades that followed, this loss of confidence was to spread like some slow, debilitating disease. No blame to Mungo Park—yet in a way he was the carrier of that sickness, despite all the hardships he himself had suffered. What had been confined to a narrow coastal strip, after him began to cover the continent, a continent part of which he had been the first European to penetrate. All that, however, is for us to consider, at the end of a century that has seen the African adventure take a wholly new turn. It was not in Mungo Park's purview. For him, landing in Falmouth on 22 December 1797, there was only triumph ahead.

Mungo Park, a portrait which appears as the frontispiece of his own *Travels in the Interior Districts of Africa* published in 1798.

"The Palaver", a presentation of gifts to the headman of one of the tribes, possibly
Mandingo, inhabiting the upper reaches of the Niger. (From *Picturesque Views on the
River Niger* by William Allen.)

Two illustrations from Mungo Park's own book about his *Travels in Africa:* (above) The Bridge over the Ba-Fing on Black River; (below) a view of Kamalia, a town he reached on the home journey in 1796.

(Above) Making and sailing canoes. (From John Ogilby's *Africa*.)
(Below) A typical view of one of many villages through which Mungo Park passed on his way to the Niger. (From *Picturesque Views on the River Niger* by William Allen.)

(Above) A view of Mungo Park's expedition of 1805. (*From La Conquête Pacifique de l'Interieur Africain*, by Gen. Philebert.)

The column of march crossing a river.

Late nineteenth-century photograph of a cross raised to one of Mungo Park's companions. The photograph has been slightly touched up, but it is evident that the cross was still standing many years later. (From *Timbuctoo – The Mysterious* by Felix Dubois.)

Chapter Eight

A Retiring Hero

The coach from Falmouth reached London early on Christmas morning, 1797. One imagines a stillness, the first filtering of light making clear the line of roof ridge and chimney, the streets still empty, the air crisp with its burden of cold. With a curious, perhaps overconsiderate, shyness, Park, arriving out of the wilderness, thought it too early to disturb his sister and her husband, James Dickson. Did he want for a while to savour the fact of his arrival, to come to terms again with the metropolis? He approached familiar gates; beyond them stretched the gardens of the British Museum. He wandered in, surely not by chance. He was a reserved man trying, one feels, to ease himself into old relationships; the gardens were under Dickson's charge and Mungo must have considered the possibility of meeting him. And there, near his hot-houses, thunderstruck, this gardener stood, bulging-eyed at the approach of an early-morning ghost. Mungo Park, risen from the miasmic swamps of Africa, torn to safety from savage and predator, come home again in a single piece and upright: a man still. Dickson can hardly have believed it. Did he express such disbelief? We have no direct record of the meeting, but it is surely possible to hear the quiet voices sliding across the frost, the controlled Borderer faces showing no more than slight smiles: "Ah Mungo, is it you? So you're back!" A handshake, perhaps. "Yes, back, Mr Dickson . . ."

But others were less reticent. For Banks, it meant vindication: a man had travelled to the Niger and come back, a man sent by him and the African Association. Into what had seemed to European eyes an almost impenetrable murk, a clear light had at last been shone. It was at once decided that Park should continue to be paid while he prepared an account of what he had seen and done, and what had been done to him; meanwhile, and swiftly, a shortened version of this account should be prepared for the Association and presented as soon as possible. The Association's Secretary, Bryan Edwards, himself the author of a book, *A History of the British Colonies in the West Indies*, devoted himself to helping Mungo Park prepare his text.

As they settled down to work, it cannot have been easy for them to ignore

the peril in which the whole country lay. For Park had come back to an embattled England. In October 1797, the Hapsburgs had made their peace with
France. And in France itself, a republican *coup d'état* had forestalled monarchist
reaction, settled in power an ineffectual and corrupt triumvirate and paved the
way for Napoleon's rule. Britain now faced that burgeoning power alone,
though still protected by her vigilant navy. It might not protect her much longer.
Napoleon, who had the previous November returned triumphantly to a Paris
that had hailed him like a coming Caesar, was planning an invasion of England.
Along the south coast, desperate preparations were in hand to repel the French,
but no one was certain and by no means all were optimistic about what the outcome would be. The tension, the feeling that the whole country was under
siege, continued throughout that winter and into the spring. Then, in mid-
May, Napoleon abruptly set sail for Egypt in an attempt to cut Britain's links
with India and the East. Despite the severity of this indirect threat to their
security, the British were able to heave a collective sigh of relief. In a little while,
they would be able to do more: they would be able to celebrate Nelson's
triumph at Abukir and the collapse of Napoleon's eastern strategy.

Meanwhile, it was at the end of the same month as that in which the French
set sail for Egypt, May 1798, that Mungo Park's "Abridgement" was presented
at a meeting of the Association, including also some geographical illumination
set out in an appendix by that somewhat dogmatic and occasionally inaccurate
expert, Major Rennell. At the meeting it was unanimously resolved that Mungo
Park had "executed the purposes of his Mission with a degree of Industry, perseverance and ability that entitle him to the warmest approbation of this
Association". He would be allowed to publish the story of his travels for his
own profit, and a subscription of those eager to buy the finished volume at a
guinea a copy was immediately opened. At the same time the meeting agreed
that it was "expedient for the present to suspend any attempt at further Discoveries in Africa by way of the River Niger" and that "Mr. Park having
signified to the Association his wishes to be employed in the business of Exploring the Interior of New Holland, The Committee be empowered to recom-
mend Mr. Park's services to the Government for that purpose".

New Holland? This was Australia, the coast of which had been a part of
Banks's own arena when he travelled on Captain Cook's first expedition. He
was the great expert on Australian affairs, acted as Government adviser, had
helped ten years before in founding the settlement at Botany Bay. What can
have seemed more plausible to him than the switching of his successful explorer
from one area of British preoccupation to another? Certainly the interior of
Australia presented as much of a mystery as did that of Africa. Its inner deserts
were still quite unknown; Banks himself was convinced that navigable rivers
must reach up to sources deep inland, and that on the banks of such useful
streams products of value to Britain would be discovered. Now he suggested
that he draw up a set of instructions for an expedition to be sent out under Park

in order to find the potential wealth he believed was there; he was prepared to take on the work at once, "such zeal do I really feel for the prosperity of a colony in the founding of which I bore a considerable share".

It seems that, before returning in the summer of 1798 to Scotland, Park agreed to lead this expedition. Back in the Border country, while Nelson destroyed Napoleon's Egyptian hopes, he settled to the task of writing down the story of his African adventures. He faced this, it seems, with some self-doubt, but nevertheless brought to it the same resolution as had carried him to Sansanding and back. He had problems of organisation, not understanding too well what he should put in and what leave out. Bryan Edwards again gave up much of his time in aiding him and editing his work; he told Banks in October that "there is such a sameness in the Negro manners and the occurrences which he relates are so unimportant that it requires some skill in composition and arrangement to make the reading supportable". Three months later, however, he was writing enthusiastically to Banks about the way Park had mastered his task, and now considered that the young Scot "goes on triumphantly".

Meanwhile, Banks's plan to send Park to Australia had foundered on an unexpected reef: the explorer's own uncertainty, even indifference. Park had been offered ten shillings a day to undertake the task, but said it was not enough. The Government, which was footing the bill, regarded its coffers and the future of Australia and offered another half a crown. Park shrugged epistolatory shoulders —he had stopped making any preparations for departure and the terms suggested did not tempt him to change his mind. With that note of priggishness that now and again peeps through in his letters, he wrote, somewhat loftily, "Pecuniary considerations, however contemptable in themselves, serve as a good interest by which to judge the importance or inutility of any office or pursuit. . . ." Banks reproached Dickson with not persuading Park to go on the Australian venture. When Dickson replied, a new explanation for Park's reluctance emerged.

"I have not in any way been a cause of Mr. Park's not agreeing with your encouragement. . . . Mr. Park is of a very closs mind and I suppose he thinks I wish him to go. So I do but shall not tell him so for this reason. When he went to Africa some of his friends were so imprudent as to say I was the cause of his being sacrificed, for they were sure he would niver return. I have found out from his sister, which is my wife, that there is some private connection, a love affair in Scotland, but no money in it. What a pity it is men should be such fools that might be of use to their country." It was neither ten shillings a day nor twelve and six that was too little, then, but rather the strain of absence that threatened to be too great. Park had discovered, or perhaps rediscovered, his Ailie, Dr Anderson's daughter. Not much is known about her, and even her name is in some doubt—was it Alice, as some think, or Alison, or Aileen? We have only Mungo's affectionate diminutive. She seems to have been attractive, with a capacity to be demurely amused which must have countered his own tendency towards sententiousness. As he struggled with the early chapters of his book, they became engaged.

At the end of 1798 he returned to London with his manuscript, and Edwards gave it the final polish, though himself now far from well. It went to Nicol, a publisher and bookseller well known for bringing out the more serious travellers' tales—he had published Cook's account—and by May *Travels in the Interior Districts of Africa in 1795, 1796, and 1797* was in the hands of the public. Those hands grabbed at it with the utmost enthusiasm. The first edition of 1,500 copies went in the first week; a second and a third edition were brought out before the end of 1799. A fourth appeared the following year. Richer by £1,000, and still with his accumulated pay largely unspent, Park travelled north again. He agreed, however, that he would "hold himself in readiness at all times to proceed again to Joliba in case Government should think fit to establish a colony on its banks, and his services be required".

Elsewhere, great events were stirring. Russians, Turks and Austrians had at last eased British isolation in the war. But the early victories of this Second Coalition had only made a different triumph possible. In November 1799, Napoleon's brother Lucien had brought the Directory to an end; by Christmas, Napoleon had become France's First Consul. In the spring of 1800, he destroyed the Austrians at Marengo. Since Russia had by then already withdrawn from the war, the Second Coalition had collapsed even more swiftly than the First. In Britain, William Pitt, beset by George III's opposition to Catholic Emancipation and with his war strategy of alliance destroyed, fell from office. Seizing his diplomatic opportunity, Napoleon began negotiations with his most resolute opponents. In March, 1802, the Treaty of Amiens codified the peace with England that he wanted. For a little while, the war had come to an end.

Far from the world's dramas, protected one hopes by his own happiness, Mungo Park had married on 2 August 1799; with his wife he settled again at Foulshiels. The two years that now passed close over him like some dark lake. He vanishes. We know he liked solitary walks and doubtless took them. His health, and particularly his digestion, had been half destroyed by his experiences. It is hard to say now whether it was the dysentery he had caught in Africa, or the calomel with which he had tried to cure it, that was the real cause of the trouble, but there was trouble and he suffered it. His mind, too, was no longer easy; from time to time he would rise sweating from nightmares, their harrowing images based on his months of captivity, on the callousness of his Moorish gaolers and the precise cruelty of Ali, their chief.

For comfort, however, he now had his wife, a tall, good-looking young woman who has been described as frivolous—a foil for his seriousness, perhaps, her delight in the superficial soothing to the deep wounds he had sustained. Slowly, he recovered, both in nerve and stamina. His restlessness and the hope, perhaps even the need, for new employment carried his attention back to London and the opportunities that offered themselves there. When Gorée was captured

by the British in 1800, Park wrote to Banks pointing out the value of that fortified island off Cape Verde, halfway between the Senegal and the Gambia. As a
supportive base for any expedition penetrating the interior it was ideal. "If such
are the views of Government, I hope my exertions in some station or other may
be of use to my country." In the meantime, he was without prospects and
"unless some of my friends interest themselves on my behalf, I must wait patiently, until the cloud which hangs over my future prospects is dispelled". One
can hear the desperation that twists and grates behind the controlled words and
perhaps Banks heard it too. It was probably at his invitation that, early the
following year, Park was once more in London, concerned in some new and
tempting Australian venture. This seems to have been much more than a mere
exploratory expedition, however, for Ailie was to have taken part in it: perhaps
he was intending to leave Britain for good and superintend some colonising
venture in a newer, faraway land.

On 12 March 1801 he wrote back home to Foulshiels, "My lovely Ailie,
nothing gives me more pleasure than to write to you, and the reason why I
delayed it a day last time was to get some money to send you. You say you are
wishing to spend a note upon yourself. My sweet Ailie, you may be sure I
approve of it. What is mine is yours, and I receive much pleasure from your
goodness in consulting me about such a trifle. I wish I had thousands to give you,
but I know that my Ailie will be contented with what we have, and we shall
live in the hope of seeing better days. I long very much to be with you, my love,
and I was in great hopes of having things settled before now, but Sir Joseph is
ill, and I can do nothing till he recovers.

"I am happy to know you will go to New South Wales with me, my sweet
wife. You are everything that I could desire; and wherever we go, you may be
sure of one thing, that I shall always love you. Whenever I have fixed on this
or any other situation I shall write to you. In the meantime, let nobody know
till things are settled, as there is much between the cup and the lip.

"My lovely Ailie, you are constantly in my thoughts. I am tired of this place,
but cannot lose the present opportunity of doing something for our advantage.
When that is accomplished I shall not lose one moment. My darling, when we
meet I shall be the happiest man on earth. Write soon, for I count the days till
I hear from you, my lovely Ailie."

"Yrs ever", he signed himself, and clearly he meant it. He was playing no
double game when he told his wife he was "tired of this place"—certainly among
London's frivolities he never cut a particularly engaging figure, nor ever showed
he wanted to. He was at his greatest ease among the sober, but happiest for the
moment, as his words suggest, on the banks of the Yarrow and with his wife at
his side.

His attitude of caution to the Australian opportunity proved the proper one,
for in the end it came to nothing. From Scotland, to which he had again retreated, Park wrote to Sir Joseph Banks, "I have always looked upon you as my

particular friend; and, as I have experienced so many marks of your favour, I thought myself bound in gratitude to inform you of such steps as I might take in life.

"I left London, as you may easily suppose, a little down-hearted: the romantic village which my fancy had erected on the shores of New Holland, as a habitation for myself and family, had completely disappeared, and I journeyed towards my native country with the painful but not degrading reflexion, that I must henceforth earn my bread by the sweat of my brow. On my arrival in Scotland, it was my wish to occupy a farm; but the high price of cattle and the enormous rents which landholders everywhere expected made it a rather dangerous speculation: in short, I was again compleatly at a stand. At this juncture a surgeon of considerable eminence died at Peebles; and, as I was tired of a life of indolence, I resolved to succeed him. I was induced to take this step, because it would afford me present employment; and in the event of obtaining something better, I could resign my situation to my younger brother or brother-in-law, both of whom are at present abroad, and who, in consequence of the peace, will be in a great measure unprovided for.

"In the meantime I hope my friends will not relax in their endeavours to serve me. A country surgeon is at best but a laborious employment; and I will gladly hang up the lancet and plaister ladle whenever I can obtain a more eligible situation."

The letter is dated 13 October 1801, and it was sent from Peebles. Two years had passed since the publication of Park's book and the money he had received from that and for his efforts in Africa was coming to an end. Of necessity, as his letter shows, and from no inner prompting or natural inclination, he had turned to his trained skill in medicine to provide a living for himself and his family. It is clear that he was not happy—he probably had less of a vocation for medicine than he had had for the ministry. Nothing he ever wrote would suggest that he regarded the world and its creatures from the standpoint of a medical man. He was, of course, efficient and humane, and often travelled the night paths of an uncomfortable countryside to the lonely cottages of those who needed him.

He did not spare himself: there is a story of his being caught far from home by night and storm, and making his way for shelter to a little shepherd's hut—there to find the man's wife in the throes of giving birth. He stayed with her all night, until her son's successful delivery just after dawn. When he left, the new father followed him down the steep path, watching his every step: "My wife said she was sure you must be an angel, and I think sae tae; so I'm just keepin' ahint to be sure I'll see you flee up!" Peasant simplicity or dry Border humour? In either case, perhaps, some compensation for a night spent without sleep.

Park, however, found his work monotonous; one senses that he felt himself being drawn back into that obscurity from which he had struggled with such energy and—one reads the fear in his letters—for so brief a time. He knew that his book had been immensely successful, that throughout Europe groups were

meeting, gatherings of the rich, the important and the self-important, all fascinated by Africa, all determined like Sir Joseph and his friends to sponsor their
own assaults on that still-mysterious continent. Wherever such projects were
discussed, his book had become essential reading. Yet he, meanwhile, sank daily
deeper into the demanding routines of a country doctor, the outlines of his
fame and his continued eagerness to serve obscured by the passing years. He
expected to be called for, and he was not—except to the bedsides of feverish
children, pregnant women, injured labourers and the dying old.

One true compensation must have been the quality of the friends he now had.
Edinburgh in the eighteenth century was the centre of a rich, varied—though
often somewhat sanctimonious and self-satisfied—intellectual life. Its critics,
philosophers and divines generated between them enough magnetic power to
attract the curiosity and interest even of the southern metropolis. It was therefore possible for Park, his own eminence hard won but well deserved, to find
himself companions of some stature, even in his Peebles exile.

Among these was Adam Ferguson, one of the creators of modern sociology,
who had been Professor of Philosophy at Edinburgh University, had written
many books and essays and counted among his distinctions a visit to Voltaire—
though that may have been a little marred by the great man's mistaking him for
some quite different Ferguson and insisting on discussing the state of Russian
education. Dugald Stewart, whose book Park had taken with him on his voyage
to Sumatra, had been Ferguson's pupil and had become his successor; he himself had been variously described as "fiery as gunpowder" and as one who
"conversed fluently but with dignified reserve" and was "possessed of a boundless flow of humour". In an earlier house of his, Burns and Walter Scott had had
the only meeting of their lives; now, at Hallyards, not far from Peebles, he
made Mungo Park welcome, bringing out a great map of Africa and, despite
the fact that he was almost eighty years old, energetically taking the explorer
step by step through his arduous journey.

The most notable of Park's acquaintances, however, was Sir Walter Scott,
whom he met only in the early summer of 1804. By this time, his second expedition was already well into the planning stage, but he found time enough for
Sir Walter's company. Scott had just moved into a house named Ashestiel, over
the ridge of Williamshope from the Yarrow, and itself on the banks of the
Tweed. He knew Mungo's brother Archibald, who was both friend and employee, and so was able to slip swiftly through Mungo's habitual screen of
shyness. Indeed, it is Scott who, among others, bears witness to the screen in
his comments on Park's coldness towards those he did not know.

Park clearly took his role as traveller with great sobriety. On the one hand,
he had, Scott affirms, cut from his narrative a number of personal anecdotes,
"circumstances which, however true, were of little or no moment, as they related solely to his personal adventures and escapes"; on the other, he hated the
oblique approach of those trying "to avoid the apparent rudeness of blunt

interrogations"—he could never work out what it was they wanted from him nor how to answer the hints and nudges of their questioning. A more outgoing man would have found little difficulty in dispensing anecdotal morsels to feed such innocuous sharks, but for Park they brought only bewilderment and irritation.

Africa, however, remained in his thoughts. It is from Scott that we learn about his nightmares, from Scott too the account of how, on one occasion finding him not at home, he discovered him dropping stones into the Yarrow, then counting intently until bubbles appeared on the surface. It was by this method, Park told him, that he had worked out the depth of the streams in Africa and so decided whether he could cross them safely. It seems very likely that if Park had remained in Scotland he would have become more and more embittered at the limitations of his life and his career. He was too young for resignation. As he reportedly said to Scott, "he would rather brave Africa and all its horrors, than wear out his life in long and toilsome rides over the hills of Scotland, for which the remuneration was hardly enough to keep soul and body together".

It is questionable, however, whether remuneration loomed really as large as that in his expectations. He would doubtless have liked to be rich and certainly to have been relieved of a medical career he did not much care for. Despite all his dourness and his genuine modesty, too, one suspects that he enjoyed his fame. But Africa had taxed him to the limit, and all his training and all the pressures of his environment would surely have made that an enjoyable experience in itself. After it, all lesser struggles must have seemed empty, childish, taking up only a part of himself. That deep strength, that inflexible will and courage, must have craved some test more demanding than the Border hills could provide. And then, the task had been unfinished: he had been forced to turn back with the termination of the Niger still a mystery. Again all his up-bringing as well as everything in his own character must have pressed him to demand a second chance at solving this centuries-old problem. At first, Ailie held him, but he had been four years married when he left for his second voyage to Africa, and one imagines that his first absorption in sustained affection and sexual fulfilment was over. Earlier preoccupations, half-repressed ambitions, seem to have begun to work in him again. For all his love of his wife, he was desperate to be off. Despite the eventual outcome, it was as well, perhaps, that the Government summoned him when it did.

PART II

THE IMPERIAL MISSION

THE PALACE, SEGO.

Chapter Nine

The Governmental Summons

Exploration had not come to an end because Park had been forced into retreat, nor had the African Association been disbanded. While Park was still in Africa, a young German named Friedrich Hornemann presented himself as candidate for an African adventure, his recommendation coming from one of those polymath near-geniuses who decorated the intellectual life of the eighteenth and nineteenth centuries. This was a brilliant university teacher named Blumenbach, originally a medical man—he had become Professor of Medicine at Göttingen when only twenty-six—but with interests that had spilled over early into other fields. Three years before he was appointed professor, he had written an influential treatise supporting the thesis that all human beings, whatever their colour or continent of origin, belonged to a single species; he had written the foreword to the German translation of Bruce's account of his Ethiopian travels; fascinated by Africa, he had followed from afar the failures and tragedies that had beset the African Association. Blumenbach's letter, and Hornemann's own level-headed approach to the problems that would face him, persuaded Banks to accept his offer.

Hornemann wanted to travel to Mourzuk in the Fezzan and from there perhaps as far south and west as Timbuctu. By the summer of 1798 he was in Cairo, in time to witness the dislocation caused by the arrival of Napoleon's army. He spent a further year preparing himself, studying the customs and language, for he intended to travel as a Muslim trader. On 6 April 1800, having reached Mourzuk, he wrote to Sir Joseph just before joining a caravan for Bornu, "Being very healthsom and perfectly acclimated to this country, sufficiently acquainted with the manners of my fellow travellers, speaking the Arabian language and somewhat the Bornu tongue and being well armed and not without courage under the protection of two great Sheriffs, I hope a good success of my undertaking." Then, like so many others before and after him, he vanished into rumour and a long silence and, as the Association learned a full nineteen years later, a miserable death by dysentery.

By the time poor Hornemann was wasting away in pain and despair somewhere deep in the Nupe country, Mungo Park was gazing moodily out at the
world from Foulshiels. But he had not, as he must often have thought then and
in the years that followed, been forgotten by the gentlemen in London. War
and politics hampered his cause, but a new and more ferocious patriotism, an
increasingly ruthless imperial drive, were ensuring that his moment would arrive
again. The fact of his near-success had not really been lost sight of, nor what
British penetration into West Africa might mean for the country's trade and
industry. Indeed, from the time that he returned to London in 1798, the interest
in exploration had not only become more general, but had also been beadily
regarded by a Government that, having taken little part in the first expedition,
was clearly not going to be left out of any subsequent attempt to establish a
European presence on the banks of the Niger.

The new emphasis on national opportunity and international rivalry only
underlined what had always been the case, that the overseas adventures of any
members of a trading community like Britain could not be undertaken without
some sort of Government involvement. Even a refusal, on the part of the Foreign
or Colonial Office, to be directly involved had to be construed as a positive act
with its own often complex significance. In the Pacific, in the south Atlantic
and elsewhere, the Government had long been involved in sponsoring exploration, its agent usually the Admiralty. Land expeditions, however, were something different, and it may be for that reason that there was at first a sort of
timidity about the authorities' involvement in it. It seems to have been Mungo
Park's successful return and the direct appeals of Sir Joseph Banks that attached
them more closely to the projects then being planned.

On 25 May 1799, Sir Joseph gave a speech to the African Association which
set out the commercial logic of what Britain should undertake in West Africa.
Having described the Association's achievements in that area, he told the members, "We have already by Mr. Park's means opened a Gate into the Interior of
Africa, into which it is easy for every Nation to enter and to extend its commerce and Discovery from the West to the Eastern side of that immense
continent. . . . A Detachment of 500 chosen Troops would soon make that Road
easy, and would build Embarkations upon the Joliba—if 200 of these were to
embark with Field pieces they would be able to overcome the whole Forces
which Africa could bring against them.

"The Trade which the Moors carry on to the Interior is always directed to
the Towns Situated on or near the River—it is said to produce an annual Return
of about a Million Sterling—much of it in Gold: The Rivers that empty themselves into the Mother Stream generally abound in this Metal, and the natives
are well experienced in the art of collecting it, in the form of Dust, near their
mouths.

"If Science should teach these ignorant Savages, that the Gold which is Dust
at the mouth of a river must be in the form of sand at a high part of the Current,

of Gravel in a still more elevated Station, or of Pebbles when near the place from whence it was originally washed . . . is it not probable that the Golden harvest they are already in the habit of gathering might be encreased an hundred fold?

"As encreased Riches still encrease the wants of the Possessors, and as Our Manufacturers are able to supply them, is not this prospect, of at once attaching to this country the whole of the Interior Trade now possessed by the Moors, with the chance of an incalculable future encrease, worth some exertion and some expence to a Trading Nation? . . . It is easy to foretell that if this Country delays much longer to possess themselves of the Treasures laid open to them by the exertions of this Association, some Rival Nation will take possession of the Banks of the Joliba, and assert by arms her right of Prior possession, should we afterwards attempt to participate in the benefits of this New Trade, or in the honor of exploring Nations which are yet unknown to Europe."

As was only natural at that period, Sir Joseph does not for a moment pause to consider what the wishes of the "ignorant Savages" themselves might be about trade with an overwhelmingly richer and more developed Europe, nor what effect rival armies several hundred strong, armed with artillery, would have on the societies across whose lands they would be forced to fight. More noteworthy, perhaps, is that, in this consideration of the future, the matter of pure exploration, undertaken for the enrichment of human knowledge, receives precisely half a sentence to itself.

Early in June, Banks approached the Government more directly in a letter to Lord Liverpool, then at the Board of Trade. With it went a memorandum that closely followed the arguments of Banks's address to the African Association, arguments persuasive enough, he must have hoped, to bring the Government to immediate action. "Should the experiment be made", Banks wrote in his letter, "I have little doubt that in a very few years a trading Company might be established under immediate control of the Government, who would take upon themselves the whole expense of the measure, would govern the Negroes far more mildly and make them far more happy than they are now under the tyranny of their arbitrary princes, would become popular at home by converting them to the Christian religion by inculcating in their rough minds the mild morality which is engrafted on the tenets of our faith and by effecting the greatest practicable diminution of the Slavery of Mankind, upon the principles of natural justice and commercial benefit."

It was not any incongruity between "the mild morality" of the Christian faith and the 200 soldiers "with Field pieces" who were to prepare the ground for its inculcation which dissuaded the Government from action, but rather the pressing needs of the French war abroad and the disputes over Catholic Emancipation at home. As we have seen, Pitt resigned over the latter; and the former came to a temporary halt after the Treaty of Amiens, which, incidentally, was signed for Britain by the same Lord Liverpool, now Foreign Secretary under Addington's premiership. In August 1802, four months after the treaty had brought hostilities to an end, Banks wrote an alarmed letter to John Sullivan, the Colonial Under-Secretary. He had read a book written by a former aide to the Governor of the French colony of Senegal, "a Book written with the Clear intention to induce the French to Colonize the whole of the Senegambia country, which view I think it is likely to promote materially. . . . Ministers should be aware of the contents, and hold in mind what will happen, which is that whoever Colonizes in that part of Africa with Spirit will Clearly be able to sell Colonial Products of all kinds in the European market at a Cheaper price than any part of the West Indies can afford . . .'

At the Colonial Office, wheels thus energised began slowly to turn. It is probable that, although he was not written to or asked for advice, Mungo Park had already been chosen to play some part in any expedition the Government would send into Africa. A year earlier Banks, looking forward to the peace then expected, had seen in it an opportunity "of sending a mission to Africa in order to penetrate to, and navigate, the Niger; and that in case the Government should enter into the plan, Park would certainly be recommended as the person proper to be employed for carrying it into execution."

To begin with, however, it was not an expedition, with all its hazards, that the Colonial Office wanted, but rather a great increase in the British presence on the Gambia estuary. Factories should be built there, protected by garrisons, and trade with the interior vigorously prosecuted. However, with the passing of another year, the collapse of the peace and new preoccupations, the Government placed such peaceful plans in abeyance. At first it was suggested that Park, this time with twenty-five soldiers for protection, should "take another trip into the centre of Africa to discover the termination of the Niger". He travelled to London to see Lord Bathurst, the Colonial Secretary, who offered him the charge of this proposed expedition. He decided that he needed time and the consent of his family before he could agree, and returned to Scotland for both. It is likely that Ailie, who had seen from closer quarters than anyone what his Peebles exile meant to him, made little protest at the proposal. In December 1803 he travelled south to London, expecting that he would very soon be on his way to the Gambia again.

By then, however, the modest plan originally proposed had swollen into a monstrous expedition intended to launch an invasion rather than an exploratory party. The Government had been approached by a Colonel Stevenson, who thought it feasible, and certainly highly desirable, for a British force to capture Timbuctu. The Government felt this was a little overambitious, but was nevertheless swept along by the colonel's military enthusiasm. Sullivan drew up a new plan, a construction of high ambition and complex detail. Taking part there would be a land force of 150 soldiers from the African Corps, 100 more from the Gorée garrison, a battalion of 1,000 to supplement these, twenty artificers, six light cannon and 200 large pistols to reinforce their normal armaments, all this power to be placed under Colonel Stevenson. To deal with the inevitable consequences of his bellicosity, a surgeon-general, four surgeons and eight surgical assistants were to accompany the force. At sea, a small frigate, a sloop and three brigs, four gunboats and two troopships, a store ship and, of necessity, a hospital ship, were to provide support. The three naval officers to command this flotilla—it was prescribed that they should be intelligent—had not as yet been picked.

The initial object of the expedition would be to throw the French out of their fortified stations at Albreda on the Gambia and St Joseph on the Senegal. Factories would then be established in Wuli and Bundu and trade agreements would be signed with these kingdoms. Colonel Stevenson would then establish and consolidate the British presence in Bambuk, while Mungo Park in a gunboat would sail off down the Niger to Segu, Timbuctu and the Hausa states, his objective to promote a "free and secure intercourse of trade with the natives".

The expedition was meant to depart in February 1804. Some of the soldiers were already on their way to Africa when Addington's ministry collapsed. It had been lent a sort of popularity by Nelson's victories off Denmark and Egypt, had been sustained by the public enthusiasm at the peace that had been signed at Amiens, but the resumption of war, and the feebleness Addington brought to its prosecution, undermined it and it fell. Pitt returned to Downing Street; Lord Camden, chiefly remembered for triggering off rebellion by his repressions of the Irish, took over Hobart's seat as Colonial Secretary. The grandiose expedition that had been planned shivered away like a mirage. As Lord Camden said, in a letter written to Banks late in September 1804, "An Expedition of the Nature and Extent of that which had (at one time) been intended, appear impracticable now; but I think much may be gained by an expedition upon a confined Scale, undertaken by a Man of Sense and Experience. With this view I have sent for and conversed with Mr. Park, and have held out (with Mr. Pitt's sanction) encouragement to him. . . . Altho' I have communicated with Mr. Park; yet, in the shape this undertaking now assumes, it bears so much the description of a Journey of Enquiry without any military attendance upon it, that it seems to me more fit that Mr. Park should be instructed as to his Enquiries and Researches by those who have turned their Mind to this subject as much as you have done, than by me . . ."

By this time, Park was back at Foulshiels. He had returned to Peebles with a native of Mogador, one Sidi Ambak Bubi, who had come to London as the interpreter for Elphi Bey, the ambassador from Cairo. This exotic companion was his in consequence of a suggestion made to him by Lord Camden that he should prepare himself for his journey into the Muslim lands south of the Sahara by learning Arabic; the Government would pay the costs of his tuition. The arrival of so very strange a stranger in the austerity of Peebles seems to have created an abiding sense of wonder in the inhabitants. In May 1804, at last convinced by Government interest that he would in fact be returning to Africa,

Park gave up his practice, took his wife and their three children back to Foul-shiels and there concentrated on his Arabic, on the study of astronomical obser-vation, which had also been recommended to him, and on considering what it was he wanted to do in Africa and how best he should go about doing it.

Not even his new friendship with Sir Walter Scott could divert him from his primary purpose. Late in September he finished work on a memorandum setting out, for the benefit of the Colonial Office, his intentions for the expedition, and was then ready to depart. There are confusing tales about his leave-taking. From Lockhart, Scott's biographer, comes a story of Park staying at Ashestiel for a farewell visit, then riding with his host back over the ridge towards Foulshiels. Scott was uneasy over Park's plans, for these still included soldiers—in Scott's opinion too few to protect Park, but more than enough to arouse hostility. But Mungo was, as always, confident. Knowing the people, he insisted that their kingdoms were not powerful enough to stop him on their own, and too inde-pendent to combine for the purpose. They were, in any case, used to travellers, to strangers passing through their domains with caravans and trains of slaves— as long as he paid his dues, no one would bother him and his men. The two men came to their moment of farewell; then Park turned his horse and jumped it over a small roadside ditch. The animal stumbled, and Scott called after him, "I'm afraid, Mungo, that's a bad omen."

But Mungo only shouted back over his shoulder, his horse now steadying into a trot, "Freits follow them that look to them." He was not a man much burdened by superstition. So far the story causes no problems, but now there is divergence, for Lockhart has Scott insisting that Park, unable to bear the parting with his wife, slipped away to Edinburgh on the pretence of having business there, and travelled from there to London without another word with his family. But there are other accounts: One, often told by the servant of the house, is that Mungo did in fact collect his courage and brave that final scene, but found it so harrowing that in the end he told Ailie that a word from her would keep him at home. She, however, good Scottish wife, shook her head: "No, go and do your duty." Still another version is less flattering to them both. It appears in a manuscript attributed to a sister of Park's, a Mrs Thomson who lived on a farm at the base of Bencleugh, and tells of how Mungo's ghost appeared to her in 1805. It refers to the scene of parting: according to this version, Mungo grew tired of the lamentations and dreadful predictions of Ailie and Mrs Thomson, clambered on his horse, called down to them, "Tell these tales to old wives!", and rode off to Edinburgh, London, Africa and death.

Whatever the truth of these last meetings, a resolute Mungo Park arrived in London early in October and within a day or so had presented his memorandum to Lord Camden. He pointed out that "worthy of particular investigation" were the trade route to and from the Niger, its safety, what might most profit-ably be carried over it and how much profit such carriage might be expected to bring. "Mr. Park would likewise turn his attention to the general fertility of the country, whether any part of it might be useful for Britain for colonisation, and whether any objects of Natural History, with which the natives are at present unacquainted, might be useful to Britain as a commercial nation."

He outlined his proposals for the actual journey—more or less those he afterwards followed—and then talks of sailing down the river "to the kingdom of *Wangara*, being a direct distance of about one thousand four hundred miles from the place of embarkation." If the Niger ended there in an enormous puddle, "Mr. Park would feel his situation extremely critical. . . . To return by the Niger to the westward he apprehends would be impossible; to proceed to the northward equally so; and to travel through Abyssinia extremely dangerous. The only remaining route that holds out any hopes of success, is that towards the *Bight of Guinea*. If the river should take a southerly direction, Mr. Park would consider it as his duty to follow it to its termination; and if it should happily prove to be the river Congo, would there embark . . . ."

He then gives reasons, none very convincing, for believing that the Niger and the Congo were the same. He ends with something of a flourish, unusual in him and possibly not his own: "Mr. Park is of opinion . . . that his expedition, though attended with extreme danger, promises to be productive of the utmost advantage to Great Britain. Considered in a commercial point of view, it is second only to the discovery of the Cape of Good Hope; and in a geographical point of view, it is certainly the greatest discovery that remains to be made in this world."

He wanted thirty European soldiers to protect him, six European carpenters to help him construct the two boats in which he planned to make his downriver ourney, presents enough to sweeten the welcome of the kings whose territories lay across his route, some twenty Africans from Gorée as artificers in his construction programme, fifty asses and six horses. This must have seemed to him a force that combined security, practicality and flexibility; in the event it would prove too small for security and too large for flexibility, while its practicality was never brought to the test. It was Major Rennell who was most urgent in warning him of the dangers that faced him, since in his theory the Niger ended in a vast, central wilderness. They met at Brighthelmston (as Brighton was still called) and Rennell urged him most forcibly not to go; for a short while, even Mungo wavered, but soon his resolution had put him back on his chosen course.

Banks too pored over the memorandum, and noted that he was well aware that "Mr. Park's expedition is one of the most hazardous a man can undertake; but I cannot agree with those who think it is too hazardous to be attempted". It was only by such a risk of human life "that we can hope to penetrate the obscurity of the internal face of Africa: we are really wholly ignorant of the country between the Niger and the Congo, and can explore it only incurring the most frightful hazards".

To provide companionship for Park, two other Borderers were now

E

recruited. One was his brother-in-law, Alexander Anderson, his friend since boyhood, who went as the party's surgeon; the other was George Scott, who had also been at school with him, had worked for several years with a noted London engraver, and was now in a secure post in the Ordnance Department, which he gave up at once to travel with the expedition as its official draughtsman and artist. Yet, with all apparently settled, the weeks continued to pass without the final, necessary official word. It was 2 January before Lord Camden at last wrote the liberating letter.

"It being judged expedient that a small expedition should be sent into the interior of Africa . . . I am commanded by the King to acquaint you, that on account of the knowledge you have acquired of the nations of Africa, and from the indefatigable exertions and perseverance you have displayed in your travels among them, His Majesty has selected you for conducting this operation." He was given the brevet commission of "a captain in Africa", and Anderson was made a lieutenant on a similar basis. He was empowered to enlist from the Gorée garrison as many soldiers as he thought proper (but "not exceeding forty-five") and he should offer them "such bounties or encouragement as may be necessary to induce them cheerfully to join with you on the expedition". He was authorised to buy asses at St Jago and hire black artificers at Gorée. When he had reached the Niger and pursued "the course of this river to the utmost possible distance to which it can be traced", he would be "at liberty to pursue your route homewards by any line you shall think most secure, either by taking a new direction through the Interior towards the Atlantic, or by marching upon Cairo by taking the route leading to Tripoli". The final paragraph gave him the far from negligible right to draw up to £5,000 for his expedition's needs.

It seems as though this commission was handed on to him by Banks and Sullivan, for, in a letter to Anderson written on 5 January, Mungo mentions having seen these two dignitaries that very morning and discovering "that it is the wish of Govt. to open a communication from the Gambia to the Niger for the purpose of trade, and they do not wish me on any account to proceed further than I shall find it safe and proper". He mentions a mysterious party— "200 pick't men"—said to be embarking at that moment in Falmouth for the expedition (one wonders whatever became of them), and informs his brother-in-law that he would be paid ten shillings a day and a Government allowance, "with a promise of their interest in your favour".

He himself had been promised "a comfortable situation at my return, and if I should die, I have asked and obtained that £100 shall be settled on my dear Ailie and family during life." Practical advice follows about what clothes to bring—eighteen shirts, he specifies, and a neckcloth for each—and the need for cash. "If you go by Peebles", he writes (and so one wonders where exactly she was living at this time) "bring me particular word how my dear Ailie is." The letter sounds a note of eagerness to be off, not unexpected after so long a wait. Mungo Park had at last been reunited with his passion.

It is clear, however, that this second voyage, so long in the discussing, was a very different venture from the first. No Government commission had given him authority and rank when he had first set out for Africa. No Colonial Secretary had permitted him £5,000 nor authorised the purchase of one ass, let alone fifty. What had been a private venture financed by gentlemen, patriotic certainly, but curious above all, had now become an act of state. Park, once the willing employee of a group of enthusiasts, was now the servant of Government, its resources his reward, but its commission the sign of his lost freedom. Not that he saw it in such terms; had they been suggested to him, he would have been the first to suspect treachery. Yet the change had occurred, as had always been inevitable, and, if it made little difference to Park and those who followed him, it would make all the difference in the world to Africa and its peoples.

For the Government, the decision to send out such an expedition may not have been as simple as it seemed. On the one hand there were the successes of its forces against the French in Senegal to encourage it, and the enormous increase in West African trade which followed from that and the British navy's European blockade; on the other, there were the demanding priorities of the war. Across the Channel Napoleon had just the previous December set upon his head the crown of the French empire that he himself had created. Against him, William Pitt, once more in office despite failing health, was attempting to reconstruct his European alliance; soon Russia and Austria would once again venture into the field against the French. Napoleon, for his part, was still actively devising plans and gathering shipping and supplies for his projected invasion of England. It would be another ten months before Nelson at Trafalgar shattered his hope that the French and Spanish navies might provide a diversion to cover that assault. By then, however, the Austrians would be reeling and the Third Coalition facing dissolution. It says something for the far-sighted objectivity of the British Government that, at the height of such a conflict, they felt able to spare money, men and ships for a venture that in the immediate future could bring them neither commercial nor military advantage. But they had the vision to do so, they had the funds to spare, and the energy; above all, they had the enthusiasm and experience of Mungo Park to draw on.

So there he is, about to travel down to Spithead, where the *Crescent* transport awaited him, and her escort sloop, the *Eugenia*. It is our last chance to see him with any clarity, before the distortions of legend blur the outlines, pound him into the two-dimensional certainties of heroism. The judgement made of him in the 1815 memoir speaks of his "enterprising spirit, indefatigable vigilance and activity, his calm fortitude and unshaken perseverance". These are not dashing virtues, and, for all his tall good looks, he was never in that sense a compelling man—as the memoir says, "not brilliant, but solid and useful". He was a prudent man, calm, even-tempered. As we gaze back across the years, our hearts sink a little: is this really all that we can discern? Heroes should be made of brighter stuff.

Through his solid Border exterior, however, a gleam or two does show. What, for example, of his optimism? He always believed that what was in hand was possible. It never crossed his mind to count what faced him and balk at the sum. This was not mere perseverance: it was an expectation of success so extreme that only the certainty of failure, the very fact of failure itself, as at the turning-point of his first voyage, could persuade him that the chance of success had vanished. There is an element of the foolhardy in this and one imagines that only his hardiness and his limitless stamina prevented his paying the price for it many years before he actually did.

He could both inspire love and give it. He cared for his parents, loved his wife. His shyness walled him in and made him seem cold and over-reserved, and his principles forced him to question the superficial value of his fame, the superficial acquaintances it brought him. But with those who by their own merit and energy broke through his barriers he seems to have been free enough, and his friends were of a quality that perhaps reflects his own. That person of wit and glitter, Lady Holland, as hostess the hub of a bright, swiftly-revolving wheel, said of him, "He has neither fancy nor genius, and if he does fib, it is dully." And it is true that if repartee and the clatter of engaging conversation were the single mark of genius, Mungo Park was not one.

He was perhaps one of those who, unable to feel free among their own countrymen, discover a kind of release among strangers. With the blacks of Africa, poor, themselves terrified of the Moors, their neighbours, their priests and their gods, he came instantly to terms. Accepting his own poverty and helplessness, he fitted in easily with theirs. Back in Britain, it is likely that he saw in the social structures that hemmed him in little more than a trap. Christianity of the more rigid kind gave him some access to the universal, but the sanctimonious note that sometimes sounds in his letters does not suggest that that is a route he often took. He was a Border Scot who had learned early that the cages built by class and education and the church were not only necessary, but to be welcomed.

Yet he was ambitious, endlessly so, and detested what his life had become when he seemed to be imprisoned in his Peebles practice. Where did that ambition come from? Was it connected with his love of poetry, with his early dream of writing? He was certainly extremely proud of his work on his own book—when Sir William Young, writing after Edwards's death, mentioned the latter's "judicious compilation and elegant recital of the travels of Mungo Park", he was immediately set upon and forced to apologise by Park himself: Edwards had helped him, he said, but the book had been his own. Does his touchiness suggest some vulnerability, or is it the proper request for respect of a man who understood his own worth? It seems exaggerated, but standards differ. What is clear is that Park had a huge appetite for a success that would satisfy him, and that the world's approbation was no substitute. It was for that that he needed to travel the length of the Niger—it was the task he had now set himself, one feels, and it had to be completed. He was an independent man, and only his own approval would seal the work he had in hand.

That he was independent we know not only from his writings, but also from the manner in which he wrote about slavery in his own book. His chapter on this sad institution's prevalence in Africa itself, and on its organisation there, ends in a sentence that at the time, and in the decades that followed its publication, caused endless apoplectic controversy. He wrote, "If my sentiments should be required concerning the effect which a discontinuance of that commerce would produce on the manners of the natives, I should have no hesitation in observing, that, in the present unenlightened state of their minds, my opinion is, the effect would neither be so extensive or beneficial as many wise and worthy persons fondly expect."

As a result of this, many passionate strugglers in the abolitionist cause labelled him a supporter of slavery. Others, who knew that Edwards, with his West Indian connections, certainly was such a supporter, thought that he had come under his editor's influence. We have the word of a Member of Parliament, George Hibbert, a West India merchant who sat six years for the Seaford constituency, that Park himself assured him "that every sheet of the publication had undergone his strict revision and that not only every fact but every sentiment was his own". We are left, therefore, with a dispassionate statement about slavery, an objective weighing-up of probable consequences, as against an over-heated expectation. Mungo Park was not a man to be driven into predetermined camps, nor to be stampeded by any collective hysteria. At the height of one of the most disturbing controversies that ever threatened the equilibrium of British political life, he was able to take a step back and say, in effect, "You cannot alter or remove a long-established institution without causing great difficulties—there are no measures that are all benefit and no loss." This is not, of course, the attitude of some dashing figure, scattering certainty like sparks from the charismatic blaze that surrounds him, but it is one likely to be true. And certainly the enforced ending of the slave trade did bring in its wake some economic dislocation, though that was soon overlaid by the general effects of European colonisation and conquest. Such balanced opinions are not likely to appeal to those battling for causes that seem to them irrefutable, but they do sound like the authentic voice of Mungo Park.

On 29 January he wrote to a friend in Selkirk that he expected to be in St Jago twenty days later, "where we must purchase 50 African cavalry, *alias* Jackasses". In a postscript breezy with the excitement of departure, he added, "I almost forgot to tell you that we have the *Eugenia*, sloop of war, for our particular convoy, and she is not to quit us until we are landed. I hope we shall see a fight between her and some of the French privateers." One forgets how young Park was, still only thirty-three, and all the current of his life rushing onward, now that the dam that had checked him for so long had burst.

There were storms and contrary winds in the Bay of Biscay, and it was not until 8 March that the *Crescent* arrived in St Jago. Park wrote to Dickson on 13 March, "If Sir Joseph enquires after me, tell him that I'm going on as well as I could wish. . . . I hope to be able to date a letter from the Niger by the 4th June". The sentence sounds cheerful and full of hope, but carries its own desperation; Park knew that he was in a race against the rains, that his wait in England through the autumn had made him dangerously late, and that, if the season turned, swampland awaited him in the interior.

On 21 March, having taken on board forty-eight asses and their fodder, the ship left the Cape Verde islands and seven days later dropped anchor off Gorée. This island just off Cape Verde had been taken by the French from the Dutch in 1677. The British had captured it during the Seven Years' War, but had returned it after the Treaty of Paris in 1763. They captured it again, a dozen years later, only to hand it back once more in 1783. It was of immense importance to the West African trade, as its position suggests, and now it was once more in British hands. There, from its garrison, Mungo Park would recruit the men who would march with him.

On 4 April he wrote to his wife, "Almost every soldier in the Garrison volunteered to go with me; and with the Governor's assistance I have chosen a guard of the best men in the place. So lightly do the people here think of the danger attending the undertaking, that I have been under the necessity of refusing several military and naval officers who volunteered to accompany me. . . .

"I need not tell you how often I think about you; your own feelings will enable you to judge of that. The hopes of spending the remainder of my life with my wife and children will make every thing seem easy; and you may be sure I will not rashly risk my life, when I know that your happiness, and the welfare of my young ones depend so much upon it. I hope my Mother does not torment herself with unnecessary fears about me. I sometimes fancy how you and she will be meeting misfortune half way, and placing me in many distressing situations. I have as yet experienced nothing but success, and I hope that six months more will end the whole as I wish."

A few days later he was once more on the Gambia. It was from Jillifree that he wrote to Edward Cooke, Under Secretary of State for the Colonial Department. At Gorée, he said, he had worked closely with the commander, Major Lloyd, and had "consulted with him respecting the proper encouragement to be offered to the troops. We agreed that nothing would be so great an inducement as double pay during the journey, and a discharge on their return. A Garrison order to this effect was accordingly made out; and in the course of a few days almost every soldier . . . had volunteered his services."

He had engaged Lieutenant Martyn, of the Royal African Corps, "on the conditions mentioned in Lord Camden's letter", and also two sailors off the frigate *Squirrel*, "in order to assist in rigging and navigating our *Nigritian Men of War*". Early on 6 April, he reported, "we embarked the soldiers, in number thirty-five men. They jumped into the boats in the highest spirits, and bade adieu to Gorée with repeated huzzas. I believe that every man in the Garrison would have embarked with great cheerfulness; but no inducement could prevail on a single Negro to accompany me . . . ." One wonders if, even for a moment, he found that last fact as chilling as we do, looking backward to tragedy over seventeen decades?

Optimism glows in his letters, the expectation of success. Was he really so confident? Was he soothing those who waited for news at home, was he comforting himself, had he simply fallen into the habit of rallying those about him, his tone of high expectation a consequence of command? It seems hard not to find his dismissal of all chance of failure almost irritating. He did what he could to ensure success, however, by taking on as his guide a man of remarkable resource and loyalty named Isaaco (Mungo Park's version of his actual name, which was Isiyaku). Combining the function of trader and priest, this Mandingo was well connected (in the natural and the supernatural worlds), knew the country and those who lived in it, and brought with him into Park's service his own hard-working followers. It was his steadfastness and their stamina that, enthused by Park's incredible determination, really made possible such success as attended the first part of the expedition.

On his last day on the coast, 26 April, Park wrote to James Dickson, "Every thing at present looks as favourable as I could wish, and if all things go well, this day six weeks I expect to drink all your healths in the water of the Niger. The soldiers are in good health and spirits. They are the most *dashing* men I ever saw . . . ." Yet, after his death, Wishaw in the memoir pointed out that they were in fact "extremely deficient both in constitutional strength and in those habits of sobriety, steadiness and good discipline which such a service peculiarly required". Park's high spirits, however, did not seem to permit him any such analysis: he felt, he told Dickson, that his detachment of soldiers made him secure from all attack, although he expected to march through the lands between him and the Niger "with presents and fair words". And then, the Niger reached, "if once we are fairly afloat, *the day is won*".

From his point of view, success was now his single option. This time he was not going to turn back; he thus allowed himself only death as the alternative— and there was no point in contemplating that. Victory, discovery, the Niger's mouth: these were the only sensible, perhaps the only bearable, results to expect. The dry season was hurrying past, each day bringing nearer the morasses, the flooded rivers, the endless humidity that accompanied the rains. But there was no point in worrying about that, either: this was the moment in which they were destined to make their start, and, late as it was, triumph remained possible. If one half-closed one's eyes and stared into the waiting distance, one might just make out its plausible lineaments. On that same 26 April he wrote to his wife.

"We set off for the interior to-morrow morning; and I assure you, that whatever the issue of the present journey may be, every thing looks favourable. . . .

The natives instead of being frightened at us, look on us as their best friends, and the kings have not only granted us protection, but sent people to go before us. The soldiers are in the highest spirits; and as many of them (like me) have left a wife and family in England, they are happy to embrace this opportunity of returning. They never think about the difficulties; and I am confident, if there was occasion for it, that they would defeat any number of Negroes that might come against us; but of this we have not the most distant expectation. . . . In five weeks from the date of this letter the worst part of the journey will be over. Kiss all my dear children for me, and let them know that their father loves them."

Chapter Ten

Column of March

What did they hope for, these loud, forlorn men as they marched off from Kayi in a straggling column on that day in 1805? It was 27 April, the heat numbing; all knew the seasons well enough to tell that in six weeks, in eight, in ten at the most, the first rains would fall. How heavy, how destructive, must their routines have been at Gorée that this journey they were now beginning should have seemed preferable. Park says nothing of the risks, of the difficulties that were piling up, the hazards of terrain and climate; he says nothing of the quality of those marching with him, accuses no one, criticises no one—either now, at the start, or later, when their destiny had begun to close on them like a fist. Yet misfortune and inadequacy appear in the first lines of his account of the journey: "some of the asses . . . stuck fast in a muddy field. . . . In a short time we overtook about a dozen soldiers and their asses, who had likewise fallen behind. . . ." Park took one road, Lieutenant Martyn and his party another; everyone was "extremely fatigued, having travelled all day under a vertical sun, and without a breath of wind". So, did these men even now begin to wish they had made some other choice? There is no record of it. They sit in the shade, one fancies their voices low, someone cursing, perhaps a languid arm waving aside the insects. Africa waits in ambush; whatever they hope for, they are doomed.

At Pisania, the asses were loaded, everything was made ready. When every pack had been weighed out, five more beasts had to be bought to carry them all. Park went to visit that apparently immortal "Seniora Camilla", still in her house and once more agreeably surprised to see him. It was 4 May before the expedition, now fully loaded and organised, set out in real earnest. What could be done by planning, Mungo Park did, numbering the asses and their loads, the beasts doubtless festive in their red paint, circus-like, all divided into groups and each group the responsibility of one detachment. One of Isaaco's guides and George Scott led the way, Martyn and his party marched in the middle, Park and Anderson commanded the rearguard. For a while Ainsley and even the brave "Seniora" travelled with them, a crowd of watchers and wavers and wishers of good luck at their sides. Then these fell back, the last farewells

were called across a widening gap, the dust drifted across the sky, then slowly
settled on an empty track. Were they confident as they turned away, did they
tell each other that Park had survived once and would again; or did they go
silently to their homes and their work, uneasy at the lateness of the season, at
Park's ambition and the rabble he had gathered to help him achieve it?

The asses gave so much trouble that by the second day some of their loads
had been transferred to the horses. On 7 May they came across the first evidence
of the region's continual wars: a destroyed village. The king of Wuli had allied
himself with one of his neighbours, the king of "Jamberoo", as Park gives it.
Perhaps this was another name for Niami, the little state lying to the west of
Wuli. In any case, it was these two in conjunction that had plundered and razed
this place. The king of Wuli himself—not the same as the one Park had dealt
with before—proved as rapacious as any other monarch who sees the chance of
easy pickings from feeble foreigners. A pair of silver-mounted pistols, ten bars
each of amber and coral and ten dollars for a makeweight did not seem to him
sufficient to constitute a suitably respectful tribute; Park had to add another ten
bars of both amber and coral, as well as fifteen dollars more, before the king's
pride was mollified. Even then, "he begged me to give him a blanket to wrap
himself in during the rains"—and, as he did whenever he could, Park obliged.

Dysentery had already begun to appear among the men, but the march
continued steadily. On 14 May, Park wrote an entry pointing up one of the
difficulties faced by those who want to trace its course: "Halted at Kussai. . . .
This is the same village as Seesekunda, but the inhabitants have changed its
name." At this place, the party found itself in trouble after some of the soldiers
had taken fruit from a tree supposed to be *tabu* (Park tells us the local word was
toong)—here actually a device for bringing spiritual authority to bear upon a
practical problem: the fruits had to be preserved for times of famine. The headman complained angrily; Park and his officers laughed at him. The situation was
different from those in which Park had found himself during his first journey;
he had muskets on his side now, and a mounted force. He was no longer a
solitary stranger sitting disconsolately in the village square, the butt of any
hectoring fanatic or rapacious chief. Now he could laugh, he could curb arrogance and challenge inhospitality, he could stand and wait for explanations.

He remained diplomatic, polite, politically generous, he understood clearly
enough that his situation was still finally one of weakness and of dependence on
the country and its people. Nevertheless his relationship with these had altered.
Before, he had of necessity been at one with those around him, his weakness
often no greater than theirs, his situation forcing him to share their own
pleasures and hardships. Now he travelled like a seigneur, a sort of nobleman,
with outriders, guides, servants, guards; an entourage. He came like a pleni-
potentiary, a representative of power, uniforms and muskets behind him; he
came, in fact, like a conqueror. His column was small and vulnerable, but it was
a column and it was the forerunner of others. He was no longer engaged in

exploration, but in reconnaissance. He had retreated from his former closeness with the people; instead, he travelled encapsuled in a portable fragment of Britain, a gentleman among officers, a leader of his countrymen. He was on a mission, his government looked to him for results, he was able to laugh at recalcitrant headmen and demand explanations from them. In short, he had lost his innocence.

Again war threatened them. Bundu's king, Sega, had been assassinated by the religious henchmen of Abdul Kader, still from his Futa Toro stronghold whirling through the region like the whiplash of Islam. On the throne of Bundu he placed his own nominee, the dead king's nephew, Amadi Pate. However, King Sega's cousin—or brother, as some claim—led a counter-revolution and retrieved the throne, allying himself with the king of Kaarta in order to secure his position. Adding to this alliance disaffected chieftains from Futa Toro itself, he was finally able to turn the tables and may even have been responsible for Abdul Kader's death—though that fierce old proselytiser was said to have been over eighty by that time. It was while these campaigns and skirmishes were at their height that Mungo Park marched his column through the region. No wonder Isaaco sacrificed a black ram on the roadway and, not satisfied that divine intercession would be enough, ordered the men to have their muskets primed and ready at all times.

Along the Gambia's banks, the crocodiles ranged for any error—Park counted thirteen side by side at one point. He climbed to the top of a low hill and gazed about him at the countryside—"a most enchanting prospect", he assures us. As a result, he named this mound Prospect Hill. In all the miles of his first journey, it never seems to have occurred to him to name a single feature. Yet here, men at his back and the commands of the Government in his pocket, not a month under way, he waves the wand of his manifest superiority and names a hill as though the continent were unpopulated, as though there were no people with a language of their own to give it any name it needed.

That day a man named John Walters died in convulsions, which Park tells us were epilepsy. By 18 May the little column was struggling its way across the river Nieriko, which bisects the kingdom of Bundu; the warmth of the water at two o'clock in the afternoon, Park notes, was 94°F. Soon they had reached Dialakato; two days later, they were halted at a village named Tambico, in vehement argument with the local chief. The ten bars of amber Park had sent him had been refused as inadequate; Park added five bars of coral, but was rebuffed in the same way. He had guns now, and battle seemed more and more probable; a horse was stolen and, when Isaaco went to ask after it, he was tied to a tree and flogged. The chief's men came for another horse, one belonging to an old man travelling with Park's column. (Horses were rare and conferred upon their owners not only mobility, but also great prestige; for a ruler, cavalry could make the difference between insecurity and safety.) The villagers themselves repulsed this insolent cupidity.

The next day, after more argument and a message to the local governor in
Dialonka, the stolen horse was returned—"I accordingly paid at different times
goods to the amount of one hundred and six bars, being not quite one-third of
what a coffle of Negroes would have paid". Perhaps we have here a clue to the
local chief's recalcitrance; earlier, Park had discovered that this man "exacts very
high duties from the coffles, to the extent of ten bars of gunpowder for each
ass-load". It was therefore the usual dues to which Park now took exception. He
was not, of course, engaged in trade, but that was hardly a matter the local
authorities would find important. He was rich, he had a caravan, he was travelling through their lands for purposes of his own, the duty was a fixed one and
other people paid it—why should he be exempt? "I . . . desired that the soldiers
might have on their pouches and bayonets, and be ready for action at a moment's
notice." Thus Mungo Park at the height of the debate. He had brought power
with him and felt free to set the levels of justice. His tone dismisses those who
disagreed as unreasonable—and who in England would say that their favourite
African explorer was wrong?

The party moved on eastwards towards the Niger. One day they managed
nearly thirty miles. At night, prowling scavengers and predators kept them uneasy, and in the darkness of 24 May an ass was killed by what Park calls "wolves",
but which were certainly jackals or hyenas. The column passed near a town in
which Park had slept on his previous journey; it had been burned down in the
Bundu wars and its central tree destroyed. He named another hill—Panorama
Hill this time, suggesting a less than poetic liveliness of imagination—and then
marched on, the landscape now broken, yet very beautiful, with abrupt valleys
falling to streams rich in fish, the nearer hillsides wooded and lively with the
game that crouched and leaped there, the distance pregnant with the possibility
of larger animals: the lions that all feared, the elephants of which the signs lay
everywhere, in footprints, broken branches, dung.

On 28 May the column halted in a place that Park names as "Badoo",
somewhere just north of where the Gambia swings to the west after its first
descent from the Futa Jallon mountains. This is perhaps Badon, some 300 miles
from their starting point, a small kingdom then loosely associated with the
Bambuk confederacy of states. From there he wrote to Banks, a brisk letter all
astronomical observation and geographical insight. Rather less abrasively he
wrote to his wife, "I am happy to inform you that we are half way through our
journey without the smallest accident or unpleasant circumstance. We all of us
keep our health, and are on the most friendly terms with the natives. I have seen
many of my old acquaintances, and am everywhere well received. By the 27th
of June we expect to have finished our travels by land; and when we have once
got afloat on the river, we shall conclude that we are embarking for England.
I have never had the smallest sickness; and Alexander is quite free from all his
stomach complaints. . . . I will indulge the hope that my wife, children and all
my friends are well. I am in great hopes of finishing this journey with credit in

a few months: and then with what joy shall I turn my face towards home!"
The note is hasty; the slatee who was to carry it back to the coast seems to have
been hovering at Park's elbow. Its optimism is that of a loyal but beleaguered
man writing to reassure his wife—it is unlikely that he himself was as sanguine
about the future, as delighted with the present. Yet he must have permitted
himself some distortion of the truth in order to maintain—as he always did
maintain—the momentum of his ambition. On the evening of the 29th, he
and his men marched on again; it was the following evening that, briefly but
ominously, the first rain they had seen since they set out fell as they were about
to pitch camp.

At the beginning of June the avarice of a ruler—or Park's Scottish canniness
over money—brought about another confrontation. The place was Diulifunda,
founded by those privileged traders enfranchised by the Mali empire; the ruler's
name Park gives as Mansa Kussan. His demands were exorbitant, repeatedly
raised and supported by threats. Park paid until he "determined to put an end
to the business; and told the king's brother that I considered myself as having
paid very well for passing through his territory". Since this time he seems clearly
to have been in the right, it was in well-founded anger that he "assured them
that Europeans would much rather run the risk of being plundered in a hostile
manner than have their goods . . . extorted from them by such exorbitant
demands". The king climbed down, with the affability of those who have tried
and done their best and failed, and the British column travelled on, to spend the
next day loyally consuming roast calf in celebration of their own king's birth-
day. Such festivity had no help from alcohol: "we were under the necessity of
drinking His Majesty's health in *water* from our canteens, yet few of his subjects
wished more earnestly for the continuance of his life and the prosperity of his
reign". It is to be hoped that George III benefited from these, among the first
loyal prayers to ascend to heaven from the interior of Africa.

Mungo Park made sure of his food supplies by buying rice; there was, he
was told, a great scarcity of it further to the east, this lack of food not the least
of the problems facing a large party trying to cross these regions at the end of the
long dry season. That, however, was beginning to break: on that same day,
Park writes, "Had a squall with thunder and rain during the night." Old James,
one of his carpenters, who had caught dysentery some days earlier but had
begun to recover, took a turn for the worse as a result of this storm. Nevertheless, the column pressed on, strung out now under the sun, the loaded asses
slowing as the heat pressed down, the men sweat-stained, open-mouthed,
shambling in the various rhythms of their discontent. Some of the time they
followed no marked route, for there was war in the direction of Futa Jallon and
Isaaco was apprehensive of their being trapped by a raiding party, horsemen
prepared to pounce on the stragglers and their acceptable pickings of food and
weapons. On 8 June the carpenter died, and on the same day five of the soldiers,
sheltering from rain under a tree, caught some disorder; by the next day, they

were suffering from "headache and uneasiness of the stomach". They were in "Satadoo" (Satadougou, although Park does not mention crossing the nearby Falémé).

On 10 June they were once again drenched by a sudden rainstorm, one of those abrupt and passionate assaults a tropical climate can make on the unwary. This was as they were pitching camp in a little town named Shrondo, and it had, Park writes, "an instant effect on the health of the soldiers, and proved to us to be the *beginning of sorrow*". The italics are one of the few signs of the bitterness, the near-despair, that Mungo Park must increasingly have felt as the days ahead paraded their endless array of misfortune, banditry and death. For, as he writes, "now the rain had set in, and I trembled to think that we were only half way through our journey". And he describes the effects of the storm: "The rain had not commenced three minutes before many of the soldiers were affected with vomiting; others fell asleep, and seemed as if half intoxicated."

The next day, twelve of the soldiers were ill; for Park, nevertheless, it was an opportunity to see the local gold-workings, and he went off to watch dust being panned in a pair of calabashes, the expert a local woman whom he had hired. This interlude was extended by a visit to the brother of that one-time patron of his, Karfa Taura; to him he gave a New Testament in Arabic. In one day, therefore, he combined Europe's interest in gold with her ostentatious piety, demonstrating once again the changes in his own role. He was no longer the humble inquirer after other people's truths: he had become the dispenser of a truth of his own.

By 13 June, he was very worried about the men he had brought: "The sick occupied all the horses and spare asses", he wrote, adding as summary a little later, "Very uneasy about our situation: half the people being either sick of the fever or unable to use great exertion, and fatigued in driving the asses." The next day, things were even worse, for he himself was ill. Still he pressed on, some of the men now delirious; on the 15th the caravan had to clamber through steep, rocky hills, the road swooping suddenly upwards, the overloaded asses slipping, some falling, sprawling on the scree and scrub, their loads scattered, those minding them tottering, sweaty-faced, finally falling themselves, the heat too great, the way too steep, their sickness like a weight upon them.

A new pest beset them, for word of their column, with its wealth and its unknown destination, had spread widely. White men had come, the bringers of riches, the makers of wonders. From everywhere flocked thieves looking for pickings, the scavengers of a poverty-stricken land in a lean season, after wars, after the destruction of towns and villages, after abduction and fire, at the end of the long drought of the year. These were not very noticeable at first, but now, as the soldiers began to fall ill, as the caravan spread out further and further, the weakest lagging, some halting, falling down for good, they began to close in. From this point on, Park and his people were rarely unattended, and few days passed without the insidious, irresistible assaults of these swift-moving robbers.

From now on, too, they had to leave more and more men behind, to die or to recover, while they themselves forced their way on towards the Niger and the relief that they hoped travel on that river would bring them.

Hinton and Sparks were left on 17 June; from the 18th to the 20th, Park himself was too ill to attend to any duties and Anderson took over from him; when they moved on again, Rowe, one of the soldiers, could not continue; on their way, rain struck at them again; on the 22nd, William Roberts, a carpenter, was left behind. So it went on, their path through a tumble of rocky hills, outcrops thrusting through greenery, all now washed more and more frequently by the rains. It is not surprising that in their condition they seemed open to attack, and, indeed, on 23 June they again found themselves threatened by an avaricious headman and some thirty of his warriors. Park's soldiers fixed bayonets and waited with daunting calm for the skirmish to begin; he himself, meanwhile, spoke to the headman. When asked who would attack the soldiers, the headman pointed to the fighting men, bows at the ready, spears bristling like a small thicket. Park was not impressed by them: "I fell a-laughing; and asked him if he really thought such people could fight." Daunted by his coolness, the headman wavered; Park pressed home his advantage with a left and a right of gifts—four bars of amber—and so won the battle without needing to give a single aggressive order.

On 27 June, the caravan crossed the river Bafing. A canoe overturned and a man named Cartwright drowned—"I used the means recommended by the Humane Society", Park tells us, "but in vain . . . ." The next day, a man named Bloor went missing while searching for an ass that had strayed; a sick man named Walter was fortunately discovered beside the path and brought back to the main party. They helped him on a little way; then he died. Bloor returned, but in his place a man named Baron disappeared. On the 29th, two more soldiers had been struck by fever. Late that day, Bloor once again vanished; one has the feeling that he had not much relished being brought back the first time.

The story of the voyage at this point reads like that of some appalling retreat, a dwindling body of men harassed at every turn by climate, sickness, bandits and predators. Anderson and Scott fell ill, as though to prove that officers were not immune. A soldier named McMillan had to be left behind; Park writes a one-sentence epitaph for the unhappy man: "He had been thirty-one years a soldier, twelve times a corporal, nine times a sergeant; but an unfortunate attachment to the *bottle* always returned him to the ranks." Park himself was failing again, though working beside his men, driving the asses, lifting those that fell, cajoling, encouraging, sometimes physically supporting the sick, reloading the pack animals when they shed the bales they carried. Lions prowled about their camp at night, and once even invaded it, forcing their own animals into a stampede, which tore down tents. One lion ran so close to the men that a guard swung at it with his sword. The next day Anderson and Scott wanted to be left behind, but this Park would not accept; a seaman named Ashton was, however, set by the wayside, a pistol in his hand, for he had become too weak to walk or ride.

On 4 July, Park nearly lost his guide, the busy Isaaco; crossing a rain-swollen river, there was a quick swirl, the twist of a dark ridged back, the long glitter of a snarling mouth. The man yelled, flailed with his arms. Blood suddenly appeared among the muddy eddies of the stream. A crocodile had snatched him by the left thigh, was dragging him away, was tugging him under. Isaaco bent, his hands reached along the slime, along the thin snout. He found one staring eye and struck desperately with his finger. The beast jerked away, its jaw suddenly slack. Calling for a weapon, a knife, the man began to stagger for the shore, spray glittered as he ran. Behind him, the water parted, the dark shape of the crocodile hung, then turned, moving with its terrible swiftness, turned and struck again. Isaaco was stopped as he strode, safety beyond his reach. But again, as he tumbled sideways, he stabbed with his fingers, found that one vulnerable point in the glittering head, jabbed into the beast's eyes with the ferocity of the dying. He was out of sight now, dragged from his element, his flesh already tearing to the creature's greed. But again the unexpected pain forced it to pull away, to release him. This time, unnerved, it turned away for good, bemused at such treatment. Bleeding, half dead with shock and pain, the guide struggled to the other shore and collapsed on its comforting rocks. He had a four-inch wound in his left thigh, one almost as long and deeper on his right, tooth marks lacerating his back. Park bound his wounds, then sent him on ahead. For the man so nearly lost, however, another was actually found. Stark-naked, all his clothes stolen from him, the discarded Ashton reappeared. Park notes laconically, "Found his fever much abated."

A three-day pause followed, while Park watched Isaaco's wounds and waited for him to be fit to travel. The men had only enough rice for two days and all but one of the party were either ill or weakened by illness. But, with their stores replenished and Isaaco's wounds beginning to heal, Park ordered a new start on 10 July. Ahead lay further ambushes, less now those of nature, rather more those of man. As Park wrote on 13 July, "we have never yet been at a place where so much theft and impudence prevails". They had possessions others coveted, they were weak, they were strangers, the worshippers of negligible gods. It is no wonder that along their route more and more human vultures should gather. From now on, it seems as though the caravan's progress was one running fight, one long, losing battle against the deft scavengers who clustered about their camps at night or darted in and away during their weary daytime marches.

On that 13 July they were in a town named Maniakoro, some 500 miles from the Gambia estuary. The next day, as they prepared to depart, the townspeople clustered round them. "They had stolen during our stay here four greatcoats, a large bundle of beads, a musket, a pair of pistols and several other things." As they rode away from the place, a man leaped from cover, dragged a bag from one of the loaded asses and scrambled away. He was run down and caught, but, while the chase was on, a second thief had taken a musket. Worst of these bandits were the sons of the king: one came to Park and asked him for snuff, and, as Park turned to answer him, another stepped up from behind, dragged his musket out of his hand and ran away. A fruitless chase among the rocks and gulleys by the roadside, then a furious return—to discover that the other gracious prince had stolen Park's greatcoat. In this way they continued, their misery completed by renewed rainstorms.

A small group of men tried to run off their pack animals, but were seen in time and chased away. A loaded ass strayed, and from some crevice a man appeared, cut open a pack, helped himself and raced triumphantly away among the rocks. There was any amount of cover on these rugged slopes, and Park, riding at the rear, could now and again see the heads of those who watched him, who calculated his strengths and weaknesses, who were following the caravan, running ahead, signalling to their colleagues, then crouching in the hollows and crannies, waiting for opportunity to beckon them to action. In such nerve-racking manner they moved through this range of hills, to come at last to the safety of the plains beyond.

Now the storms were more and more frequent, one on the night of 16 July so heavy, so terrifying in the power of its thunder, the whiplash of its lightning, that Mungo Park fled from his tent, expecting it to be struck at any moment. The next day, on their march, an ass was stolen; the following morning, however, Park must have found some satisfaction in riding down a thief who had just snatched away a greatcoat. He shot him in the leg, almost shot him again, but was stopped by the man's appeals: "Do not kill me, white man!" It is a cry that would have echoes in the century to come, but for the moment one can only sympathise with Mungo Park. The local guide wanted to kill the man, and with some difficulty was persuaded not to. The thief himself, his leg broken and streaming blood, scrambled in terror up a tree, where Park was happy enough to leave him. Again, when one of the sick had been robbed of his coat, Park made the thief return it at pistol point. But another coat was taken, and a knapsack, by different men. Park and Scott flushed out a straggle of robbers from the rocks and so took back some of what had been stolen; meanwhile, six muskets, a pair of pistols and a knapsack were dragged from one of the asses. Small victories, petty defeats; a greater was the loss of another man, a sick man whom they were sure the bandits had killed somewhere in the woods behind them.

Again and again the rain drenched them, driving down on them like missiles, like blows. The animals were failing now: Scott's horse foundered, then two of the asses. Men were falling out, collapsing from weakness and fever, only to return, sometimes thirty hours later, stripped and robbed. The party came to a river and decided to float across on a raft, but had not enough men with the strength left to carry logs to the water's edge. They crossed at last, with the aid

of hired men who carried their baggage over. Then, however, they were too
weak to drag it up the eastern bank. Another man, a soldier named Beedle, was
left to die. Scott collapsed, and Martyn shortly after him—the disasters seem
almost monotonous in their relentless series. Park knew by now that word had
gone ahead of them, that everywhere people would be waiting for their share
of his ailing *coffle*, that they had been told that the caravan "was a *Dummulafong*,
a thing sent to be eaten". Nevertheless, Park, his own horse with packs on its
back, trudged on, driving one of the asses; he sent two of Isaaco's men back to
fetch the officers, not the last time that the energy and industry and endless
trustworthiness of that party of guides was to help save lives.

There was some respite in a town called Bangassi, where the ruler proved
unusually benevolent. The place was already within the jurisdiction of Mansong
of Segu, to whom the king of Bangassi paid tribute. This he was about to send
to Segu, in the charge of his son, and suggested that Park might travel with that
caravan. Perhaps injudiciously, Park said he would rather press on as soon as
possible instead of waiting until all the tribute gold had been collected; his men
were, many of them, sick and not fit to travel and, although he gives this as a
reason for marching further, it makes an equally good argument for staying
where he was welcome, protected and fed. On 26 July, a corporal named Powal
died; when the caravan left the next day, another soldier was too ill to travel.
Three men, named Frair, Thomson and, perhaps inaptly, Hercules, soon afterwards lay down and refused to go on; a quarter of a mile further a carpenter,
James Trott, did the same. Park himself was now ill again, feeling very weak
and faint, but still on foot, still leading his loaded horse and driving an ass. That
night, before they were able to pitch tents, the evening rains drove down on
them, drenching them and soaking the merchandise and provisions they carried.
Lions again troubled their pack animals, which dragged out the pins tethering
them and huddled near their drivers for protection. That night Park sent a note
to those who had returned to Bangassi. He addressed them as "Dear Soldiers",
told them he was sorry to hear they had gone back to that town, informed them
that with the letter three strings of amber had been sent, "one of which will
procure rice for forty days; the second will purchase milk or fowls for the same
time; and the third will buy provisions for you on the road till you arrive at the
Niger".

Did it cross his mind that they might well travel in some quite different
direction? Might stay where they were for a leisurely month? To him the destination is self-evident: the Niger awaits them, the splendid journey down its
long current to the sea. It must have occurred to him that his men were less
clearly motivated, but he does not for a moment entertain such an idea. They
will wait in Bangassi until fit, the king will supply them with a guide, they will
travel on to Bamako. The party will re-group, travel to Segu, embark on the
final phase. Nothing can alter these intentions, drawn up in the optimistic
atmosphere of London, but here, amidst the actual difficulties and disasters of the

march, sustained only by his inflexible will. Nothing would stop Mungo Park now except his own death; every other man in his company might fall or desert, might buckle and collapse and, sweating, die, but he would continue, inexorably committed to what had become the single, particular purpose of his life. Whatever one might think of the purpose, there is an overwhelming grandeur in that commitment. Not many have had the fortune to discover the task that gives value to their lives; very few of these have had the strength to carry it out to the very limits of the possible. Those few are heroes. Time or our own commitment alters our view of their achievements, but, good, evil or irrelevant, the achievements stand.

On 30 July Park abandoned another man, William Allen, as usual paying the local headman for his keep. He records his regrets on this occasion in a more particular manner than usual: "he had naturally a cheerful disposition; and he used often to beguile the watches of the night with the songs of our dear native land". There was rain both day and night now, and a constant watch for thieves; one night the recovering Martyn shot at and perhaps hit a man making off with a musket. What might have been a worse disaster was a disagreement with Isaaco, who, whether by accident or furious design, hit out at a pair of soldiers during a river crossing. One threatened him with a bayonet; Anderson prevented bloodshed; Park reprimanded Isaaco; and the consequence was that the caravan was left for a while without his support and that of his men, upon whose continuing strength and ingenuity Park had increasingly relied as his own men had failed, deserted or collapsed.

Unrelentingly, however, Park led what remained of his party to the east, all of them sometimes going without food for a whole day, trudging through the rain, through the increasingly treacherous mud, sleeping in wet clothes on the wet ground, the nights lowering, the dark pressing on them, the rain hissing through leaves or drumming on the earth, their sleep ringed around by the howling of jackals. Men fell, asses were picked off by predators, watch fires failed as the rain doused them, thieves hovered in shadow, bit by bit depleting the reserves they carried, the clothes they laid by, the weapons they put down. Only, it seems, the swift return of Isaaco, loyal despite his pique and their condition, saved the column from a final disintegration.

William Hall, Lawrence Cahill, William Cox, J. Bird, Michael May—the list of those collapsing or dying lengthened day by day. On 10 August William Ashton, once saved, began to fail again. But, much worse for Mungo Park personally, he now had to watch his wife's brother and his own close friend, Alexander Anderson, weaken with every mile. At a village named Dadabu he found "Mr. Anderson lying under a bush, apparently dying. Took him on my back, and carried him across the stream . . . ." It was not the only load Park carried: a little later he notes, "Found myself much fatigued, having crossed the stream sixteen times". They were 550 miles from their starting point, but had covered nearer 700.

Scott recovered, but Ashton died, and a soldier named Dickinson. Not a single European was now fit enough to lift a load; each day, as Park walked wearily on, he had to pass the sick and the dying, lying where they had fallen or had flung themselves at the roadside. On 12 August, he records, "At half-past twelve o'clock Mr. Anderson declared he could ride no further. Took him down and laid him in the shade of a bush. . . . I sat down to watch the pulsations of my dying friend." But Anderson, after all, had it in him to rally; Park helped him into the saddle of his horse and led it on towards the nearest village. They were on their own by now, the whole caravan scattered and disorganised. Isaaco and his men were far ahead, far behind came the straggling sick, those of them with strength enough to hobble on. Behind them again lay the discarded and the dead. Between Isaaco's people and Park stretched the disconnected pack train, the animals in groups, some with white men staggering beside them, others again with white men drooping in the saddle. Thus Park had no help when, suddenly, "coming to an opening in the bushes, I was not a little surprised to see three lions coming towards us". One fancies the comment over-restrained in the circumstances, but given Park's response it may not be. For he dropped the bridle of his horse and walked towards the lions until they were within range of his musket. He then fired at the one in the middle. "I do not think I hit him; but they all stopt, looked at each other, and then bounded away a few paces, when one of them stopt, and looked back at me. I was too busy in loading my piece to observe their motions as they went away. . . ."

He now found himself in an area of deep, eroded stream-beds, a maze of gullies in which he lost his way. Afraid of falling down some sudden, unexpected cliff, he halted for the night beside a sick man named Jonas Watkins. Park lit a fire, wrapped Anderson in his cloak, then watched the two sick men all night. Two others came up during the early hours of the morning, but Anderson slept soundly through their arrival. The next day Park led them to the haven of a village named Kumikumi, following the trail of their asses, which had reached it the evening before. There, Anderson rested. Jonas Watkins, however, died, another sacrifice to ambitions he almost certainly hardly recognised and did not share.

On 15 August there was a break in the bombardment of misery that Park had been suffering; for in a small town called Dumbila he met again the man who had led him to safety on his first voyage, the slave trader Karfa Taura. He was now living in a place Park names "Boori", perhaps the gold-rich area of Bure in Futa Jallon to the south. It was, in any case, six days' journey from his home to Bamako, but news of Park's caravan had reached there. On the morning after hearing of it, he had set out. He had not found them at Bamako, so had started searching to the west until he met them. "He instantly recognised me", Park writes, "and you may judge of the pleasure I felt on seeing my old benefactor." It is a moment of humanity, breaking through the carapace of responsibility and the onslaught of disaster, an echo of the earlier Park, that lone wanderer so vividly aware of everyone he met.

Scott now disappeared, Park waiting for him, expecting every day to see him, then despairing of him. (It was not until six weeks later that Park received certain news of his death.) When he left Dumbila on 18 August 1805, only one of his men was fit to drive an ass. It did not prevent them from rushing to the nearest village as soon as camp was pitched that night, drinking in the dry of some hut, perhaps buying a woman, while Park spent the night herding the pack animals and making sure they did not ravage the villagers' corn fields. On the 19th he pushed on, Anderson carried in a litter, one of his sergeants delirious, until, clambering over a ridge, "I went on a little before; and coming to the brow of the hill, I *once more saw the Niger* rolling its immense stream along the plain!"

Chapter Eleven

"On Board HMS *Joliba*"

Park's situation was far from the one he had planned: sixteen weeks had been spent in reaching the Niger, rather than the optimistic six he had predicted to his wife; three-quarters of his soldiers had died, and he had but one carpenter to build the boats he needed in order to sail downriver. No wonder he felt that "the prospect appeared somewhat gloomy". He nevertheless expressed his pleasure at having maintained good relations with most of the people he had met: "in conducting a party of *Europeans*, with immense baggage, through an extent of more than five hundred miles, I had always been able to preserve the most friendly terms with the natives". Perhaps it was his optimism that fuelled his determination, for certainly he had had his problems with the people of the land; it is true, however, that he had not had to fight and that in many places he had been treated with courtesy and offered at least some co-operation. "In fact", he concluded, "this journey plainly demonstrates, first, that with common prudence any quantity of merchandise may be transported from the Gambia to the Niger, without danger of being robbed by the natives; secondly, that if this journey be performed in the dry season, one may calculate on losing not more than three or at most four men out of fifty . . . ."

Clearly he felt that such a loss of life was more than balanced by the commercial advantages of by-passing the desert routes and the Moorish trade monopoly. Alas, his own journey had not been made in the dry season and the loss of life in his party was far heavier. "Of thirty-four soldiers and four carpenters, who left the Gambia, only six soldiers and one carpenter reached the Niger", he wrote, describing the party that at last filed down into Bamako, at the river's edge.

On 22 August, their supplies were loaded on canoes for the first, river-borne stage of the journey to Segu. Park, nursing Anderson, travelled with them; Martyn led the rest of the men and the pack animals along the bank. Sometimes the canoes dashed through the flung spray and torn water of rapids, at others they glided easily past low islands. On one of these, wide-eared, splay-legged, there stood an elephant. Park writes, "I was very unwell of the dysentery;

otherwise I would have had a shot at him, for he was quite near us." One wonders why—they could hardly take the elephant aboard, nor stay to butcher it on the mud flat. Commerce, Christianity, and now the useless slaughter of large animals—for all his bravery and all his principles, Mungo Park carried with him the whole gallery of ideological arrogance and careless self-indulgence that was to mark so much of Europe's dealings with the world.

The headman of Marabu, the small town where they disembarked, sent a bullock to the now reunited party, but refused to meet them himself, "conceiving that if he ever saw a white man, he would never prosper after". His gift, too, was less straightforward than it seemed: jet-black, the beast was a bad omen, and Isaaco, wise priest as well as loyal guide, would not allow it to be butchered. Meanwhile, the Niger having been reached, Park honoured his agreement with Isaaco and paid him the value of two slaves, as well as promising him all the asses and horses once they arrived in Segu.

This seems a proper recognition of what the Mandingo guide and his men had meant to the expedition. While the whites faltered, swayed in their saddles, fell in the swoons of fever by the wayside and one-by-one died, Isaaco took the burdens of their journey largely on his own shoulders. His men were honest and endlessly industrious, his own efforts were tireless and apposite, his advice was almost always sound. He approached local dignitaries, he picked out the daily route, he guarded the animals and their packs, he saw that everything was unloaded at night and loaded up again in the morning. When he felt it necessary, he also interceded with the local gods by way of sacrifice and incantation. Park was the enthusing spirit of the expedition, but Isaaco and his men were the willing and muscular flesh. As for the soldiers Park had recruited, they turned out on the whole to be little more than trappings, the imperial decoration giving fragile substance to Park's dream of profitable commerce, London's dream of ultimate control.

On 28 August, Park sent Isaaco on to Segu; with him travelled gifts for the king, Mansong, and a message for his chief minister which politically pointed out that further rewards awaited signs of the king's helpfulness. Park himself, meanwhile, seemed to be weakening daily under recurrent bouts of dysentery. He tells us that, "as I found that my strength was failing very fast, I resolved to charge myself with mercury. I accordingly took calomel till it affected my mouth to such a degree that I could not speak or sleep for six days. The salivation put an immediate stop to the dysentery, which had proved fatal to so many of the soldiers." Indeed, they were still dying, for on 6 September yet another soldier, a man named Thomas Dyer, succumbed to fever. It took a thousand cowrie shells to persuade the invisible headman, still skulking nervously in his hut, to allow the dead man to be buried anywhere on the lands he controlled.

On 8 September Mansong sent his minstrel, his "singing man", to bring Park and his men, with all their baggage, to Segu. Eight days later they landed at Sama Markala (Park's "Samee") and the minstrel, Bukari, travelled on to see

Mansong in Segu. Three days later, Isaaco arrived at their camp; although
Mansong was friendly enough, he said, whenever he had told the king anything
about the white men and their journey he had begun "to make squares and
triangles in the sand before him with his finger", signs intended to avert evil
fortune. "Isaaco said, that he thought Mansong was rather afraid of us; particularly as he never once expressed a wish to see us, but rather the contrary."
Nevertheless, in the days of waiting that now passed, Mansong's minister
accompanied by four of his chiefs came to visit Park, and the king sent him a
plump and, better still, auspiciously milk-white bullock.

On the minister's second visit, Park made plainer the purpose of his journey
and why it was in Segu's interest for Mansong to let him pass and even to help
him in his project. "You all know", he told the Bambaran dignitaties, "that the
white people are a trading people; and that all the articles of value which the
Moors and the people of Jenne bring to Segu are made by us. If you speak of a
good gun, who made it? The white people. If you speak of a good pistol or
sword, or a piece of scarlet or baft, or beads or gunpowder, who made them?
The white people. We sell them to the Moors; the Moors bring them to Timbuctu, where they sell them at a higher rate. The people of Timbuctu sell them
to the people of Jenne at a still higher price; and the people of Jenne sell them
to you. Now the king of the white people wishes to find out a way by which
we may bring our own merchandise to you, and sell everything at a much
cheaper rate . . . ." If Mansong let him pass so that he could make sure nothing
obstructed the navigable course of the Niger, "the white man's small vessels
will come up and trade at Segu, if Mansong wishes it".

Two days later, the minister brought the monarch's answer: "Mansong
says he will protect you. . . . If you wish to go to the east, no man shall harm you
from Segu till you pass Timbuctu. If you wish to go to the west, you may
travel through Fuladu and Manding, through Khasson and Bundu. The name
of 'Mansong's stranger' will be sufficient protection for you." This impressive
and probably by no means vainglorious declaration of Bambaran power must
have reassured Park considerably; the minister also passed on Mansong's permission for him to build his boats wherever he wished—"name the town, and
Mansong will convey you thither".

On 26 September, with two more men lost, soldiers named Seed and Barber,
Park and the rest of his party set out in canoes for Sansanding, the town where
he had chosen to construct the boat he would need for the last, the important
part of the journey. On the way downriver, he became almost delirious with
the heat—it took the arrival of Isaaco to rig up "a sort of shade over our canoe
with four sticks and a couple of cloaks", after which Park's condition improved.
The next day they arrived at Sansanding, having to beat their way through the
crowds gathered there to see them land. Death still lingered about them, however; early in October two soldiers named Garland and Marshall succumbed,
one to fever, the other to dysentery.

Park now waited for Mansong to supply him with the canoes, promised earlier, that he intended to fit out for his dash downstream. As the days passed and no canoes appeared, he took space in Sansanding's great market to sell the goods he had brought and so make enough money to buy two boats himself. This made some of the other merchants so jealous that they offered Mansong rich presents if he would kill or expel these interlopers. "Mansong, much to his honour, rejected the proposal, though it was seconded by two-thirds of the people of Segu, and almost all Sansanding." Business was almost overpoweringly good—one can see why the other traders were so anxious; at one time Park had three tellers counting the cash as it came in. On one day he took 25,756 cowries, no negligible amount when one recalls that during his first journey he had found that he and his horse could subsist on 100 a day (though the exchange rate he calculates would make what he had now earned only a little more than £5).

On 16 October Mansong's emissaries at last brought him a canoe, but Park found that one half of it was rotten. He sent for a new half; it did not fit the sound half he had. While 1,600 miles to the north Nelson destroyed Napoleon's fleet off Trafalgar, Park sent further gifts to the king—"two blunderbusses, two fowling pieces, two pair of pistols, and five unserviceable muskets"—in the hope of being sent a canoe he could use. Four days later, Isaaco appeared with yet another half-rotten canoe, but this time its good parts might with labour be made to fit those he already held. With the assistance of a soldier named Bolton, Park now began to hammer and patch, taking out what was rotten, repairing what was holed, joining the pieces that were strong, then reinforcing those joints until all question of risk had been eliminated. In that heat he worked every day for eighteen days; one can see him, the brown water just beyond him, a handful of bemused spectators watching in immobile fascination, his arm raised in effort, Bolton crouching beside him, the sweat bright on their faces, the arm about to descend, a mallet already swinging towards the waiting peg, all this transfixed for a split second, held there, imagination's photograph, clear for the particle of a second and then gone, a vanished micro-dot in the blurred mosaic of history. Martyn, meanwhile, caroused, a bad-lot officer come all this way to continue his barrack pleasures. We have his own word for it.

On 1 November he wrote a letter to a friend named Megan at the garrison in Gorée. "Thunder, Death and Lightning—the Devil to pay: lost by disease Mr. Scott, four carpenters and thirty-one members of the Royal Africa Corps which reduces our numbers to seven out of which Doctor Anderson and two of the soldiers are quite useless, the former from one disease or other has been for four months disabled: we every day suppose he'll kick it. . . . Excellent living since we came here (August 22nd) the Beef and Mutton as good as was ever eat. Whitbread's Beer is nothing to what we get here." And, a few days later, the scribbled postscript: "Dr. Anderson and Wills dead since writing the within— my head is a little sore this morning—was up late last night drinking Ale in company with a Moor who has been at Gibraltar and speaks English—got a little tipsy—finished the scene by giving the Moor a damned good thrashing."

Thus the lieutenant, paradigm of a hundred thousand uniformed bully-boys to come. Meanwhile Park worked on, possessed by the possibility of success; at the end of his eighteen days of carpentry and joinery, of sewing and caulking, he had "changed the Bambarra canoe into His Majesty's schooner *Joliba*; the length forty feet, breadth six feet; being flat-bottomed, draws only one foot water when loaded".

But he had worked with tragedy beside him. On 28 October he writes, "At a quarter-past five o'clock in the morning my dear friend Mr. Alexander Anderson died after a sickness of four months." He adds that "no event which took place during the journey ever threw the smallest gloom over my mind, till I laid Mr. Anderson in the grave. I then felt myself as if left a second time lonely and friendless amidst the wilds of Africa." Even now, however, he had apparently no thought of turning back, of not venturing the vast length of the unknown river. He might have, and without blame. The force he had been given to accomplish his task had been ripped from him by the climate and diseases of the region. He had worked day and night, gone without food, without comfort, without sleep. He had survived malaria and dysentery. No task had been too menial, no diplomacy too tortuous, no hostility threatening enough to daunt him. He might have retreated without dishonour; he had the dead to vouch for the truth of his misfortunes. He does not mention retreat, seems never even to contemplate its possibility. He had reached this point on his first journey and turned back, so that he knew it was an option open to him. One suspects, however, that precisely because he had turned back then he had no intention of doing so now. He was not a person to be defeated twice at the same place.

Nevertheless he certainly realised that, once he had started on his long sail down the Niger, there was no other point at which he could turn back. Ahead of him lay nothing but hostility, as he had learned during his last stay in Segu. Timbuctu lay in the hands of Tuaregs; Jenne remained disputed territory. What he did not know, perhaps, was that there was a new ferment among the Muslims of West Africa, that in the lands all about him a process was beginning that would culminate in numerous religious and revivalist wars. Radical movements were arising, total movements, revolutionary in their aims, intent on building new societies that would be Muslim in principle, practice and personnel. Many an aspirant to power would use the slogans of Islam to elevate himself, only to fall victim to the zeal of some new revivalist—whether genuine or self-advancing.

In the Hausa lands to the east, where the Niger sweeps southward to the sea, a teacher of radical views, Sheikh Uthman ben Fudi, had already arisen, using Arabic, Fulani and Hausa to put his message to the people. The people, for their part, were ready for news: twelve centuries after the Prophet was, as many believed, the time of the Mahdi, "The Expected One", "The Guided One", the Messiah whose coming would usher in the last short, golden age before the world's end, a redeemer whom North African Muslims more than most have been prone to identify, at various times during the last thousand years, in the person of some local teacher, leader or revivalist. With his headquarters in Sokoto, Sheikh Uthman had soon established a nucleus of power rivalling that of the nominal ruler of the area, the king of Gobir, a state centred halfway between the Niger and Lake Chad. It was precisely during the period of Park's first voyage, between 1796 and 1798, that the king of Gobir had begun his harassment of these zealots. As they continued to become more and more powerful, however, so his anger had increased; six years later, he had ordered the community to disperse. In February 1804, the sheikh had proclaimed *jehad*, his holy war. Now, as Park made ready to go on board, the lands past which the lower Niger ran were loud with conflict.

Nor was this turmoil without its effect far beyond the Hausa regions. The teachings of Sheikh Uthman found a response throughout West Africa. In Runde Siru, near Jenne, there was already active a teacher, Ahmed Lobbo, who would bring to Massina the same radical changes as Sheikh Uthman was bringing to Sokoto. As yet, he still herded other people's cattle while he pondered the Koran and the wisdom of the Prophet. It would be not until two years later that the first overt disagreements would appear between him and the political authorities; he was to wait until 1816 before declaring his own *jehad*. But he was symptomatic of a new fervour—and one that boded little good for any Christian interloper.

On 15 November, Isaaco returned from Segu with a message from Mansong: the king would like his European guests to depart as soon as possible, before news of their intentions filtered to the east and brought to life Moorish hostility. The next day, Park finished his final preparations. Forty-four men had marched, happy, indifferent or drunk, from the Gambia estuary eight months before. Only five were left to make the attempt to follow the Niger's course: the intemperate Lieutenant Martyn, three privates, one of whom was delirious, and Park himself. With them were two black men, slaves, and a guide named Amadi Fatuma. Later, a third slave was added to their number. It seems a forlorn party to attempt the wide sweep of an unknown river.

On 17 September, Park wrote to Lord Camden; he headed his despatch, "On board of HM schooner *Joliba*, at anchor off Sansanding". He gives some details of what had befallen them, of the situation that faced them. He wrote, "From this account I am afraid your Lordship will be apt to consider matters as in a very hopeless state, but I assure you I am far from desponding. With the assistance of one of the soldiers I have changed a large canoe into a tolerably good schooner, on board of which I shall set sail to the east, with the fixed resolution to discover the termination of the Niger or perish in the attempt. I have heard nothing I can depend on respecting the remote course of this mighty stream, but I am more and more inclined to think that it can end nowhere but in the sea.

"My dear friend Mr. Anderson, and likewise Mr. Scott, are both dead; but although the Europeans who are with me should die, and though I were myself half dead, I would still persevere, and if I could not succeed in the object of my journey, I would at least die on the Niger. If I succeed in the object of my journey, I expect to be in England in the month of May or June, by way of the West Indies."

Two days later, still at Sansanding, he wrote to his wife. "It grieves me to the heart to write anything that may give you uneasiness; but such is the will of Him who *doeth all things well*! Your brother Alexander, my dear friend, is no more! He died of the fever at Sansanding, on the morning of 28th October. . . .

"I am afraid that, impressed with a woman's fears and the anxieties of a wife, you may be led to consider my situation as a great deal worse than it really is. It is true that my dear friends, Mr. Anderson and George Scott, have both bid adieu to the things of this world; and the greater part of the soldiers have died on the march during the rainy season; but you may believe me, I am in good health. The rains are completely over, and the healthy season has commenced, so that there is no danger of sickness; and I have still a sufficient force to protect me from any insult in sailing down the river to the sea.

"We have already embarked all our things, and we shall sail the moment I have finished this letter. I do not intend to stop or land anywhere, till we reach the coast; which I suppose will be some time in the end of January. We shall then embark in the first vessel for England. . . . I think it not unlikely but that I shall be in England before you receive this. You may be sure that I feel happy at turning my face towards home. We this morning have done with all intercourse with the natives; and the sails are now hoisting for our departure for the coast."

Whatever there was of optimism in his situation he had filched for his wife's comfort. Did he believe his chances were really so good? Certainly he thought he had some chance—one long fling down the current, covering who knew how many hundreds of miles of rapids, of mud flats, of mazy streams where crocodile lurked, of slow tides under hostile walls, of gloomy jungle overhang, of mangrove swamp or steep defile, to come out at last on some huge, labouring estuary, with the waiting sea beyond. It had to be possible—he knew cargoes travelled to the Hausa lands far to the east. One feels that the battle had become personal now, this desperate attempt to drag the Niger out of African darkness and into the light of European day. It was between him and the river; science, geography, commerce, patriotism and the Cross, all had ceased to matter as much as this strange tussle between one inexorable man and the uncaring water, which would carry his schooner as indifferently as any merchant's over-laden canoe.

So it must have been with some optimism that, on that 19 November 1805, he took his seat under the protective awning of bullock hides, cover against both the sun and hostile missiles, gave his signals to his men and watched the crowded bank recede. The long, narrow shape eases out into the current, the bows turn and steady, Mungo Park twists round perhaps, waves to an acquaintance, to the faithful Isaaco, to some representative of the king. The boat settles in mid-stream; across the water someone calls a late farewell. Mungo Park nods, the slanting sunlight catches the brightness of his hair. Then he has gone, moved further, out of our sight and into mystery, into legend.

Chapter Twelve

The Last Gamble

Consider Park's situation, and that of his companions. They were afloat on a current that led away into areas totally unknown, in directions that could only be guessed at, that had indeed been guessed at in a welter of contradictory speculation, a river of which the only certainty was that it would carry them into regions both unfamiliar and hostile. No one knew better than Park that the lands they were about to pass through were inhabited by fanatics prepared to imprison and even kill any European on sight. Above all, no one had the slightest idea where, if anywhere, this river ended.

In 1754 D'Anville had proposed, reasonably enough, that the best way of finding out about Timbuctu would be to send there *"quelque personne habituée au climat"*. Now such a person was on his way—there could be few Europeans more habituated to the climate than Mungo Park—but religion and Tuareg occupation put Timbuctu itself out of bounds. It had been one of his great ambitions to see it, but he would have to forgo this achievement in order to pursue a greater one: the discovery of where the Niger came to its—dramatic or anticlimactic—finish. The British consul in Mogador, the traveller and adventurer Grey Jackson, had written of a party of seventeen Africans of which he had heard; they had, he claimed, travelled by river from Jenne to Cairo, carrying their craft at the many shallows, passing, it was said, 1,200 towns and cities on the way, each with its domed and minaretted mosque, to come out at last on the majestic brown width of Egypt's river. Was that where Park would find himself in the end?

Or was Major Rennell right in his conviction that deep in the interior of the continent there was a vast lake that endlessly received the Niger's waters? If so, Park and his companions were hurrying downstream into a waiting trap. Once on that lake, with hundreds of miles of forest and mountain, dozens of states and tribes, between them and the coast, they would be faced with an impossible journey to reach safety. Or was Park correct, in a hypothesis he had derived from a West Africa merchant named Maxwell, that what was Niger at its source was Congo at its outflow? Martyn had written to his friend at Gorée, "Capt. Park has made every enquiry concerning the River Niger and from what he can learn there remains no doubt but it is the Congo." In that case, he faced a journey of well over 2,000 miles through territories about which he was in total ignorance. There was no possibility that was not hedged and barbed with hazard, no direction that did not suggest disaster.

From Sansanding Park had written to Banks, "With respect to my future views, it is my intention to keep to the middle of the river, and make the best use I can of winds and currents till I reach the termination of this mysterious stream." It is likely that he kept to his intentions, at least according to the abbreviated tale told later by Amadi Fatouma, Park's guide and a man he described as "a native of Kasson, but one of the greatest travellers in this part of Africa". From his narrative one gets an impression of the boat's flashing down the stream, the towns and villages sweeping past, from each issuing its little group of hostile and pursuing war canoes. They halted at Silla to take on one more hand, a slave bought at that place, the extreme point of Park's previous journey, then travelled on, passing Sebi, where three canoes came after them "armed with pikes, lances, bows and arrows, etc., but no fire-arms"; then passing Rakbara, where three more had to be repulsed, then sailing on past fabled Timbuctu, again in a racket of musket fire, the dark shapes of hostile canoes closing in, then swinging away, finally repulsed, left behind. . . .

But at this point the clarity of the story fades and softens. Fifty years later Heinrich Barth reached Timbuctu and met there a Tuareg chief named Awab who told him of the Christians who all those decades ago had come down the river in their large boat—his tribe's wincingly suspicious attitude to Barth himself was, he explained, a direct result of their passing but brutal contact with Mungo Park. Not that, even in Awab's account, Park had been to blame. He had landed at Kabara, Timbuctu's riverside port, and there attempted to make contact with the inhabitants. Was the old ambition still working then, Timbuctu the lure that caused Park to change his mind and step ashore after all? If he did, he was soon on his way again, only to be attacked a little lower by Tuareg boats, gathered there at the news of his arrival.

Amadi Fatouma says that three canoes attacked near Timbuctu; however many it was, Park broke free. According to Awab, word was then passed swiftly downriver that the Christians should be stopped. Somewhere near Bamba (where Park was said to have stopped an hour or two, apparently to purchase supplies), a neighbouring Tuareg tribe, the Igwaraden, came after these strangers in their canoes, were savagely mauled, but rallied and attacked again near the narrows at Tosaye. And Amadi Fatouma agrees that in passing Gourma-Rarous "seven canoes came after us, which we likewise beat off"; later, he says, sixty canoes attacked them, but Park's little schooner was well supplied with muskets and crewed by men now beyond the limits of desperation. They shot and shot again, and loaded and shot, until their pursuers turned away.

Martyn, narrow in his courage, kept on and on firing—through the insubstantial gauze of the narrative one senses his anger, his blood-lust, his demented
aggression, the bully-boy pushed outside normality, insecure but striking back.
Amadi "took hold of Martyn's hand, saying, 'Martyn, let us cease firing, for
we have killed too many already.'" Martyn, thus balked, would have killed
him too had not Park stopped him.

Lower down the river, Barth found further stories still remembered and
told about Park: a chieftain named Kara, whose people lived on an island in the
river, volunteered the information that "a Christian had come down the river
in a large boat with a white tent and the river being then full, had passed without
any accident the rocky passage ahead of us". He had, however, been attacked by
a neighbouring tribe at a place called Zamgoy. At Gao, that ancient city, once
capital of the Songhai empire, Barth met an old man from whose friendly
chatter "I could not but conclude that he had come into close contact with the
Christian who so many years ago navigated this river in such a mysterious
manner; but, unfortunately, he was of weak understanding, and I could not
make out half of what he said to me."

But somewhere near Gao, Park and his companions seem to have run into
danger so extreme that they were almost destroyed. Was this at Ansongo, some
seventy miles downstream? According to Awab, the *Joliba* went aground at a
place he called Ensymmo—Barth believes this was indeed Ansongo. According
to the Tuareg chief, his people here attacked with such ferocity that two of the
Europeans were killed. And, still in these regions, Barth met an old man who,
speaking of Park, "gave me an accurate description of his tall, commanding
figure, and his large boat". He too spoke of a Tuareg attack near Ansongo, but
emphasised the vigour of Park's defence, for, as Barth put it, "the intrepid
Scotchman shot one of his pursuers, and caused two to be drowned in the
river".

Clapperton, too, some twenty-five years earlier, had had it in writing from
the scribe of the Sultan Bello of Sokoto that after Park's boat had halted in
Timbuctu, where the whole party was given hospitality by a prince named
Babal-kydiali, "they went on towards the country of Soghy till they came to one
of its towns called Gharwal-gaoo. There the Tuaricks met and fought them
severely till three were killed, and two only of them escaped with the vessel."
Nothing here about going aground. Amadi, however, does mention a time
when "going along we struck on the rocks". He says nothing of any attack,
however, and perhaps this was a different time. There is, in fact, no correlation
to be made between his account and what Barth and the other later travellers
were able to learn. Awab, however, did give Barth one odd detail, describing
an iron hook which, he said, was used by Park to thrust away both hostile
canoes and troublesome hippopotami. And Amadi confirms that on occasion
these enormous animals caused concern—"A hippopotamus rose near us, and
had nearly overset the canoe . . . ." (That the memory of the hooked instrument,

probably devised on the model of a boat-hook, should have survived half a century indicates the impact that Park's voyage made on those who lived on the river banks.)

At one point, Amadi Fatouma was taken prisoner while on shore buying provisions. This was on an island where he had been sent to look for milk. Mungo Park seems to have acted with his usual resolution, taking as hostages merchants who had come out in their canoes to sell him their rice and fruit and fowls. Thus checked, the islanders sent Amadi back, and Park released his prisoners. Amadi then adds a sentence that makes one believe the incident truly reported, for it smacks of the authentic Mungo Park: "After which we bought some provisions from them, and made them some presents." Park had always reacted with similar magnanimity after such small victories as circumstances had forced him to fight for. One cannot imagine Lieutenant Martyn doling out gifts after such a crisis.

The contradictions pile up and multiply. Different accounts are circumstantial, they give the names of people and places, but they do not tally. Did Park land anywhere? It seems it was not his intention, and Amadi said that the canoe was stocked with provisions, salted and fresh, so that they could sail down the river "without stopping at any place, for fear of accident". Yet several accounts say that Park did land; when he did, he was either well received or he was attacked, according to which source one believes; if not attacked at once, then his stopping provided his enemies with an opportunity to prepare a riparian ambush. One story even has him abruptly sailing upstream, past Timbuctu, as though intending to return to Sansanding, a manoeuvre that has been construed as a ruse to throw the waiting Tuareg into confusion.

What is clear is that it was with the most forceful determination that he made his colossal bid for success, his reckless attempt on mystery. Amadi does not mention it, but from Ansongo to Bussa dozens of rock-toothed rapids make navigation almost impossible and the few who have attempted this stretch of the river seem usually to have been relieved at their survival. Yet Park seems never to have hesitated, never to have thought of giving up his plan. The canoe, cobbled together in those eighteen days of effort, and dedicated, with dogged patriotism, to a distant Britannic Majesty, bobbed and wallowed and churned its way down those hundreds of miles, its desperate occupants blasting aside those who again and again tried to halt them, the waters flat and placid or white-flecked and dangerous, the banks low and muddy or rocky and tall, villages hostile, friendly or indifferent, towns jumbled and battered by history, all glimpsed for a moment, then left behind for ever, the river a sort of tunnel now made tolerable only by the hoped-for sea which, like daylight, would one day glint in welcome, would widen and open and offer them the safety of its indifferent freedom. Was it his single-mindedness that finally destroyed Park? His difficulties, it has been suggested, were often of his own making—the Niger was a trade route and those who used it paid their dues to the chiefs whose

F

domains they passed, just as caravans did on land. Was it Park's determination
not to stop that aroused legitimate hostility in those who lived, at least in part,
off the duty they levied from river traffic? Perhaps—but if the *Joliba* halted in
Timbuctu and Gao, were the dues not paid? On the whole, it is unlikely that
Park went ashore, but Amadi did, as his own account shows. He says that, on
the occasion when he had been released from his short imprisonment, twenty
canoes came after Park's boat, the occupants calling out, "Amadi Fatouma,
how can you pass through our country without giving us anything?" Park
"gave them a few grains of amber and some trinkets, and they went back
peaceably". Was this the only occasion on which this happened? If Park shot
first and asked questions later, as has been alleged, why did he not shoot on this
occasion?

The contradictions pile up, multiply. Court, when consul in Mogador, sent
information back within eighteen months of Park's trip, saying that Park had
not paid the Tuaregs the customary tribute, so that these tribes were affronted.
When they took to their own boats to protest, however, Park did not allow
them near him but put up an immediate barrier of defiant shot. In 1826,
Gordon Laing, his intention to sail down the Niger from Timbuctu, was attacked
while on his way there by Tuaregs who, he claimed, took him for the same
Christian who had sailed past the riverside peoples in an insolence of musket
fire. He wrote, "How imprudent, how unthinking! I may even say how selfish
it was in Park, to attempt to make discoveries in the country at the expense of
the blood of the inhabitants. . . ." Giving up his intention to take a boat and
follow Park, an adventure he now considered too dangerous, Laing nevertheless travelled on to Timbuctu, where, unable to avoid his fate, he died.

Park in his earlier captivity had formed his own opinion of the Moors. He
knew something of their religious feeling, had seen them at work in raid and
robbery along the upper Niger and on the banks of the Senegal. He wanted
desperately to reach the Niger's mouth; almost as desperately, he wanted to
avoid becoming a second time the prisoner of Tuaregs, Berbers or Arabs. It is
possible he did not realise that the Niger was subject to dues and tolls like any
other trade route. He expected to meet Moorish hostility and was in a mood to
construe any approach as an attack. He had prepared himself for only two possibilities: success or death. Thus keyed up, it is likely that he saw in the remon-
strations of riverside officials echoes of Ali's tyrannical claims and was determined to brush them aside.

This attitude in someone so obviously rich—he was white, heavily armed and
in a large boat—would not unnaturally have angered those who had approached
him legitimately; those who had in fact come out to plunder and kill needed no
further stimulus but a Christian stranger's presence. Park's intransigence would
have brought both factions together, infuriating the authorities and legitimising
the murderous intentions of the fanatics. A swift, and swiftly increasing, ripple
of hostility would have moved along the Niger's course, sometimes following,

but often ahead of Park's improvised schooner. As Awab's story demonstrates, it was possible for one tribe to send a message to another lower down the river in time for them to attack these hurrying strangers.

What, then, was the outcome? Again, one is faced with contradiction, distortion, guesswork, suspicion. According to Amadi Fatouma, he spent his last two days with Park teaching him a few necessary words and phrases to help in those lands that still lay between him and the coast. When they landed at Yauri, his own task had come to an end. The last duty he performed was to give Park's presents to the local emir and to buy provisions for those who were continuing the journey south. But, the day after Park left, Amadi was, he said, flung into captivity. The chief of the riverside settlement off which Park had anchored had complained to the emir that the white men had left without giving either him or the ruler anything. "The king immediately ordered me to be put in irons; which was accordingly done . . . . The next morning early the king sent an army to a village called Boussa near the river side . . . . Mr. Park came there after the army had posted itself; he nevertheless attempted to pass. The people began to attack him, throwing lances, pikes, arrows and stones. Mr. Park defended himself for a long time; two of his slaves at the stern of the canoe were killed; they threw everything they had in the canoe into the river, and kept firing; but being overpowered by numbers and fatigue, and unable to keep up the canoe against the current, and no probability of escaping, Mr. Park took hold of one of the white men, and jumped into the water; Martyn did the same, and they were drowned in the stream . . . ." One slave remained alive; he stood up—one thinks one sees his terrified face raised towards the crowded bank, his arms abjectly spread—and asked them to stop their attack. "Take me and the canoe, but don't kill me", he begged them. Amadi says that he himself was kept in irons for three months, but that, when he was at last released, and given a female slave in partial compensation, he spoke with the man who had survived. "I asked him if he was sure nothing had been found in the canoe after its capture; he said that nothing remained in the canoe but himself and a sword-belt. I asked him where the sword-belt was; he said the king took it, and made a girth for his horse with it."

The story seems clear, and comes to us certified by the suffering of the man who tells it. But there are problems in it: for instance, the fact that Bussa was fifty miles downstream, with rapids between it and Yauri, so that it is unlikely that any army would have caught Park up once he had taken his day's start (although, if the rapids were so bad that travellers were forced to carry their craft forward overland to safe water, the force of this objection is diminished; certainly later travellers pronounced these reaches of the Niger barely navigable). Bussa, in any case, was a state independent of and in a condition of some rivalry with its northern neighbour; no army from Yauri would have been allowed to cross its borders without a great amount of dealing and arranging. A minor discrepancy is suggested by the only one of Park's notebooks to survive, that

containing the logarithms he used for navigation: it apparently shows no signs
of having ever been in water.

There is also the question of where precisely this ambush, this final intervention, actually occurred. There are the Tsulu rapids, but they are nearly
fifty miles upriver from Bussa. They could have been reached by the Yauri
warriors, but then there would have been no need for Amadi to mention Bussa
at all. And Bussa does seem to have been the place: the scribe of Sultan Bello of
Sokoto wrote, in the account he gave Clapperton, "They proceeded towards
the east till they arrived at Boussa"; but now a new element appears, for, he
continues, at Bussa "the inhabitants fought and killed them, and their ship is to
this moment there". So according to him it was not the people of Yauri, but
those of Bussa, who set up that ambush. Early this century, however, a Dr
Cameron Blair offered yet another possibility: in 1901, while he was quartered
on Jebba island, he met two very old men who, unhappy at European beliefs
that Park had been killed, told him that, on the contrary, when Park was coming down the river towards Bussa the people there tried to warn him of the
dangers that faced him by hurrying up the banks and signalling him to stop.
Park ignored them—which certainly rings true—and simply continued on his
way, thinking that he was faced once more by local hostility. In the rapids he
met his death when his boat struck and capsized and all who travelled in it
drowned.

The rapids suggested by this account are the Bubaru rapids, ten miles below
Bussa. Was it there that Park's last scene was played? But if it was, who saw it?
Who took that sword-belt, that undamaged notebook, from the canoe? No
village stood there: neither fishing nor trade prospers where white water roars
past gleaming rocks. And Clapperton, who tells us that he was shown the
actual spot where the canoe struck, takes the time to mention that, even if Park
had come through Bussa safely, he would certainly have perished at the Bubaru
rapids, on a sharp stone slab that local people called *Mutu Kabari*—"Dead Man's
Grave". It was not on that rock therefore that the Scot and his companions died.

But could it have been at Bussa itself? It is true that when the river there is
low the tiger-teeth rocks stand ready to claw for prey. And by late February or
early March the river is low. Can Park's journey have taken so long? A dozen
or so weeks to cover some 1,200 miles—it makes an average of only fourteen
miles a day. Yet we do not know whether Park's little group travelled every
day; if some of the stories are true, Park stopped at Sebi, at Kabara, at Gao; at
many other places, Amadi went ashore to replenish their supplies. At each of
these halts time would have to be taken for courtesies, for the handing out of
gifts and tribute, for haggling in the market-place perhaps, and the transport-
ation of what had been bought or presented. They had missed the best of the
current by several weeks, for the highest water is early in October; for long
stretches the Niger is at the best of times a dawdling river, trapped in a wide
maze of swamplands and islands, shredded to the point of bewilderment into

a twisted complex of languid streams. Three of the men had been ill before the journey began; it is not inconceivable that, either for that reason or because of damage done after one of the many running battles with the Tuaregs, Park felt it necessary to halt somewhere and wait for fever to pass or wounds to heal.

However, by a tradition noted in 1913 by the District Officer at Yelwa, a man named Clarke, "when the . . . day [after Mungo Park's death] broke, night immediately came on again". There was indeed an eclipse in 1806, but it occurred on 16 June, too late for this chronology. It is a case of two marvels having been compounded into one, just as the silver medallion presented to the emir of Bussa by Richard Lander over twenty years later has, in popular memory, been drawn into the earlier and more magnetic story. It is believed to have been a gift to Kisaran Dogo, then ruler of Bussa, from the white man who rode in his canoe down from the mysterious beginnings of their great river.

The transferred darkness of an eclipse; the wishful attribution of that silver gift to Mungo Park—at a deeper level, perhaps, such alterations in history point to a collective mood. If it was not the people of Yauri who killed Park, if it was not the Bubaru rapids that overturned his boat, how did he die? Clapperton in 1826 could walk from Bussa to where, in the easternmost of three channels, he could see the place at which the canoe had struck. Low banks, not more than ten feet high, hemmed in a swift stream running over the ominous darkness of slate. He marked the spot for any other traveller to pick out—it lay, he wrote, on a line that, running through a double-trunked white tree standing solitary on a small, flat island, was drawn directly from the house of the sultan. Similarly, the Lander brothers said that the place where Park died was not more than a mile from their lodging. The reliable accounts therefore agree: it was hard by Bussa that the *Joliba* came to its sudden ending, it was there that those who had sailed her so far finally gave up their last ambition.

How did they die? Still confusion and contradiction perplex us. At Wawa Clapperton heard that, when the canoe struck, the whites tried but failed to struggle ashore, drowning there under the eyes of a population too frightened either to help or to attack. In the boat, riches were found, and books and papers, and salted meat. But, as to the meat, "the people of Boussa who had eaten of it all died, because it was human flesh . . . they knew we white men ate human flesh". Once again the distorted images of slavery appear in the buckled mirrors of rumour and superstition: the white men's need for the black was so exorbitant that Africans could explain it only by cannibalism. At that time, in 1826, most people believed that Park's canoe still existed; many asked Clapperton if he were on his way to fetch it.

The emir of Yauri wrote to Clapperton to tell him that, far from having been an accident, Park's death had been caused by the people of Bussa. At the time, so Clapperton heard, he had wanted to punish them for it, but had been unable to. Mohammad Gomsoo, one of the principal Arabs in Sokoto, told Clapperton that he had been near Yauri in 1806. When Park left Yauri, he said, the emir had sent messengers after him to warn him of the rapids. This they could not do, either because they could not catch the canoe up or because Park refused to listen (a story confirming an earlier one told by Abdel Gassam, a Mecca-bound pilgrim from Timbuctu, who said that the emir sent boats after Park to warn him: "However, the Christians went on and would not suffer the Sultan's people to come near them, and they all perished"). According to Mohammad Gomsoo, however, it was no accident that concluded the story, for from both banks of the river an attack was launched on the white men, "upon which they threw overboard all their effects; and the two white men arm in arm jumped into the water, two slaves only remaining in the boat with some books and papers and several guns".

The transferred eclipse, a moment of darkness in Bussa's history, the lowering gloom of tragedy; the presentation of the silver medallion, symbol of friendship, foisted on Mungo Park, altering to trust what may have been enmity, what was at best indifference. Why such alterations in the facts? Clapperton, twenty years after the disaster, found the people of Bussa strangely evasive. They would not speak of what had happened. "Everyone in fact appeared uneasy when I asked for information, and said it had happened before their rememberance, or that they did not see it." The Lander brothers, four years later, found that response unchanged. Was it the collective guilt of a community self-accused of murder?

All were agreed that the boat drifted ashore. Why did Park and his companions not drift ashore with it? What forced them to leave it, to take to the uncertain security of that rock-riven current? It had not overturned—the recovered book is not water-stained. If they had struck, had been in difficulties, yet had not overturned, would not the good people of Bussa, their town not a mile distant, have witnessed this and made some effort to help? Can one really believe that they stood thunderstruck, allowing fate to work out these strangers' destiny? What if they did? The canoe came ashore—there exists as testimony Park's navigational book and a hymn-book, once Alexander Anderson's, which the Landers found at Wawa and returned to the dead man's family. Richard Lander, homeward bound after Clapperton's death, found himself cleaning Park's guns for the headman of Wawa and heard that ammunition too had been recovered. Not, one fancies, from an overturned canoe.

The possibility of accident recedes. Over that scene there drifts a blue-white haze of gunsmoke; arrows whisper through the misted air, the strong shafts of spears whirr and waver. From the banks there come the calls of hatred, of defiance and a summoned courage. Was the battle caused, as Richard Lander thought, by the Bussa people's over-swift reaction to these pale voyagers, strangers from the north—did they believe them to be Fulani warriors, forerunners of that revivalist army trying to spread the newly cleansed word of Islam through these backsliding regions? The *jehad* was two years old, the fighting widespread; here to the south, however, the people were not sure what to expect. Did they imagine that Park and his companions were outriders of that holy band, come to chastise them? Lander tells us that the people of Bussa "had only *heard* of that warlike nation", the Fulani, though they knew them to be on the move. Yet is it really possible that they had never seen the Fulani, whose nearest villages were at most only two or three days away? It seems unlikely. So too, then, must the possibility that they mistook the white strangers for these not so distant neighbours.

On the other hand, there is the disappointment of that riverside chieftain in the emirate of Yauri. Was his the echo of a similar anger further up the Niger, the rage of men who see their right to levy tribute defied, who watch their chance of plunder vanishing downstream? If Awab's people could pass a message eastward from Timbuctu, the emir of Yauri could alert the sultan of Bussa. Amadi's story has a right to be taken seriously: he was, after all, there at the time. He seems to have been inaccurate about the place where the attack took place and about the people who mounted it; on the other hand, he has the excuse that he was shackled, locked away, so that the story came to him as hearsay. Yet surely, if that was the case, he loses his credentials as the eyewitness, the man who took part.

Richard Lander decided on the evidence that, despite Amadi's testimony, Park and the emir had parted on good terms. Between that ruler and the people of Bussa, on the other hand, the feeling was far from friendly. Why should Bussa punish a man who had done Yauri harm? They were as likely to welcome him. News of Park's neglect to pay the various duties levied by the Tuaregs further north was not likely to have reached a people who are said to have had no direct knowledge even of their neighbours, the Fulani. Somehow, the proposed sequence of events does not strike true—the emir in assumed outrage sending a messenger downstream, the men of Bussa massing on the bank, ready to commit their neighbours' murder: what reason had they to do Mungo harm?

What of a third possibility: that Park shot first, came down the river, blazing away at anyone who came near him? It does not sound like the pliable Mungo Park who had, through all those weeks of weariness and sickness, through all the thieving and repeated tragedy of death, kept his caution, his diplomatic control, his essential friendliness. Yet he was at the end of a long journey, he had struggled with sickness, with the dangers of the river, with the endless hostility of the people who lived on its banks. If the people of Yauri sent canoes after him to warn him of the rapids, if the people of Bussa came upstream to turn him aside from the dangers that awaited him, he might well have mistaken their intentions, assumed their gestures threats, their cries of warning the brutal screams of warriors. He was a man whose will had narrowed to a single overwhelming determination from which he would allow nothing to turn him aside. He seems still to have had the hot-headed Martyn with him, a man more likely to shoot at the first sign of hostility, or what might be construed as hostility, than was Park himself. It would have taken only the one shot, perhaps. The people on the banks, frustrated in their efforts to help, furious at this aggressive obtuseness on the part of those whom they had made such an effort to befriend, and underneath possibly nervous of such outlandish strangers, might well have reacted with ferocity. It would not have needed many of them to see that shot as a challenge. Perhaps someone was hit, fell, shouting and holding his shoulder. Twenty yards away his cousin or best friend, watching him collapse, seeing the sudden brightness of blood, would have flung his spear before thought could prevent him. Such an action would have confirmed all the suspicions of those in the canoe. In a moment, the battle would have been under way, one more weary battle in Park's long struggle to reach the sea.

This time, however (we can invent the scene), it was not to be the same. Behind their barricade of shot, the voyagers come hurtling down the water, to find themselves suddenly among the black blades of the rocks, the long slabs of slate under the swift current. There comes the moment of shock, the canoe hanging for a second, trembling with the water's force; then a slow scraping, a sudden freeing, the boat slewing to one side, perhaps, then catching again, tilting. From the banks sounds a high ululation of triumph, a raucous call of defiance and anger. The arrows and the spears march in their high arcs across the air. Like cruel hammers they strike at woodwork and goat-skin canopy; they fall with a scattering of spray in the streaked water; with a malevolent thud they bite deeply into flesh.

So there it is, the final convulsive action: Martyn and Park, linked or each heroically bearing a companion, their bodies momentarily outlined against sky and water as they climb high on the canoe's side and hover there in the split second before destruction. Martyn bawls some curse lost in the hiss and tumble of the water. Park looks steadfastly ahead, his eyes clear, the light catching the fire of his hair for the last time. Before him the river unwinds, unwinds; its miles unreel in his head, in all the bitterness of thwarted expectation. He strains for the sea, but its brightness does not appear. The river vanishes. He jumps. He and the river become one.

Crossing a swamp on the Kebali route (an illustration from *De L'Atlantique Au Niger* by Aimé Olivier). The French illustrator has modernized Park's clothing, but he has a good feeling for jungle vegetation.

Mungo Park insulted by the Moors (an illustration from *The Story of Africa and Its Explorers* by Robert Brown). Despite the privations of travel, Park remains properly attired in this fanciful late-nineteenth-century version.

Chapter Thirteen

The Colonial Consequence

So Mungo Park vanished. The world waited; in place of news, it had to make do with rumours. In Mogador Alexander Court, Jackson's successor as consul, heard confused accounts, no more than hints, and sent a man to Timbuctu to try and find out more. In Bombay, in 1809, a newspaper carried a story about a pilgrim from Ethiopia who had spoken in Mecca of Park having met with a violent end. From the banks of the Niger itself, Court's representative brought back a letter written by one of his informants. The Christians, it said, had passed Jenne and Kabara, but some had died on the way. The four who remained "went and killed a Shariff . . . by the side of the Nile, and they fell in with the Touarks at Bounba [Bamba], and they fought and slew some of the Touarks—and they went on till they passed to Henbara, which is ten long days Journey from Tombuctoo, and I have heard no more of them but this. I don't know if they are dead or alive. God only knows. . . ."

This was received by Banks in 1810. As early as July 1806, Major Lloyd, the commander of the Gorée garrison, had been asked to mount an investigation, but he had been able to learn nothing more. Park had travelled down the river, he had passed Timbuctu and been attacked there, perhaps for not paying duty, had possibly fought again lower down the river, and had then vanished. Court passed on to Banks in London a later report, which spoke of a party of travellers seen on what he called "the Second Grand Cataract of the Niger" during the summer of 1808. He felt that this party could only be Park's group. He did not satisfactorily explain what they had been doing in the intervening three years.

The Napoleonic wars had had their repercussion in Africa, and there was now a British governor in Senegambia. It was he who, early in 1810, authorised Park's old guide Isaaco, the merchant Isiyaku, to make an investigative journey to the Niger in an effort to find out what had really happened to the explorer and his companions. Isaaco set off for Segu, travelling through the effects of the still-continuing local wars. His own family had been forced to flee as a result of invasion and battle. He too, like Park, seems everywhere to have been subject to the caprices of rulers and the depredation of thieves; unlike Park, he knew the people and the language well, was one of them, had his counters ready.

It was late in August before he reached Segu and could be received by "Dacha, King of the Bambarras". He describes the scene, one Park himself never witnessed: "On my entrance in the first yard I found a guard of forty men, young, strong and without beards. On entering another yard I met another guard, well-armed and very numerous, lying in the shade. A little farther on I found the king sitting; there were four broad swords stuck in the ground, on each side and behind him, which had been given him by Mr. Park." The king, however, had no information to pass on and Isaaco went on to Sansanding.

In a village near that town, he at last came across the one informant who could tell him what he wanted to know—Amadi Fatouma himself. "I sent for him; he came immediately. I demanded of him a faithful account of what had happened to Mr. Park. On seeing me, and hearing me mention Mr. Park, he began to weep; and his first words were, 'They are all dead'. I said, 'I am come to see after you, and intended to look every way for you, to know the truth from your own mouth, how they died'. He said they were lost for ever, and it was useless to make any further enquiry after them . . . ." Then he told Isaaco his story of the journey, the difficulties encountered, his own imprisonment and Mungo Park's death.

Isaaco turned back to Segu, but sent eastward an emissary, a Fulani, "to get me the belt by any means and at any price, and any thing else he could discover belonging to Mr. Park". The belt was, of course, that sword-belt now serving as a girth for the emir's horse. While he was away, Isaaco remained in Segu. The king amused himself by sending his army out on a retributory expedition to the Hausa lands, but his notions of distance were somewhat vague; when the army reported that such a journey was too long for the army to make safely, he ordered them to attack Massina instead. Since this kingdom lay next to his own, it simplified the logistics wonderfully.

It was eight months before Isaaco's faithful and hard-working representative came back from those inhospitable distances that had so daunted the Segu commanders. "He brought me the belt; and said he had bribed a young slave girl belonging to the King, who had stole it from him; and that he could not get any thing more, as nothing else was to be found which had belonged to Mr. Park or his companions." With the belt, this report and Amadi Fatouma's short chronicle, Isaaco returned to the coast, despite the rainy season and the pleas of the king of Segu that he stay. It was two years since he had set out from there, but he brought with him the firm news everyone had expected, and dreaded: Mungo Park was dead.

Later travellers tried, as we have seen, to discover more about Park's end; they also attempted to hunt down physical evidence of his having been in Yauri and in Bussa. When Clapperton was in those regions, the boat in which Park had sailed was believed still to exist, although he could never get near it. This was, he felt, the consequence of the deliberate evasiveness of a guilty population. There had been papers, he heard, but they had been dispersed; there had been books, but they had been taken away by an imam in flight (these were bad times for the religious). The Landers did find that hymn-book of Anderson's at Wawa; over fifty years after the disaster, J. H. Glover (then a lieutenant but later knighted and a governor of Lagos) rediscovered and bought the book of navigational calculations, once used by Park and now in the museum of the Royal Geographical Society. The Landers chased the will o' the wisp of Park relics through those riverside towns and villages, but all clues, mistaken or deliberately falsified, led only to "the bitterness of hope suddenly extinguished". They were given a gown which they were told had belonged to Park, and exchanged one of their guns for another, English-made, also said to have come from the stranded canoe. Both these were lost on their return journey. In Yauri, there is a staff, silver-tipped and now a part of the emir's regalia, that is said once to have belonged to Park. There is no other physical evidence that he was ever in those regions.

There were rumours now and then, supposed sightings of a tall man, red-bearded, English-speaking. Heroes when they die become the seeds of legend. His family believed unswervingly, it seems, that he remained, a prisoner, for-lorn, knowing himself forgotten and thus no candidate for rescue, somewhere deep in the dangerous recesses of West Africa. His second son, Thomas, was the person who, next to Ailie, held most tenaciously to this conviction. In 1827 he left England, bound ostensibly for the South Seas. Instead, he appeared later that year on the Gold Coast. From Accra he wrote to his mother, who seems to have remonstrated with him for this hot-headed pursuit of his father: "I was in hope I should have been back before you were aware of my absence. I went off—now that the murder is out—entirely from fear of hurting your feelings. . . . Besides, it was my duty—my filial duty—to go, and I shall yet raise the name of Park. You ought rather to rejoice that I took it into my head. . . . I shall be back in three years at the most—perhaps in one." Impassively, the trees of the forest stand, planted in the darkness of their own eternal shadows. The Niger flows softly through its cluttered delta to the sea. The boy turns north, the gloom closes behind him, Africa snaps shut like the jaws of its own predators. There are some passing remarks by Richard Lander, a mention of fever, a glimpse of the young man naked, clay-smeared, attempting to live like an African, his body seen for a moment hanging from a sacred tree; then little more. For him too the end was silence, disaster and death.

The nineteenth-century explorer stood at one of those curious points of inter-section where social philosophies that are apparently contradictory manage for a brief moment to meet. Representing on the one hand the extremes of indivi-dualism, of private idealism, personal ambition and single-minded physical endurance, the explorer was on the other the passive instrument of historical and economic forces he almost certainly neither noticed nor understood. In the twentieth century, this passivity has become much clearer to all of us; the technocrat-explorer, strapped into his tiny capsule on the tip not only of a vast rocket, but also of a multi-million pound, government-sponsored programme, has had his area of freedom so whittled away that it no longer deludes anyone. If he himself has any illusions on the point, the controlling voice whispering constantly in his ear, the electronic monitors checking his every physical function, will very swiftly dispel it. Even at the moment when a human being first stepped down on the surface of the moon, he was forced, by the patriotic and commercial interests that had sent him there, to mouth an array of platitudes, the insignificance of their content matched only by the inflation of their language.

We look back therefore to Mungo Park and those like him and see in their activities a liberty, a personal commitment and an individual achievement that we can only envy. Alone, we say, they mastered wilderness, storm, disease, starvation and hostility. Unsupported, they struggled for the truth. The information they sent back to the centres of their civilisation illuminated a great darkness, stretched human awareness and made enormous additions to the extent of European knowledge. Many, like Park himself, died heroically in pursuing these ideals. Yet we know, distanced as we are from those events and thus cushioned against the immediate impact of triumph and disaster, that, if it had not been for Europe's new wealth, for its increasing population and its exacerbated nationalism, it is unlikely that Mungo Park would have been on the Niger at all.

It was Britain's jealousy of France, and not a disinterested desire to learn about the world, that lay behind Park's second voyage; it was Britain's commercial ambitions that lay, perhaps more covertly, behind his first. Both were made possible by Britain's wealth, in its turn the product of slavery overseas and the disinheriting of the peasantry at home. The enclosures driving people from the land and into the cities, there to offer their labour at wages forcibly and inhumanly low, the new machines increasing their productivity, the overseas plantations providing an endless flow of capital—this was the background, from the 1780s on, to that splendid explosion of geographical curiosity that, in the hundred years thereafter, sent a medley of heroes to and fro across the world. In Africa the first of these—as it were—institutionalised explorers, by his second attempt on the Niger openly recognised as such, blessed by governmental support, military rank and the Colonial Secretary's own instructions, was Mungo Park.

Yet the man was there: there was a real Mungo Park, pensively walking his own rain-soaked hills when at home, or, deep in Africa, his hair wild, his skin flayed by the sun, marching in rags through that threatening bush, whisking down the long river's current to his death. There is a fundamental difference, however, between the living man experiencing the world at first hand and those who experience that world through him, through his account of it. For them, he was finally no more real than the regions he traversed and the people he met, a character existing in a shadowy realm between fiction and verifiable fact. He was in some ways less, dispatched like a projectile by a belligerent and expanding society. This turned him into a sort of lackey, the representative of a million armchair explorers, an endless array of broad-stomached would-be entrepreneurs, agents, middlemen and merchants. As an individual, he had no significance, and the reality of his experience was of no significance, any more than was the subjective reality of the peoples whose lands he crossed. In the last analysis, it did not matter who he was, what he did, how he travelled or whom he met—the important thing was that he was there, catspaw of an overwhelming European curiosity, evidence of an ever-increasing British power.

A flood of popular books hurried this process of stripping all true individuality from the explorers. In time, Park merged with Stanley, with Speke, with Livingstone, to become a single, admired and heroic invention, a sort of waxwork draped in the national flag: "The Explorer". Other countries chose their different heroes in the same way and for the same purposes. The consequence was that their very different achievements flowed together into one appalling yet titillating struggle against a savage humanity and a ferocious environment. Another composite appeared—"Africa", a concept robbing that enormous and variegated continent of all reality. Jungle, desert, mountain and savannah swam into one disagreeable continuity; Zulu and Hausa, Kikuyu and Mossi, all the nations of Africa, all the peoples and sub-divisions of the peoples, all the cultures and languages and religions, were forced by the European imagination into one mould. Out of it stepped the "native", the "savage", offering the blood of sacrifice to grinning gods, dancing in lunatic abandon around flames and, as like as not, making a meal of his enemies.

The explorers themselves had no such view of Africans, no simple picture that rejected African reality and denied to Africans their full humanity. We know what Mungo Park's view was, but Clapperton, in Sokoto on the journey that was to kill him, set it out in detail: "The people of England . . . erroneously regarded the inhabitants as naked savages, devoid of religion and not far removed from the condition of wild beasts, whereas I found them, from my personal observation, to be civilised, learned, humane and pious."

Not many, however, were really interested in his personal observation. He had vanished in "The Explorer", a lay figure upon whom might be draped the collective fantasy of his nation and his race. Above all, it was believed by the vast majority, he typified the best qualities of his people. Explorers were, of course, not typical at all, but rather eccentric, single-minded almost to madness, their ambition often built upon an implacability so extreme that in almost any other context it must have seemed unbearable. They were a tiny and obsessed group, survivors through diplomacy and toughness, their curiosity both meticulous and insatiable. It was necessary, however, to believe their qualities virtues and those virtues typical, since it made more credible the claim that they were the representatives of the society that had sent them. In the end, therefore, the value of each individual explorer became not personal to him at all, despite all the statues put up after his death, but instead became part of the value held in common by the people who had, so to speak, elected him to make their journey.

His success, or the heroism of his defeats, confirmed these in their dream of national or racial perfection. The explorer, behaving in a typically British (French, German, Italian, American, Swedish—but above all, *white*) fashion, had circumvented all the traps of man and nature to establish his, and thus his country's and his race's, presence in this or that dangerously remote spot. Conversely, when he failed and died in his failure, then the intractability of jungle, desert or mountain and the ignorant hostility of their inhabitants had brought him to an ending so appalling, and borne with such courage, that it emphasised again his—and thus his country's and his race's—inviolable moral superiority. The whites became undefeatable, for victory was natural, and defeat always a victory.

In this way, long before the dusty columns toiled behind Tricolour or Union Jack deep into the African interior, as in so many other militarily uninviting areas of the world, the explorers had won many of the essential battles. Regarded by almost all their fellow countrymen through a veil of prejudice and expectation itself partly created and constantly renewed by their exploits, everything they did seemed to a Europe convinced of its own merits abundantly and self-evidently right, utterly and unquestionably glorious. As a result, a self-regarding system was created, a round of constantly reinforced self-satisfaction that made it impossible to consider what such expeditions achieved from any other point of view—from that of the people who lived in the countries thus explored, for example. Before anyone could do that, he would have to challenge the whole mood, the whole ethos and enthusiasm, of the nineteenth-century Western world. In its turn, such questioning would demand the setting-up of quite different criteria from those already established for determining what civilisation actually was. It was a great deal to ask from a majority; paradoxically, if anyone could have managed it, it was the explorers themselves, singular characters whose most potent experiences occurred in countries far from their own and in societies to which, however uninviting they seemed, they had to adapt if they were to survive.

For the millions who, in their own homelands, constituted the audience for these adventures, the superiority of their own civilisation, attested by the successes of the very heroes they were watching, was too obvious even to be discussed. It was the condition of the lives they lived, embedded in the very structures, ambitions, habits and presumptions of their middle-class existence. And it was middle-class, for much nearer at hand than in the tree-shadowed interior of Africa lay another colonised and unconsidered nation, the nation of the labouring poor. It was not they who defined the nature of civilised conduct, not they who organised the expeditions that sent Europe's representatives out to shed their light in the world's benighted places, not they who drew much benefit from the exploitation that followed. To the arbiters of taste, they too were no more than a mass of undifferentiated and almost unknowable sub-humanity, presently useful, yet potentially dangerous. "The awful thing is the vast extent of misery and distress which prevails", wrote Greville in his diary in 1832, "and the evidence of the rotten foundations on which the whole fabric of this gorgeous society rests"—a discovery forced on him only by his duties as Clerk of the Privy Council faced with a cholera epidemic. "Is it possible for any country to be considered in a healthy condition", he went on to ask, "when there is no such thing as a *general* diffusion of the comforts of life . . . but when the extremes prevail of the most unbounded luxury and enjoyment and the most dreadful privation and suffering?"

His view is the more powerful because expressed by so conservative an aristocrat, a man unconvinced by the arguments for democracy, an opponent of electoral reform, a determined élitist. Yet in the end he is brought to ask no fundamental questions about the social, economic or political structures that have created so appalling an inequality, and burdened so many with so profound a poverty in order that a few might remain so inordinately wealthy. For Charles Greville, with his sinecures and his race-horses, the world remained a very pleasant place, and it was the Charles Grevilles of the West who determined the nature of its civilisation. Not that the labouring classes did not eventually come to share in the euphoria that white exploration engendered—patriotism became as much the opium of the masses as ever religion did, and, after all, they too were white and Christian, clearly superior therefore to those who were pagan and black: it was splendid to be able to stand shoulder-to-shoulder with the rich and despise the heathen African, whom *all* white men outranked. But it was not they who determined the nature of the world they lived in; that was decided by the Grevilles, while the lower classes lived in it, for all their vast numbers, almost on sufferance.

Yet neither the poor nor those whom circumstances had given the advantage over them seemed prepared, except in a few rare cases, to alter this oppressive system. It stood, as self-evident as some phenomenon of nature, its success so clear that it seemed beyond the reach of relevant criticism—especially as the only available criteria were those it had itself established. In other words, the accepted standards of civilisation, those standards that placed Western man on the very pinnacle of achieved evolution, that endorsed his every activity and legitimised his every desire, were so all-pervading and so unhesitatingly accepted that to question them would have been an act not of philosophical speculation, but of revolution—even, so closely were they bound up with established religion, of blasphemy. A civilisation so widely and willingly endorsed, so beyond scepticism, ceased to be one among a number, but instead became singular: it became Civilisation.

"Civilisation" had as the natural consequence of this singularity a monopoly of the highest levels of art, adminstration and religion, of science, technology and ethics. It was therefore Europe's duty to press its benefits upon those benighted millions unfortunate enough to have been denied them. If one takes the most humanitarian and imaginative of all the opinions on the subject that were prevalent at the beginning of the nineteenth century (and matters were not to improve as the century advanced), those expressed by the liberals who in 1807 formed the African Institution—men like Wilberforce and Macaulay—one finds that, for all their protestations of human equality, they had not the slightest intention of treating Africans as anything more than beneficiaries at best. The Institution was to sponsor the learning of African languages, it declared in its 1809 *Report*, and fit them up with an alphabet so that they might be decently written down. Was this in order to learn what the African had to say? No, indeed—it was "with a view to facilitate the diffusion of information among the natives of that country". It was "the instruction of the African in letters and in useful knowledge" that the Institution had in mind—these were the ways in which it intended "to cultivate a friendly connexion with the natives of that continent". Africans could be exploited or they could be educated—that is, they were either serfs or children. In this way there was created a hypocritical rationale of empire which placated the benevolent, while, if the hard-headed men of politics or commerce knew better, they hedged about their knowledge with the rhetoric of patriotism.

The distortions and comforting self-delusions thus introduced have done and continue to do incalculable harm. What is now called racism, but was then considered so self-evident that it did not even have to be named, was clearly an element determining the way Europeans regarded their far-flung explorers and pioneers. The popular stories drawn from the accounts these brought back, lurid abridgements of what were originally records of careful and objective observation, swiftly reinforced such feelings of racial superiority. This in turn provided a moral basis upon which colonial administrators could take their stand, a basis that again reinforced in the peoples of the white homelands their comfortable conviction that they were created by God and nature to be the world's masters. So the unselfconscious attitudes of the eighteenth century, which led as easily to the acceptance of blacks as to their persecution, were hardened and deepened by the experiences of the nineteenth century to emerge as the rancorous prejudice of today. There were, of course, many other streams feeding into that great sewer (not all of them—I speak as a Jew—concerned with colour); but one tributary certainly, despite the humanity of many of those involved, comes trickling down to us from the grand peaks of courage upon which the explorers unfurled their flags.

There were of course, as we have seen, always those, not all of them cynics, who understood clearly enough that empire's primary cause was commercial necessity: the drive for captive markets, for an assured flow of primary products, for a cheap source of raw materials. The cultural and racial aspects were of no importance to them, since in their view military power gave European nations the simple right to conquer and exploit. For them, the land was in essence empty, and the people on it no more than another natural resource. They questioned neither motive nor action; commercial considerations dominated all they did, at home or abroad. Whether the people left behind took this view, however, or considered European expansion as a function of their civilising destiny, they united in seeing the explorer as the instrument of a collective will. There was no point in his representing their virtues, if he did not do so in the interests of the European purpose—however that was construed. This view was most forcibly held by, and often provided the main motivation for, those whose responsibility it had been to invest private or even governmental money in some voyage of discovery. In the end, therefore, the explorer too, like the lands and people he reported on, ceased to have any separate and particular existence, ceased in short to be an individual. He too, in other words, fell victim to the processes that made him necessary, and so became an object, a thing.

In this view, of course, many explorers unconsciously acquiesced. They were, after all, white, citizens of their countries, patriots as well as adventurers. Mungo Park on his second voyage, suddenly an officer, a column of soldiers behind him, clearly knew that he had taken on a public role, a nationalistic responsibility. He saw himself with pride as the outrider of commercial expansion, as a scout for future colonisation and as the spokesman for the distant interests of the king and his gentlemen in London. He accepted eagerly the duties of one supported by the British Government. Not only that—he now appeared as God's interpreter, handing out his Arabic New Testaments to anyone who might be swayed by them.

Like others, however, he had his own view of himself. In his own eyes he could not appear merely as an object, the pawn of social forces and economic interests, nor as an entertainer, a gladiator locked in mortal combat with a whole terrifying continent for the delectation of an audience of European blood-and-wonder addicts. Men rarely do things for purely abstract reasons, though religion, politics and patriotism all have their martyrs. It is hard now to capture even in part what really motivated Mungo Park. There was, clearly, a strong element of ambition in what he did. The new interests of society—commerce, industry, science—demanded new people. As a result, they provided opportunities denied to earlier generations trapped in the more stratified society of the past. The professions, the forces and the church still maintained the old hierarchies; around them, however, there had developed this new turmoil, the consequence of sudden wealth. In that turmoil, such men as Stephenson and Watt, Cook and Mungo Park could see and seize their opportunities. As a child he had

G

wanted fame, had wanted to write and to see his name perpetuated. Exploration made it possible. At the edges of the world, class, money and education became irrelevant; only survival mattered. When Clapperton died, his servant Richard Lander became the traveller, the man who spoke and wrote and described, and who later received the accolades. When Lander returned to West Africa, it was as an explorer, his own man.

But there was another element in Mungo Park. It does not often appear, yet must have been within him, held to himself, a romantic heat deep below the controlled surface. He had read and still remembered the ballads of the Border, fiercely emotional tales concerned with the ravages of greed, ambition and sexual desire, with family pride and individual honour. He had written poetry himself. He had the mind and the spirit to become a crony of Walter Scott's. It was in this private element, surely, that the roots of his obsession with the Niger lay. He had, one senses, personalised his struggle with that great river. Its secret was its treasure, its own length the guardian dragon, he the knight who would filch that gold and carry it home. Only death would prevent his success. We know the passion of his involvement by the sacrifice he made for it. We do not see the passion in him, because he was a Lowland Scot not given to hysteria or histrionics. We realise it is there from the fact that in the end it overwhelmed him. It drew him from his wife and children, it hurried him on through sickness and disaster, it drove him out on that river in a patched-up canoe with only the tattered remnants of his party about him. Finally, it killed him.

The empires he heralded have collapsed. Where they once stretched, European languages and institutions lie scattered like debris after an explosion, recognisable here and there, in other places twisted and scorched out of recognition. Yet the attraction of the explorers does not wane, their exploits retain their grandeur and their names are not forgotten. It seems mysterious: why should we still be so aware of Livingstone and Burton, of Cook and Scott and Mungo Park? Clearly, nostalgia plays its part. The safe part of the world was smaller then, adventure beyond those limits more easily come by. Not only that: such adventure seemed integral to the world's development. There was a point to the solitary journey; something previously unknown might be learned. Danger did not have to be sought for its own sake in such artificial projects as a single-handed sail around the globe. Instead, one could test fear and endurance, one could exercise one's curiosity, and still remain within the mainstream of European activity. Such journeys, however exciting, were not undertaken for excitement alone; both participants and audience took it for granted that something serious was going on.

There must also be nostalgia in the European heart for the newness of that nineteenth-century world. A century and a half ago there were huge areas of this planet in which anything might have existed, enormous territories—almost the whole of Africa, much of South America, the frozen regions of both south and north, much of the Pacific—where white men had never penetrated. Every journey to an unknown land might reveal undreamt-of wonders, monsters beyond nightmare, riches enough to swamp even European avarice. Each new account of an explorer's experiences was snapped up by a public anxious to be, for one moment, reduced again to the status of children, wide-eyed and joyfully defenceless under the impact of the unexpected, the magical.

Nostalgia nevertheless has its darker side. For one senses too a hankering after the political simplicities of that earlier period, for the certainties of a time when the whites, wielding gold, guns and the Cross, took what they wanted from the world. It was agreeable to discover that, whatever your status might be at home, on the worldwide scale you were an aristocrat. Anyone who even now visits Third World countries is in danger of being seduced by an automatic servility, particularly in those cities where whites once ruled with unselfconscious arrogance. The old obsequiousness diminishes as the generations change, but its persistence is an indication of how deeply Western power affected those who became its prisoners, its servants, its minor officials. Like the whites, they too measured themselves against that power and saw themselves as microscopic, ineffectual and tainted. By contrast, the whites not only owned power, they *were* power, were its corporeal, personified reality; no wonder they strutted then, no wonder that many of them look back with longing to the days when it was true.

But there is more than nostalgia in the admiration we retain for men like Mungo Park. We care for their courage, since every such story makes possible our own heroism. What they endured is endurable, can be suffered and survived by human beings just like us. It extends our capabilities and, though we may not want to put it to the test, it warms us—our admiration for them spills over into a certain careful, half-acknowledged approval of ourselves.

At the same time, there is a wistfulness in the way we look back at them. They knew what they were doing. They stood four-square on the values of their own culture, their own people. They had no doubts about their role. They were not, as many of us have learned to become, outsiders. As a result, they knew clearly what they had to do and why it had to be done—they had their road to self-fulfilment. They could pick out for themselves a visibly difficult but precisely defined objective—as does, for instance, an acrobat or tightrope walker. Like these, only an intense dedication, an unwavering effort, carried them through to success, while elsewhere an audience in whose name such feats were being attempted gasped and clapped—and paid the bills.

In other words, despite the half-glimpsed forces that worked on them, despite their own ambivalent motives, the explorers were free men. They had picked their own tasks and gone their own route to achievement. No one had ordered them to make their journeys; they were volunteers to the last man (and woman—from Hester Stanhope through Mary Kingsley to today's explorers of Amazon and Himalayas, the line runs with admirable clarity). Cramped in our cities, hemmed in by hierarchy, necessity and greed, we reach out in their direction as though the sight of their arrogant enterprises and the vast arenas on which they were acted out will heal us. Packed away in our housing units, oppressed by schedules not worked out by us, we flee to the imagination's loneliness in which a Mungo Park endlessly confronts his destiny. He managed what has been denied us, what we have denied ourselves—he reached the very limits of himself, used up every particle, stretched for his own chosen achievement so far beyond the bounds of practicality that in the end he died. In this, he stands for what we cannot be, yet know we might have been, ought to have been. Somehow we have lost, may even have spurned, the freedom that blazes about him. As we watch, he seems to recede, to fall away, tiny, infinitely bright—or is it we who are being dragged from him? Dwindling, he is still to be glimpsed, he will never vanish altogether—the lost, the enthralling, the infinitely desired, totally unattainable alternative.

The German geographer Reichart, in his *Ephemerides Géographiques*, published in Weimar as early as 1808, had without once setting foot in Africa successfully collated the information already gathered about the course of the Niger. It flowed east as far as Wangara, he declared, then swung to the south, after which "it makes a great turn from thence towards the South-west till it approaches the northern extremity of the Gulf of Guinea, where it divides and discharges itself by different channels into the Atlantic. . . ."

Equally ingenious, another theorist, James M'Queen, used information gleaned from the Mandingoes and Hausa working on his Grenada plantation (including one man who claimed to have rowed Park himself across the Niger), as well as the published accounts, to work out in a similar fashion the great river's course. It was he who realised very quickly that Bussa, far from being, as had been thought, only a little way downstream from Timbuctu, was actually hundreds of miles from the city, a calculation that immensely lengthened estimates of Mungo Park's last journey. M'Queen traced various tributary streams that fed into the main river from the recesses of the Sudan, and then, having eliminated the alternatives, showed clearly that "in the Bight of Benin and Biafra, therefore, is the great outlet of the Niger".

Since his first announcement of this theory followed eight years after Reichart's, it might have been considered that the Niger mystery was solved. Few people, however, took much notice of these stay-at-home explorers, their logical analyses inevitably appearing somewhat bloodless after the tales that real travellers had brought home of wilderness, arrow-flight and fever. It is true, of course, that theory must if possible be verified and that in geography this involves the journey of some trustworthy witness. Where was such a witness to be found?

J. Wishaw, who wrote the memoir of Park that appeared in the 1815 edition of his travels, thought that the lesson both of Park's and Houghton's fate was to "demonstrate the utter hopelessness of such undertakings, when attempted by solitary and unprotected individuals". A military presence, he felt, would always be necessary—as long as it was "strictly limited to purposes of security and protection—since such a force was bound to "inspire the Africans with greater respect for the European character". More interesting, however, was his idea that for the next group of explorers it might be "better to employ *Mahometan* travellers. . . . There is reason to believe that individuals sufficiently intelligent for an expedition of this kind, and whose constitutions would aslo be well suited to the climate of Africa, might be found without much difficulty among the Mahometan inhabitants of Hindostan." Alternatively, he felt, English-speaking soldiers of the Royal African Corps might be sent out, and indeed such a scheme was for a short while actively planned.

That no force of this kind was ever despatched owed more to the hidden implications of exploration than to its overt purpose. What was truly seen, if it was not a white man's eye that saw it? Even more importantly, how could the white man impose his existence, on areas where none of his kind had ever been known, except by his physical presence? The underlying rationale of exploration could not be served by mere emissaries, by delegates. Isaaco made the journey to Sansanding; in terms of exploration, this was meaningless. He was a Mandingo. The fact that he and many others had made the journey many times before did not in the slightest diminish Mungo Park's claim to have been the first to make it. He was the first *European* to travel that way, and that is what counted.

Similarly, Isaaco sent his Fulani envoy all the way to Bussa to collect Park's sword-belt. But who was that man, wrestling for those eight mysterious months with the problems of his own journey? He disappears from Sansanding; eight months later, anonymous and perhaps a little out of breath, he reappears. The only questions history asks of him are those concerned with Park. But what had he seen, what peoples had he met, how far away was Bussa? No one cares to hear about these things from him. He vanishes, a nameless local, intelligent and trustworthy enough to be sent successfully on an eight-months mission, but of no consequence when it came to the task of deciding where the Niger flowed. Of course, he was no objective observer, knew neither the calendar, standards of measurement, nor English; yet he stubbornly fulfilled his by no means uncomplicated task, travelling some 2,000 miles to Yauri and back in order to do so. Can one really doubt that he, or another like him, would have been fit after suitable training to record the course of the enormous river he followed? Yet he makes no appearance in the ranks of African explorers, and the same would have applied to soldiers of the African Corps or "Mahometan inhabitants of Hindostan". Exploration was a white affair; it was primarily not an aspect of science, but an aspect of politics and economics.

M'Queen, sitting far away on his West Indian island, understood all this very clearly. By the time he came to repeat his theory in a book published in 1821 he had moved a long way beyond mere geographical exploration. Instead, his patriotic ambitions led him to consider what the Niger might mean to whoever controlled it. Bussa, he felt, was the key: "on this commanding spot let the British standard be planted", he declared. There, it would "become the rallying point of all that is honourable, useful, beneficial, just, and good. . . . The resources of Africa, and the energies of Africa, under a wise and vigorous policy, may be made to subdue and control Africa. Let Britain only form such a settlement, and give it that countenance, support, and protection which the wisdom and energy of British councils can give, and which the power and resources of the British empire can so well maintain, and Central Africa to future ages will remain a grateful and obedient dependency of this empire. . . . Thus the Niger, like the Ganges, would acknowledge Great Britain as its protector, our king as its lord." For one citizen at least the reasons for British involvement in Africa were clear—and, in the terms of his day, both honourable and desirable. There is no reason to believe that gentlemen in Whitehall, however inefficiently they might come to terms with their ideals, felt very differently on the subject. And it is surely for these reasons above all that in the end neither armchair analysis nor local delegation would do; the whites had to go themselves.

It was symptomatic of the changed attitude to exploration that the impetus to examine Africa that had been provided by a private gentleman, Sir Joseph Banks, should now as he aged become the responsibility (shared officially with the Colonial Office) of a governmental grandee, the Second Secretary of the Admiralty, John Barrow. The Admiralty, of course, had been the prime sponsor of seaborne exploration, particularly in the Pacific, so its involvement in Africa was not very surprising. A traveller himself, author of a popular book about southern Africa, Barrow not only enthused others but also stood as an authority in his own right. (His eminence was not always matched by his judgement, his contempt for theorists being such that he dismissed Reichart's ideas as "entitled to very little attention".) In 1816 he sent Captain Tuckey up the Congo, in a ship named after that river, in order to determine once and for all whether here was indeed the Niger's outflow to the sea. Tuckey, unused to the tropics and the victim of a serious liver complaint, soon failed and died; with him perished the expedition's botanist, its zoologist, its anatomist and a large percentage of its non-specialist personnel. Having learned nothing about the Niger, the *Congo* sailed home with only the ship's surgeon left to assist her master.

Almost at the same time, a force of 100 men marched east from the Gambia estuary, its commander a Major Peddie. He died shortly after the expedition's departure; his second-in-command died a little later; a surgeon named Dochard and eight soldiers struggled on to Segu, while what was left of the rest marched back to the coast. Having met Isaaco, Dochard too returned to the Gambia, compounding this venture's total lack of achievement with his own death shortly afterwards. Another expedition, under a Major Gray, fared little better.

While they were stamping up and down in Mungo Park's footprints, a three-man party under Major Ritchie attempted to cross the Sahara from Tripoli, a route that Barrow had been persuaded to favour. Ritchie and one of his companions died; the survivor, Lyon, a naval lieutenant, made his way back to the Mediterranean coast, his passage marked by a succession of convivial gatherings. Through what seems to have been an alcoholic haze compounded by the distracting rhythms of the local dances, he gleaned the information that the waters of the Niger "by one route or other . . . join the great Nile of Egypt". This conviction, however, was challenged by Gordon Laing, himself later to fall victim to Moorish ferocity; while travelling through the uplands of Futa Jallon he realised that these were simply not high enough to provide the kind of impetuous flow that would carry the Niger across the vast plains of central Sudan and northwards into Egypt.

In 1822 there set out from Tripoli what was officially known as the Mission to Bornu. A retired naval surgeon named Oudney, bored with his Edinburgh practice, volunteered to traverse the Sahara and so became the expedition's nucleus. He himself suggested as his companion a man who was to be the next in the long line of distinguished Scottish explorers, Hugh Clapperton. One of twenty-one children, Clapperton had been a cabin-boy at thirteen, a deserter from the Navy, had served in a privateer, had nearly married an Amerindian princess, had rejoined the Navy and risen to the rank of lieutenant, and had then, when he was twenty-nine and the French wars were over, been put on half-pay. To these two, who knew each other, trusted each other and worked well together, there was later added a third, Major Dixon Denham, an appointment that almost at once created one of those triangular situations beset by bickering, arguments about status and a lack of clarity about who gave orders to whom.

Denham, a touchy man who felt himself outnumbered—"any proposition coming from me is generally negatived by the other two", he wrote to his brother—at one time retreated as far as Marseilles. Nevertheless, supported by a shipwright named Hillman, a tough and imperturbable man, and their black servant, Columbus, they eventually travelled south, over the bones of slaves who had perished on their way from the Niger towns. In February 1823 they saw Lake Chad, probably the first Europeans to do so since Roman times. However, their dissensions grew, Denham hinted that Clapperton had had homosexual relations with an Arab and went off on travels of his own, fever struck all four Europeans, and, though three of them recovered, Oudney's sickness lingered on. Nevertheless, he and Clapperton decided to travel on to Kano and Sokoto; on the way, Oudney died.

Denham explored the area around Lake Chad, while Clapperton, alone, made his way to the capital of the now triumphant Fulani people. Entering Sokoto, in the frock coat and epaulettes of his dress uniform, on 16 March 1824, he remained there for three months; it was during this period that he gathered much of the information he was later to pass on concerning the fate of Mungo

Park. He also was given a certain amount of contradictory and plainly false information about the further course of the Niger, but tales of war to the south dissuaded him from following as he wanted to the river's banks to the sea. It was on 10 July that he and Denham, by this time rivals and enemies, met again; refusing to speak to each other, they communicated only by notes. Eleven months later, they had returned to Britain. While vast areas south of the Sahara had been drawn into the orbit of the known—Barrow was delighted that "we now know where the great kingdoms of Mandara, Bornou and Houssa are to be placed on the map"—the question of the Niger seemed more confused than ever.

It was now that the over-confident Laing set out, enthused perhaps by his curious marriage with the daughter of Hanmer Warrington, British consul in Tripoli, who while permitting and even officiating at the ceremony refused his permission for the couple to consummate it until Laing's return. He arrived in Timbuctu, the first European to do so, at a time when Tuareg and Fulani were struggling for its control. Perhaps for that reason, perhaps because of the Muslim revival general in those regions at the time, Laing was imprisoned, brutally treated and even tortured. Only two days after he was at last allowed to continue on his way towards Segu, he was murdered.

A mere three months after arriving in England, Clapperton was off again, determined this time to reach Sokoto from the south. It was his strong conviction that in this way he would complete the map of the Niger's course, but his main purpose, in the eyes of the authorities, was the note he carried to the ruler of Sokoto requesting him to end his participation in the slave trade. With Clapperton travelled his personal servant, a peripatetic Cornishman named Richard Lemon Lander. Having left home at the age of nine and served a variety of masters in different parts of the world, Lander had developed a delight in travel which must always have been natural to him. He was strong, broad-shouldered and cheerful, had had experience of much of Europe, of the West Indies and of southern Africa and was, it seems, wonder-struck at the size and mystery of that continent: "There was a charm", he wrote, "in the very sound of Africa, that always made my heart flutter . . . the awful obscurity in which many of the interior regions were enveloped; the strange and wild aspect of countries that had never been trodden by the feet of a European, and even the failure of all former undertakings . . . united to strengthen the determination I had come to . . ." Given the chance of setting off with Clapperton, therefore, Lander was not to be put off even by the temptation of "a more lucrative situation in one of the South American republics". It is an interesting sidelight on his lively but uneducated intelligence that, of all the early explorers in West Africa, he is the only one who seems to have been impressed by the art of its peoples, in particular by the wood-carving of the Yoruba.

They landed near Lagos, at Badagri, were entertained for several alcoholic days by its chief, then took to canoes for the first miles of their inland journey, thus actually embarking on what Clapperton at least had come there to find, the point where the Niger flowed into the Atlantic. A mangrove-bounded stream, however, meandering through swamplands, was not perhaps what he was looking for and he ignored it. On 7 December 1825 he and his companion began their overland march. Clapperton, not yet fully recovered from his previous journey, soon began to fail; Lander suffered from heatstroke; the rest— Captain Pearce, the naval officer who was Clapperton's second-in-command, Dawson, a seaman, and the medical officer, Morrison, who might have looked after them—all one by one went down with fever. Morrison turned back after a few days; Dawson died. Clapperton by now was having to be carried in a litter. On 27 December, Pearce died and three days later news came that Morrison too had not reached the coast alive. Clapperton and Lander were now the only Europeans left, their companion and interpreter a Hausa known as Pasko, a tiny, dishonest lecher, a one-time slave, later a sailor with the British Navy, later again in the service of Belzoni, one of the many Europeans who died while attempting to reach Timbuctu from the Arab lands of the North African coast. Engaged by Pearce, Pasko survived to aid and plague in equal measure first Clapperton, then Lander.

They spent seven weeks in Katunga, the capital of the northern Yorubas, before travelling on to Wawa and Bussa. It was on this journey that Clapperton noticed the Bussa people's curious evasiveness on the subject of Mungo Park's death and became convinced that it was there that the earlier Scottish traveller had reached his final catastrophe. Distracting the attention of both travellers, however, was a mountainous widow named Zuma, enormously wealthy (she owned 1,000 slaves) and enormously fat, who, while they remained in Wawa, had no hesitation in offering herself as the mate, first of Lander and later of Clapperton. "Her hair", Lander informs us, "used to be carefully dyed with indigo, and of a rich and vivid blue; her feet and hands stained with hennah and an extraction of the goora-nut, produced alternate streaks of red and yellow; and her teeth were also tinged with a delicate crimson stain." All this, in addition to her breasts, which Lander simply called "tremendous", combined to make her in the Europeans' eyes a vast, overwhelming grotesque. Lander says that she "took it into her head to fall desperately in love with me, whose complexion, she affirmed, rivalled her own in whiteness". Every day delicacies and provisions of all sorts flowed into their hut; every day, she herself would come and visit him. There, for hours at a time, she "would gaze intently on me, while the most amorous glances shot from her large, full, and certainly beautiful eye, which confused and disconcerted me not a little . . . for I had been a wanderer from my childhood, and had had but few opportunities of mingling in the delightful company of the gentler sex in my own country, and consequently was excessively bashful in coming in contact with ladies, whether in the country of the Hottentots or the birthplace of the widow Zuma." More than bashfulness restrained him, however, for he confessed that he was "positively afraid, from the warmth and energy of Zuma's embraces, I should actually be pressed to death between her monstrous arms".

Clapperton, meanwhile, rather enjoyed being the bystander at these amorous meetings; his lofty amusement, however, did not survive the widow's transferring her desires to him. For Lander having regretfully refused the role of lover—he pleaded his delicate health, as well he might—Zuma turned for consolation to his master. He, on his way to Bussa, was confounded to discover her, at the head of her personal army, an overpowering sight in her golden cloak and scarlet boots, determined to accompany him. Wawa's chief, who had had his own intermittent political problems with Zuma, immediately took Lander hostage; this would eventually force Clapperton to return and he, so the logic ran, would inevitably entice the widow back. Once safely in Wawa, separated from friends and allies, she would be unable to make much trouble for its chief. Lander, who had originally been left behind because of sickness, soon escaped from his somewhat half-hearted imprisonment. He rode to Bussa, where he was remarkably well received, but missed Clapperton. That officer was establishing the accuracy of the chief's predictions by returning as swiftly as he could to Wawa. Sure enough, where he went, Zuma was sure to go; but finally, thwarted in all her hopes, she threw herself at the feet of her merciful sovereign and was duly forgiven. The saga of love and desire was over; Clapperton and Lander continued on their way, the former never again to meet "the generous, the kind-hearted, the affectionate, the ambitious, but above all the enormous widow Zuma".

War now circumscribed their efforts, fever limited their ambition. They made their way to Kano, where Clapperton again left the still-ailing Lander and paid his second visit to Sokoto and its sultan. Holy war had turned political; Sokoto was now at war with Bornu. Clapperton's intention to travel to that state and present gifts to its ruler—oddly, not only the New Testament and the Psalms of David in Arabic, but also Euclid's *Elements* and a history of the Tartars —seemed to Sultan Bello of Sokoto an unfriendly act. The gifts were confiscated and he himself was regarded with the cold suspicion reserved for spies. Lander, still very sick, joined him on 23 December. The two men, both by this time wearing the local robes, now found themselves trapped in Sokoto, at least while the war lasted. Time abruptly halted, space closed in. They were bound in boredom; only occasional shooting expeditions altered their restricted routine.

Early in March, Clapperton was struck by a debilitating attack of dysentery. A month later, he was so diminished, so reduced, so appallingly weak, that it was clear that he was beyond recovery. Lander scribbled an account of his final instructions, an unpunctuated, pencil-written note in which the dying man's words are interwoven with Lander's own comments: "Richard I am going to die I cannot help shedding tears has he had behaved like a father to me since i had been with him . . . bear yourself up under all troubles like a man and an english man do not be affraid and no one will hurt you . . . take great care of my journals and when you arrive in London go to my agents and tell them to send directly for my uncul and tell him it was my wish that he would go with me to the colonoal office and delever the journals that they might not say their were anything missing my little money my close and evrything i have belongs to you . . . writ down the names of the towns you go throw and all purticulars and if you get safe home with the journals i have no doubt of your being well rewarded for your truble."

For a fortnight after Clapperton's death, Lander was himself too ill to leave his hut. At the sultan's suggestion, he finally made his way back to Kano, half-dying of thirst on the way, the vast party of Mecca-bound pilgrims with whom he was travelling demonstrating their fervour by refusing all aid to a Christian. He tried to reach Fundah, where he had been told the Niger ended, but war again foiled him. It was not until he was once more in the land of the Yoruba that he met with assistance, courtesy and friendship. Indeed, in Katunga the king wanted him to make his home there, offered him four of his daughters as inducement, suggested that he might be the chief minister, the commander-in-chief—whatever he chose. It may be that, if rats, caterpillars and especially dogs had not featured so prominently on the menu—"I by no means relished the huge luncheons of roasted dogs which were served twice a day", he was to write later—Lander might have lived out his life there in aristocratic contentment. However, he continued to the coast, which he reached on 21 November; he had been in the interior for two whole years.

Conditions on the coast were brutal, bloody and superstition-riven. Slaves, if they did not swiftly find buyers, were simply drowned. The Europeans there were Portuguese, to whom he stood as representative of the nation that had drained away the livelihood of their own. The chief, wealth-corrupted and obsessed by the paranoid suspicions of all tyrants, lived by black ritual and open violence. Lander himself was forced to drink the cup of poison which would prove him innocent if he survived—a *post hoc* judgement that to everyone's astonishment went in his favour. Eventually, he was taken off by an English brig and arrived in London at the end of April 1828.

Across the Channel, meanwhile, there had returned from Africa in romantic triumph the French traveller René Caillié, a man who from his youth had been obsessed by the mysteries of Africa, and whose enthusiasm had been reinforced by Mungo Park's account of his own travels. All through the previous decade he had been making efforts to follow in Park's footsteps, despite the new and implacable barrier that the rise to dominance of the Fulani and their Muslim fundamentalism had placed in the way of Christian penetration of that area. Caillié determined to get around this problem by posing as a Muslim, and in 1824 offered himself to a Moorish tribe living on the north-eastern fringes of Senegal as a convert anxious to learn more about his new religion.

Thus armed and prepared, he made several attempts to gain official sanction and support, but in the end decided to rely on his own savings. He set off up the valley of the river Nuñez, between Sierra Leone and the Gambia, his only scientific aid the two pocket compasses he carried. These and his notebooks were all that distinguished him from any other Muslim pilgrim. Scurvy halted him when he reached the lands of the Bambara, but after six weeks, during which "the roof of my mouth became quite bare . . . and my teeth seemed ready to drop out of their sockets", he began to recover. It was, however, five months later before, at the beginning of 1828, he was once more able to take up his journey. He accompanied a trader to the town of Jenne, where the rich Moorish merchants were only too pleased to help him. He had, he told them, been captured when very young by Christians; now he was on his way to Mecca to reclaim his heritage.

Towards the end of March he embarked for the journey downstream to Timbuctu on a boat engaged in the river trade and subject, therefore, to the capricious levying of tolls by the Tuaregs who still lived along the Niger's bank. Fortunately, in this hundred-foot-long craft filled with merchandise, passengers and crew, it was not too difficult for him to hide himself and his suspicious complexion. At last, on 20 April, he arrived, unfettered and undetected, unlike the earlier and unhappier Gordon Laing, in that city that had for so long exercised European curiosity. Despite his delight at his achievement, he seems to have felt some disappointment—legend always glitters more magnificently than reality. He wrote that "the sight before me did not answer my expectations. I had formed a totally different idea of the grandeur and wealth of Timbuctu. The city presented, at first view, nothing but a mass of ill-looking houses, built of earth. Nothing was to be seen in all directions but immense plains of quicksand of a yellowish white colour. The sky was a pale red as far as the horizon: all nature wore a dreary aspect, and the most profound silence prevailed . . ." He roused his old enthusiasm sufficiently, however, to remark that "there was something imposing in the aspect of a great city, raised in the midst of sands, and the difficulties surmounted by its founders cannot fail to excite the imagination".

Ironically, although he himself was taken without question to be a Muslim, the hut he was given faced that in which Laing had been quartered, and he was often told, for his amusement, how that unfortunate traveller had been insulted and maltreated during his stay. One assumes that so constant a reminder of the fate he risked did much to keep him within the limits of his role. He was even told in detail how Laing had been killed—choked by a turban held between two of those who had offered themselves as his guides. He was shown the places where the murder had occurred and where the dead man's body had been flung. Conscious of the fragility of his own situation, he gave no sign of any emotion except curiosity and even, it may be, admiration. As a result, he managed to survive all that threatened him, finally travelling on in great hardship as a beggar. Under the contemptuous protection of a group of Moorish merchants, he crossed the Sahara to Fez. From there he made his easier way north to Tangier and eventually arrived in Paris, to proclaim his feats, write his still-exciting memoirs and claim the rewards for his three years of masquerade, danger and privation.

In January 1830, Richard Lander set off a second time for West Africa. Despite Clapperton's death-bed prediction, he had not been rewarded for the journey he had made from Sokoto to the coast, nor for bringing to safety the records of Clapperton's expedition. Now, and since he had married, it was agreed that while he was away his wife should receive £100 a year; when he returned he would be given a further £100—no great outlay for a man Barrow had described as "the fittest person to send". The punctuator, grammarian and literary overseer of his travel tales, his younger brother, John, went with him—as a volunteer, naturally travelling unpaid. At Badagri, which they reached on 22 March, local preparations to do away with 300 slaves by way of a celebration meant that they avoided the most belligerent of the ruler's attentions. With Pasko once more in attendance, they struck inland, their instructions this time to make absolutely certain where the Niger reached the sea.

They were welcomed with the greatest friendliness by the king of Katunga, but first Richard and then John fell ill. As soon as they could, however, they thrust further inland and by the time they reached Bussa both were more or less recovered—just as well, perhaps, since among those welcoming them there was the vast Zuma, the widow of Wawa, finally exiled by a chief grown tired of her endless plots and insurrections. It was now that they were handed Park's old nautical almanack; in their disappointment at discovering that it was not the notebook they had hoped for, they left it there. Among the loose papers still caught between its covers were a tailor's bill and a dinner invitation dated 9 November 1804: "Mr. and Mrs. Watson would be happy to have the pleasure of Mr. Park's company at dinner on Tuesday next, at half-past five o'clock. An answer is requested . . ."

After an excursion to Yauri, where they discovered Anderson's hymn book, the Landers returned to Bussa in an effort to obtain a canoe. They were as determined as Park had been to follow the river all the way to the sea. Late in September, they finally embarked, in craft that did not have their full confidence, but on a journey the first stages of which at least had been guaranteed by the diplomatic efforts of the ruler of Bussa. Crews would travel only a short distance downstream, before having to be discharged and new men hired. At Rabba they were met by the riverside chief, representative of his ruler and himself termed "The King of the Dark Waters". After long negotiation, they at last were able to buy a boat of their own, a punt-shaped craft fifteen feet long and four feet wide.

The journey was, not surprisingly, punctuated by hazard. They found that, although their companions spoke five African languages between them, none of these were of any use among the strangers whose lands they now passed through. Of these, many were prepared to attack them, or at least to try and steal their belongings—unknown, representative of no understood power, they were of course fair game. Nature, too, with its rocks and spits of sand, its gargantuan hippopotami and voracious crocodiles, made its own efforts to thwart them. Three of their five African companions had to be almost forced to continue the journey. Nevertheless, day by day, they made their southerly progress, carried on towards discovery by the energy of the stream.

On 25 October they saw "a very considerable river, entering the Niger from the eastward"—it was the Benue, the great tributary flowing down from the Lake Chad regions, and at first they believed it to be an arm of the Niger itself. The strength of the current against them soon disabused them of this notion. It was shortly after this that they came as close as they ever were to being killed; making camp, they were confronted by a band of fully armed warriors about to attack them. Tribes on opposite sides of the river were in dispute and their unexpected arrival had been instantly construed as aggression, invasion and threat. Unharmed, the Landers walked towards arrow-point and spear. There was a moment of tension, bow-strings tautened, death crouched for them like a lion—and then, abruptly, the situation turned about, the weapons dropped, the chief knelt before them. Their unfamiliar whiteness had unmanned the war-party and, far from blood, all they now wanted was forgiveness. Never was it, one imagines, more happily granted.

The Niger widened. The silence of great waters stretched about them. On the occasions when they landed, they noticed a subtle alteration among the people. Here and there they heard English words, they saw bottles of rum, once a man dressed in the redcoat of a British soldier. The inner part of Africa, influenced from the north by the peoples of the desert, was behind them; they were approaching the lands that lay directly behind the coastline, drawing their European influences from the ships that traded there. Indeed, the people of these kingdoms had never heard of Bussa and Yauri, nor even of the Yoruba. They looked southward; Africa to the north was as mysterious to them as it was to Europeans.

Just as it seemed as though their current was carrying them unhurriedly to success, disaster checked them. Near Kirree, at the point where the Niger begins to break and flower into the complex spread of its delta, they were set upon by pirates; Ibo canoes "of amazing size" and "prodigious dimensions", each rowed by some forty people, turned, pursued and rammed them. They were dragged from the water, stripped and imprisoned. Their possessions were destroyed or stolen. After so nearly completing their task, it seemed as though they too would be defeated by the unaware guardians of mystery. They were finally sent as captives to the king of the Ibo, a tiny, self-confident man in a scarlet tunic and brass anklets, grown rich on the proceeds of the slave trade.

He in turn sold them to the king of Brass, a "wretched, filthy and contemptible place" situated on the estuary of the Niger. It was thus, as prisoners in a forty-paddle royal canoe, passing the tentacular pillars and arches of the mangrove swamps, half-stifled by stench and heat, that they covered the last miles of their journey. They were now merchandise, the property of Brass's ruler, whose hope it was that a white man's ransom would bring a fair return on his investment. John Lander having been kept by the king as hostage, Richard went aboard the *Thomas*, a Liverpool brig anchored a day and half's paddling down the estuary. If he imagined, however, that the Red Ensign would now assure their safety, he had reckoned without the realities of the mercantile marine of the day. The *Thomas*'s master, Captain Lake, had lost men with fever and seemed himself "in the very last stage of illness". He was not a man with charity to spare for strangers.

"If you think that you have a —— fool to deal with, you are mistaken; I'll not give a bloody flint for your bill, I would not give a —— for it". So Richard Lander reports his response. He himself, he says, felt overwhelmed by humiliation: "I had promised the price of our ransom should be paid by the first of our countrymen that we might meet with . . . to be thus refused . . . would, I know, degrade us sadly in the opinion of the natives . . . ." He was right. He asked his guide to take him to Bonny, where he knew there would be several British ships, but King Boy, the minor chieftain who had charge of him, shook his head: "This captain no pay, Bonny captain no pay, I no take you any further".

He departed, leaving Richard on board, John imprisoned. Lake would not budge; he refused not only to pay the Landers' ransom, but also to pay pilotage. As a consequence, his mate, a man named Spittle, was seized while taking soundings above the estuary bar. Lake, however, whether villainous, miserly or merely without money, seems at all events to have been determined. He decided to sail, pilot or no pilot, mate or no mate, with John Lander or without. If Lander could not make his own way aboard, he would have to stay wherever he was; Lake would pay nothing for him. Richard spent his whole time watching out for his brother; Lake assured him he need not bother himself, since John was certainly dead. "If he had been alive he would have been here by this time; tomorrow morning I shall leave the river."

The next day, however, the wind was too strong for the *Thomas* to depart, and the day after King Boy brought John Lander on board. There now settled upon the situation an armed stalemate, with King Boy demanding fifty bars for the release of the mate, Spittle, while Lake in turn held him prisoner and roared out his refusals. "Give me my mate, you black rascal", he yelled, like some character in a Robert Louis Stevenson fantasy, "or I will bring a thousand men of war here in a day or two; they shall come and burn down your towns and kill every one of you; bring me my mate!" Cowed, King Boy fled; before the hour was up, the mate was back on board.

After two desperate attempts to clear the estuary mouth, the *Thomas* at last was able to make her way out to sea. In Fernando Po, the Landers took ship for Rio de Janeiro. On the way, fever struck down the crew, and the Landers themselves, with three men to help them, had to work the ship. In mid-March they finally arrived in Rio; in another three months they arrived in England. Under the date, "Friday, June 10th", Richard Lander wrote, "Having left my brother at Portsmouth, I arrived in London this morning by the mail, and reported our discovery to Lord Goderich, His Majesty's Colonial Secretary".

When the Landers' book appeared, Barrow welcomed it, despite the fact that it destroyed his own theories about the Niger. "The long sought for termination of the Niger has now been discovered, and by a very humble but intelligent individual...." Richard received 1,000 guineas for the book; this was just as well, for from his government he had only his promised £100; when, because of the continued appalling state of his health, he asked for a pension, a year later, they paid him the same amount again. Thus, in a sort of diminuendo, the story of the long effort to determine the Niger's course came to an end. It had claimed the lives of many, wrecked the health of others, made no fortunes. Its heroes, some vain, some petty, had nevertheless all in their own ways been gigantic.

In a world strapped together by simple communications, where no one with a short-wave radio need ever be for long out of contact with a friend, where antibiotics and sulpha drugs allow the traveller to march like some invincible figure out of legend through the miasmic threat of fever and disease, where aeroplane, hovercraft and jeep have left few regions truly inaccessible, it is hard to imagine what their exploits entailed. These men would, for all practical purposes, leave their own planet, to wander in loneliness and unremitting danger through territories totally alien to any they had ever known, living with people whose religions, foods, clothes, houses, priorities and expectations could hardly have been guessed at before they were experienced. They would march away into a silent wilderness; behind them the dust would slowly fall and settle, the bushes at the edge of the forest would shake for a while, then stand still under the great press of sunlight. The weeks would pass, the months, the years. Wherever they were, no one could help them, no one could rescue them, no one could bring or send them comfort. When they returned, they might be welcomed by the fanfares of patriotism and the ready gold of the curious. When they failed to return, as Mungo Park did, years would pass before the terrible silence into which they had stepped would at last begin to shred. Only then, through the rents in that vast curtain, would those who had loved them perceive the outlines of their last disaster. They may have been free men, these extraordinary explorers, but many of them one after the other paid the full and terrible price of their freedom.

And what was the consequence of their efforts? Europe gained knowledge, but it was not knowledge disinterestedly gathered for its own sake. Governments and wealthy individuals had sponsored the explorers and they looked for some return on their investment. The main thrust of the British effort was up the Niger, the burden of its organisation lying at first on the shoulders of a Liverpool merchant named Macgregor Laird. In 1832 he sent two steamships, especially built for the task, northwards from the delta. Fever destroyed them and, of the forty-eight Europeans who had set out, only ten returned. Their guide was among those who died: Richard Lander, who above all had proved the venture's feasibility. In 1841 the British Government sponsored a second expedition; again fever took a third of the European members. For the rest, the journey was made more difficult by local hostility, whipped up by the traditional European traders afraid for their livelihoods.

It was not until a third expedition—again under Macgregor Laird's sponsorship and supported by the Government, but led on the river itself by a naval surgeon named Baikie—that the now accepted use of quinine managed to protect the Europeans. The year was 1854, the expedition's ostensible purpose to try to locate Heinrich Barth, then on his extraordinary journey to Timbuctu and through the middle Niger regions. He was not encountered and made his own way home, but the Benue was charted, trade links were forged and, above all, not one of the whites died. Africa's last barriers were giving way.

There were by now three prongs to the fork of European penetration in this part of Africa. The first, which demanded both British energy and British money over many decades, was the creditable and humane endeavour to stamp out the trade in slaves. The second was the introduction of more and more British goods, partly to take up the economic slack caused by the cessation of the slave trade. The third, inevitably, was the Christian religion, the tenets of which were carried into the most remote areas by the devoted stamina of hordes of missionaries, some of them from the beginning African themselves. In 1864 the first bishop of the Niger Territories was consecrated, his name Samuel Adjai Crowther, a liberated slave who had been educated in England.

The attempt to destroy the slave traffic and the complementary drive to increase British trade, the whole aided by a sort of devout fifth column of Christian converts, generated its own power and produced its own logic. If the flow of slaves was to be stopped up, kings and chieftains who insisted on living off it had to be replaced by rulers more amenable and humane. If traders were to penetrate the interior, they had to be protected from robbers and river pirates. It was thus, for example, that the British discovered their moral right to capture Lagos in 1851, placing on the throne there the particular claimant who had promised to cease trading in slaves. Since the very fact of such alien support undermined the authority of the sponsored king, however, the British were finally forced to the last extremity of control—Lagos became a Crown Colony ten years later. African defensive violence brought with it its own logical consequence of retribution, invasion, conquest and annexation. So, after many campaigns, went the Ashanti nation, defeated in 1874, annexed after much belligerent shadow-boxing some thirty years later. Lagos was followed by the Niger Coast Protectorate. The Yoruba took British protection, the Ibo were again and again shown the dreadful results of attempting to thwart British power, Benin paid the price of temerity. To the north, the Royal Niger Company pursued its profitable and sovereign way, making treaties with the descendants of those who had in their varying manner welcomed Mungo Park, Clapperton and the rest, and keeping the ambitious thrusts of France at bay. At precisely the turn of the century, what had always been only a quasi-private enterprise was taken over by true officialdom: the protectorate of Northern Nigeria was formed. The Niger Coast region became the Protectorate of Southern Nigeria; Lagos remained as before. The divisions, however, proclaimed differences without distinction: all three were administered by the Colonial Office.

And the lands through which Mungo Park had trudged, once lonely and in rags, then dragging behind him that long line of dying soldiers, what had become of them and their multifarious kingdoms? There it was France that dominated, once she had recovered from the Napoleonic wars and their defeats. At first, her merchants could do no more than trade through posts set up at centres of caravan or river traffic, some of these with long histories of European involvement. But West Africa, too, felt the weight of France's renewed ambitions under Napoleon III. At the orders of a vigorous governor, Faidherbe, strong presences were established in Galam and in Khasson, Futa Toro was occupied, the coastal kingdom of Cayor beset. Faidherbe, once an officer in the engineers, had a logical mind. In 1863 he set a memorandum before the emperor, suggesting that the time had come to consolidate French interests in Senegal. Gambia should be taken from the English by barter—Gabon, Assinie and Dabou were to be part of the parcel offered in exchange—after which "all the sources from which the trade of these coasts is drawn would be completely in our hands".

The grandeur of Faidherbe's plans found France in no condition to respond; Napoleon III was already in decline, his juicy dreams of empire dried into grotesque, autumnal husks that, at the first touch of Prussia's wintery storms, were plucked away and tossed into oblivion. It was almost twenty years before French vigour erupted again into a new and more effective colonialism; it was even later, in 1890, that the formation of the Comité de l'Afrique Française gave this renewed imperial ambition a political base at home. In its first manifesto, this committee stated with arrogant clarity, "We are witnessing a spectacle unique in history: the actual partition of a little-known continent by certain civilised nations of Europe. In this partition, France is entitled to the largest share . . . ." It had been essential to move swiftly in the past to extend French influence in Africa. "Such initiatives seem more and more necessary today, when we face the problems of acquiring the rights of the first occupier in Central Africa . . . ." France responded to this patriotic call. By the turn of the century, Senegal was hers, and all the lands east of Senegal, almost to the banks of the Nile. She held Algeria, and all the lands south-eastward as far as Lake Chad. Her ancient trading posts on the coast of Guinea still existed, still clawed wealth out of West Africa. The "union across the Sudan of French Congo, Senegal and Algeria–Tunisia", urged by the Comité, was complete.

This then, and not the plotting of the Niger's course, was the real conclusion of Mungo Park's imprecise intention. Nigeria was British, the Gambia was British, Senegal was French, the wide belt of central Sudan was French. The British were elsewhere, too—on the Gold Coast, and in Sierra Leone, that erstwhile heaven for freed slaves—while the Germans struggled for their share in the Cameroons. Rigid frontiers, decided in the conference rooms of distant capitals, struck abruptly across the maps. The European penetration of West Africa was at last complete, accepted and codified. There is no question that for Mungo Park such a conclusion would have coincided with his wildest, most optimistic expectation. He had no doubt that the civilisation of Europe would bring with it an infinity of benefits for the peoples of Africa, just as he realised that colonisation and trade in that continent would bring vast profit to the peoples of Europe. That a hundred years after his dreadful death his courage and misfortune should have been vindicated in such a fashion would have seemed to him just. It was, he would have said, precisely to achieve something of the kind that he had made his hazardous effort.

The empires have crumbled now. Overstretched and wrecked by its own bloody rivalries, Europe trembled into a swift senility. War was its disease; by the time that that plague was cured, its natural consequence of poverty had become irreversible. The very condition of Europe's economic survival was its relinquishing of the colonies that had symbolised its strength. Withdrawal from colonial power brought new health—for some at least. Those who had been most extended have taken longest to recover. The paradox is that, in the stories of such heroes as Mungo Park, this conclusion has had no diminishing effect. Legend had long separated the heroism of the explorers from the cool commercialism of the later administrators. With the link between them forgotten, the revulsion with which many of the latter are now regarded does not extend to the former.

We have tacitly agreed to overlook or disregard the explorers' motives. For us, Mungo Park was simply what he did; his achievements lie in the manner of his survival and of his death. Others marched behind the banner of his heroism and stole the lands he had been the first European to see. That he would have approved of such theft does not diminish his heroism. In the end, after all, it is quite alone that we see him, far from the flags and the hypocrisy of empire. He sits over a bowl of *kous-kous* and smiles at the village women whose charity has provided it; he staggers down the swirling mazes of his fever; he suffers imprisonment and robbery, ridicule and the rapacity of tyrants; straight-faced, he survives the frivolity of fame to return to wilderness and danger. Across the decades we see him exhorting the sick and dying, bending again and again under loads others are too weak to lift, disguising his own sickness to hearten his companions, outfacing predators and thieves, recalcitrant subordinates and greedy

kings; at last he sets out, leader of a handful of survivors, unbroken, guided by
his own inflexible will, to chance the compassion of the river that obsessed him.
That compassion turned from him at last and the river took him, as perhaps it
was always bound to do. His motives are history, as are the empires that his
achievements led to. His courage, like his death, remains his own.

Bibliography

Ajayi, J. F. A., and Crowder, M. (eds), *History of West Africa*, vol. 1, London 1971.

Ayandele, E. A., *African Exploration and Human Understanding*, Edinburgh 1971.

Barth, H., *Travels and Discoveries in North and Central Africa*, London 1857-8.

Bascom, W. R., and Herskovits, M. J. (eds), *Continuity and Change in African Cultures*, Chicago 1959.

Blake, J. W., *European Beginnings in West Africa, 1451-1578*.

Boahen, A. A., *Britain, the Sahara and the Western Soudan*, London 1964.

Bovill, E. W. (ed.), *Missions to the Niger*, London 1964.

Bovill, E. W., *The Niger Explored*, Oxford 1964.

Caillié R., *Travels through Central Africa to Timbuctoo*, London 1830.

Cameron, H. C., *Sir Joseph Banks*, London 1952.

Clapperton, H., *Journal of a Second Expedition into the Interior of Africa*, London 1829.

Davidson, B., *Africa in History*, London 1974.

Davidson, B., *Black Mother*, London 1968.

Fage, J. D., *A History of West Africa*, Cambridge 1969.

Gibbon, L. G., *Niger—The Life of Mungo Park*, London 1934.

Gwynne, S., *Mungo Park and the Quest for the Niger*, London 1934.

Hallett, R., *The Penetration of Africa to 1815*, London 1965.

Hallett, R., *The Record of the African Association*, London 1964.

Hargreaves, J. D. (ed.), *France and West Africa*, Cambridge 1969.

Harris, J. E., *Africans and their History*, New York 1972.

Harris, P. G., "A Note on Mungo Park and the Upper Niger", *Journal of the Royal Africa Society*, vol. 35, 1936.

Johnston, H. H., "The Niger Basin and Mungo Park", *Scottish Geographical Magazine*, vol. 23, 1907.

Lander, R., *Records of Captain Clapperton's Last Expedition in Africa*, London 1830.

Lander, R. and J., *Journal of an Expedition to Explore the Course and Termination of the Niger*, London 1830.

Langley, M., "The Last Journey of Mungo Park", *History Today*, vol. 21, 1971.

Lloyd, C., *The Search for the Niger*, London 1973.

Lupton, K., "The Death of Mungo Park", *Nigeria Magazine*, no. 72, 1962.

Maclachlan, T. P., *Mungo Park*, London 1898.

Owen, R., *The Saga of the Niger*, London 1961.

Park, M., *Journal of a Mission to the Interior Parts of Africa*, London 1815.

Park, M., *Travels in Africa*, London 1954.

Parry, J. H., *The Age of Reconnaissance*, New York 1964.

"Sabiad", "Did Mungo Park Die at Boussa?", *West African Review*, vol. 223, 1951.

Shepperson, G. (chairman), *The Exploration of Africa in the Eighteenth and Nineteenth Centuries* (seminar), Edinburgh 1971.

Sillery, A., *Africa—A Social Geography*, London 1961.
Thomson, J., *Mungo Park and the Niger*, London 1890.

There are in addition valuable manuscript sources in the British Library, the library of the British Museum (Natural History), the Public Records Office, and the National Library of Scotland, Edinburgh.

Index

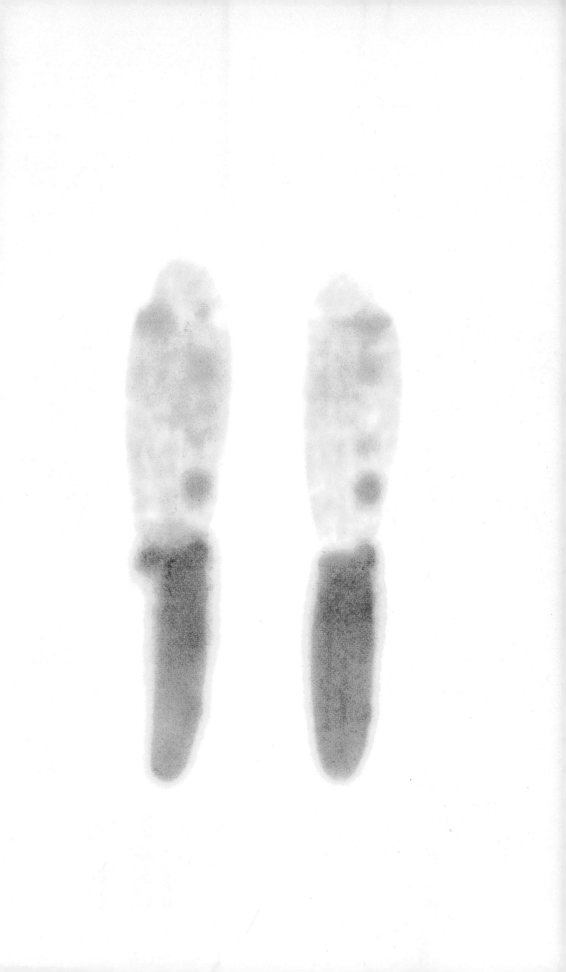